ACTING P[

"Robert Cohen's book, *Acting Power*, follows the tradition of his other book, *Acting One*, and has been the veritable bible for acting teachers for the last quarter century." – *David Krasner, Emerson College*

"This book, above all else, is an attempt to explore the qualities of acting power… to suggest to you, the actor, an approach toward not merely good acting but powerful acting. Great actors display the power to frighten – and the power to seduce – and can shift between the one and the other like a violinist can her notes." – *From the Preface*

The first edition of *Acting Power* was a groundbreaking work of acting theory that applied sociological and psychological principles to actor training. The book went on to influence a generation of theatre and performance studies students and academics, and was translated into four languages.

This carefully revised twenty-first century edition (re)considers, in the context of today's field:

- questions such as "should actors act from the inside or the outside?" and "should the actor live the role or present the role?"
- contemporary research into communication theory, cybernetics, and cognitive science
- brilliantly illuminating and witty exercises for solo study and classroom use, and a through-line of useful references to classic plays
- penetrating observations about the actor's art by more than 75 distinguished professional actors and directors.

Cohen's elegant and rigorous updates emphasize the continuing relevance of his uniquely integrated and life-affirming approach to this field. The new edition draws on his extraordinarily rich career as teacher, scholar, director, translator, and dramaturg. It is a recipe for thrilling theatre in any genre.

Robert Cohen is a prolific playwright, play reviewer, and translator, and directs professionally at American Shakespeare festivals. His 17 books include five on acting, a subject he has taught in over a dozen countries. He is currently the Claire Trevor Professor of Drama at the University of California, Irvine.

ACTING POWER

The 21st Century Edition

Robert Cohen

Routledge
Taylor & Francis Group

LONDON AND NEW YORK

21st Century edition published 2013
by Routledge
2 Park Square, Milton Park, Abingdon, Oxon OX14 4RN

Simultaneously published in the USA and Canada
by Routledge
711 Third Avenue, New York, NY 10017

Routledge is an imprint of the Taylor & Francis Group, an informa business

© 2013 Robert Cohen

First edition published by Mayfield Publishing Co. 1978

British Library Cataloguing in Publication Data
A catalogue record for this book is available from the British Library

Library of Congress Cataloguing in Publication Data
Cohen, Robert, 1938-
Acting power : the 21st century edition / by Robert Cohen.
pages cm
Includes bibliographical references and index.
1. Acting. I. Title.
PN2061.C58 2013
792.02'8--dc23
2012037409

ISBN: 978-0-415-65846-1 (hbk)
ISBN: 978-0-415-65847-8 (pbk)
ISBN: 978-0-203-07599-9 (ebk)

Typeset in Goudy
by Saxon Graphics Ltd, Derby

Printed and bound in the United States of America
by Edwards Brothers Malloy on sustainably sourced paper.

FOR LORNA COHEN
vivere est cogitare

CONTENTS

ACKNOWLEDGEMENTS

I am deeply grateful to many people who have proved invaluable to the development of this book during the 40 years since its first inception. Chronologically, this began 45 years ago when I crossed paths in a corridor with my colleague Lewis (Creel) Froman, then a Professor of Political Science on my campus, and he suggested I read Paul Watzlawick's *Pragmatics of Human Communication*. The book opened my mind to entirely new ways of conceptualizing human interactions, and spurred me to read the works of Erving Goffman, Eric Berne and other social science specialists. Had he not made the suggestion, this book would never have been written. I then reached out to the National Science Foundation, which gave me a grant to study lie detection and what it might reveal about the acting process (next to nothing, as it turned out), and to the eight brave undergraduate drama students who signed up for what I called an "Acting as Communication" class, and thereby allowed me to experiment with them in creating a "cybernetic acting theory" that privileged future-oriented interactions over actors delving into their own psyches. And then came Lorna Buck, who became Lorna Buck Cohen while I was hammering out the pages of the original text, and who gave me both undeserved confidence and well-deserved criticism as she read my sentences hot from my Smith-Corona, and then Lans Hays, at Mayfield Publishing Company in Palo Alto, who accepted the finished manuscript and published it the following year. After that, I became deeply indebted to Maija-Liisa Marton, who wrote to me from Helsinki asking if she could translate the book into Finnish, and then Andras Marton, who translated it into Hungarian, followed by Mall Klaassen and Jaak Rähesepp who translated it into Estonian and Cipriana Petre who translated it into Romanian; all of these wonderful people have given the book – and more importantly its concepts – an international readership, which has vastly expanded my own ongoing research.

For this current edition, I am most deeply indebted to Lorna Cohen, once more, and to my former student Tyler Seiple, each of whom took the role of faithful and honest critic while offering valuable edits and suggestions during my extensive revision process. And my profound gratitude extends to publisher Talia Rodgers, at Routledge, for her enthusiastic support and extraordinarily helpful comments, and her equally lively editorial assistant, Sam Kinchin-Smith. To all of these talented and wonderful people, I am permanently grateful. Bless you all.

PREFACE TO THIS EDITION

This book is the first – and will be the last – revision of my 1978 text, *Acting Power*. That book was initially to be titled: A Cybernetic Acting Theory. Fortunately, I changed my mind before it was published.

Since then, I have refined and targeted my work to broader audiences in successive editions of *Acting One, Acting Two, Acting in Shakespeare,* and *Acting Professionally,* along with acting chapters in my books *Theatre* and *Working Together in Theatre,* and in a variety of essays in several theatre journals. The books, first published by a then-obscure company in Palo Alto, California, have, over the years, captured a broad international readership, which has led to invitations to teach acting in over a dozen countries.

Acting Power is quite different from my other acting books, however. It was not originally intended to be a textbook (although it was ultimately published as one), but as a theoretical study of the acting process, with the intention of providing actors and their teachers with an integrated acting approach, or what I call an "alignment," between the various and seemingly opposite approaches of emotion and control. It sought – and still seeks – to find the link between an actor's spontaneity and her technique, her imagination and her discipline, and, in most cases, her quest for a measure of "realism" within the performance of a variety of "styles." It is also aimed at finding the points of connection between the actor's fullest embodiment of her character on stage or in front of the camera, and her ability to satisfy – indeed to thrill – audiences that come to see her performance. It seeks to create what my late colleague Jerzy Grotowski called a "dialectics of human behavior" as it might exist in a theatrical or film performance, and a satisfactory way of dealing intellectually with the many contradictions and controversies wrestled over by theatre artists and acting theorists – most notably by Konstantin Stanislavsky and Bertolt Brecht – in their various productions and writings.

This new edition does not change any of the ideas in the earlier one, but it certainly augments them. It includes my findings and discoveries during my 35 years of subsequent practical work as an acting teacher and professional director, which provided me with qualifications I did not possess at the time I wrote the original text. It also includes my new research in both acting theory and the cognitive sciences, which I have continuously conducted since the first edition's appearance, and with sustained attention since the 1980s when I created the bi-annual graduate course in acting theory that I continue to teach today. We have learned a great deal in these intervening years, particularly in the area of brain research, which has led to new understandings of the complex neurological activity in connecting emotions and actions. The discovery of mirror neurons that lie at the heart of interpersonal communication and empathy has been particularly revelatory, as has the mapping of operations and interconnections of the senses – mainly hearing, seeing and touching – along with the other facets of the human thought processes that underlie great performances. These, and my own discoveries about the art of acting after three-plus decades of actually teaching it, have been incorporated on every page of this new edition of *Acting Power*.

What is unchanged between this edition and the previous one, however, are the following points, which were in my first preface, and which I quote verbatim:

> There is bad acting, there is good acting, and there is great acting. And we can all tell the difference when we see it, even if we can't exactly define the difference.
>
> Most actors try very hard to become good actors. This is laudable, of course, but it is not enough. One must try to become a great actor. Why? There are two reasons. The first is a professional one. Only great actors can develop, over the course of many years, a suitable and successful professional career. If you are good, very good, you can get cast from time to time, perhaps even regularly if you make yourself continually available. But nobody will be *dying* to cast you, and in a business as competitive as the theatre (or films or television) it is having people dying to cast you that is, over the long run, pretty much what it takes to ensure a permanent career.
>
> It takes directors, producers, and casting directors who will think of you when you're not around, who will take the trouble to hunt you out and negotiate with others for your services. That means that you are more than a good actor; it means you are an exciting actor, one who has the capacity to quicken their pulse and enliven their imagination and, if theirs, an audience's as well. The only alternative to being a great actor is to be selling yourself day by day in what is clearly going to remain what it is today: a buyer's market. And this is a difficult way to have to spend your life.
>
> The second reason is even more important. It is the artistic reason. Most professional actors – most interesting actors anyway – do not perform solely for money, or fame, or exhibitionistic exploitation. They are actors because they have a tremendous need to act; a powerful urge to express themselves creatively and skillfully in a medium of high

artistry – a medium with a twenty-five-hundred-year history and with a brilliantly exciting present. Merely good, competent, "B plus" acting will not satisfy this – either for actors or for their audiences. After all, there does not have to be a theatre. Theatre is not like government service, primary education, or agriculture. People can live perfectly good lives without theatre, and in many parts of the world they do live without it. Theatre only exists, and only continues to exist, because of great plays, great performances, and great actors. "Greatness" is what creates audience demand; "greatness" is in the theatre's very lifeblood. Without greatness, and the striving toward it, theatre would simply cease to exist.

What separates the "great" from the merely "good?" It is not easy to say, perhaps not even possible to define in absolute terms. But I think it can be approached.

Philosopher William James suggests that "the difference between the first- and second-best things in art absolutely seems to escape verbal definition – it is a matter of a hair, a shade, an inward quiver of some kind – yet [it] is miles away in point of preciousness." [1]

What is greatness in acting? It is not necessarily becoming a "star" or playing lots of leading roles. There are great actors in every medium who specialize in small parts, locally seen, and who offstage are self-effacing to the point of anonymity. But they have power: the power to excite the emotions, the intellect, and the very physiologies of the audiences who see them. They have the power to make audiences want to see them again, and directors want to cast them again – or steal them away from other directors. They have the power to entertain, to move, to dazzle, to fulfill, and to inspire. They are men and women of wide-ranging powers; they are, if you ask someone, "Great!" "Powerful!"

This book, above all else, is an attempt to explore the qualities of acting power; to take aim at that "inward quiver" which James mentions, and to suggest to you, the actor, an approach toward not merely good acting but powerful acting. Great actors display the power to frighten – and the power to seduce – and can shift between the one and the other like a violinist can her notes.

I am aware of a certain presumptuousness in this attempt; a presumptuousness in my writing of it, and in your thinking about it. We live in an age of professed egalitarianism, where "coolness" and "looseness" are publicly preferred to the apparent arrogance of transcendence. But art is not egalitarian. Art demands, or requires, the very best of every aspirant; it accepts only the maximum effort. An actor who wants to be part of the lifeblood of the theatre – the theatre of today and the theatre of the future – must set his or her sights at the highest, at greatness itself. Nothing less will really do.

NOTES FOR THIS EDITION

- I have "illustrated" this book with what I believe to be pertinent quotations largely by actors (and a few directors) distinguished for their work on the stage or in film, and most often in both of these media. About half of these quotations are from the original edition, a few from actors who have by now seen the fall of their final curtain. The other half are from actors of our current century, and whose careers continue to blossom.

- I have used a few well-known plays – A Streetcar Named Desire, The Glass Menagerie, Man and Superman, Death of a Salesman, Hamlet – as reference points for some of my discussions, since I believe these are works with which most of my readers will be acquainted, or can quickly become so. Similarly I use, as I did in the first edition, Mike Nichols's The Graduate as perhaps the most well-known film of the last fifty years, even among readers born decades after its 1967 release – a conclusion I reached only after polling my undergraduate drama students in 2012.

- Since this book is mainly about generic people (mostly actors) instead of specific ones, it includes a great many pronouns. In the first edition, as customary at the time, I used masculine pronouns when referring to actors in general (e.g. "The actor learns his lines…"). To compensate, I have used feminine pronouns when referring to actors this time, employing male pronouns occasionally when referring to other theatre personnel or, of course, specific male individuals. I have avoided the use of the word "actress" except when, in identifying the authors of the inserted quotations, I have labeled them by sex, nationality, and name (e.g. "American actress Meryl Streep"). I hope the next generation will come up with suitable non-gendered pronouns that will refer to human beings of both sexes, and retire the phrase "his or her" to its deserved demise.

- This book includes a considerable number of exercises. Some are designed for classroom use, and some can be done by the reader alone in her study – or even in her head. A great many of them, however, are really "fantasy exercises," which I don't really expect anyone to actually perform, but believe may prove useful for readers to contemplate, and to *imagine* themselves doing. Reading them, in any case, may clarify the practicality of some of my more theoretical statements, or so I would like to think.

- As my professional background is almost entirely in live theatre, my references in this book are mostly to acting on the stage – but the principles I discuss herein apply equally to acting in film and television, to which I frequently make reference. So when the reader comes across the phrase "on the stage," this can be equally interpreted as "on the set," or "on the soundstage" – and the words "play" and "script" can also refer to "film" and "screenplay." Since the vast majority of professional actors today seek careers in all performance media, I do not believe it necessary to identify them separately at every turn. For those interested in the specific acting techniques useful in film and television, I am happy to recommend two fine books by past and present colleagues of mine at the University of California, Irvine: Ian Bernard's *Film and Television Acting* (second edition) and Richard Brestoff's *The Camera-Smart Actor*.

INTRODUCTION
THE ACTOR'S VIEWPOINT

"You're really driving four horses, as it were, first going through in great detail the exact movements which have been decided upon. You're also listening to the audience, as I say, keeping if you can very great control over them. You're also slightly creating the part, insofar as you're consciously refining the movements and perhaps inventing tiny other experiments with new ones. At the same time you are really living, in one part of your mind, what is happening. Acting is to some extent a controlled dream. In one part of your consciousness it really and truly is happening... To make it true to the audience ... the actor must, at any rate some of the time, believe himself that it really is true ... Therefore three or four layers of consciousness are at work during the time an actor is giving a performance."

British actor Sir Ralph Richardson[1]

Alignment

Power comes from alignment. You can easily hold twenty plates in your hands, but you cannot hold twenty ping-pong balls, even though the ping-pong balls are far smaller and lighter than the plates. That is because the plates can be aligned, and the ping-pong balls cannot.

If you want to hold twenty plates in your hands, all you have to do is stack them. Then you simply pick up the bottom plate and the rest will follow. You need only concentrate on the bottom plate – provided you have stacked the plates correctly to begin with.

It is the same with acting. An actor cannot concentrate on her situation, characterization, style and theatricality individually, one-at-a-time, as though these elements of her craft were so many individual ping-pong balls. She must stack them so that one rests upon another, so that by handling one of them correctly she can carry all of them at the same time.

The bottom plate is the character's pursuit of a *goal* (or *objective*, or *intention*, or *want*, depending on the actor's terminology) within her immediate *situation*. This demands the actor's total concentration, and all of her conscious, controlled energy, which is tightly focused on winning that goal.

The elements of characterization, style, and theatricality are critical, but they must all be "stacked" on that bottom plate in perfect alignment for her performance to be seen as whole. Then they can be handled with confidence. The actor is propelled by her situation; by her pursuit of one or more goals. In focusing on her situational goals, she can play character, style, and theatricality simultaneously and automatically. Stacking them atop her situational objectives gives her total and undivided attention during her performance. It is by thus *structuring her consciousnesses* that the actor can drive Ralph Richardson's multiple horses without falling off – or falling apart.

A structuring of consciousness

Goal, situation, character, style, and performance must therefore be aligned at the moment of performance. The actor cannot be expected to think in a rotating alternation of each of these five "consciousnesses," nor can she divide her overall consciousness, like a pie, into five separate slices. She must, on the contrary, coalesce these multiple consciousnesses into a single, highly focused, concentration. If her separate consciousnesses can be made to feed into each other, they will multiply rather than fragment the actor's concentration, and allow her to perform with five times rather than one-fifth her strength and power. Finding a structural alignment for the actor's thinking must therefore have the highest priority in an actor's training.

To this end, a five-leveled model of acting consciousness is pursued throughout this book.

Playing the character's *goal*, i.e. playing to *improve your character's situation*, is the first level. It is the foundation of acting. At this level, the behavior of the actor is "pulled" entirely by the goal she wants to win, the ideal future she seeks, and the victories she actively pursues. This is the life level of acting, whereby the actor creates a human being with human aspirations. It is the *aspiration* of the character – what she hopes for, dreams for, works for and sacrifices for – that propels the character beyond her present self and towards her imagined future, which she may or may not reach. This is playing "out of the self," which is the title of Chapter 1, or, in Stanislavsky's famous term, "living the part."

Playing the character's *interactions* is the second level. Acting is something you do with *other* people – usually other characters in the play, often characters that inhabit your own character's mind, and eventually before an audience. These interactions differ greatly, but only if they are interwoven into alignment will the actor succeed in being seen as both "truthful" and "brilliant." Playing interactions means playing "into the other," which is the title of Chapter 2. It is every bit as important as playing out of yourself – indeed, it is far more important.

Playing the author's *character* and playing the production's *style* are at the third and fourth levels. Here the actor's behavior is drawn from scripted and directed sources; from the playtext, from the director's blocking and coaching, and from the actor's own research. These are at the *dramatic* level of acting, whereby the actor creates a dramatized human being whose intensities are dramatically interesting. These subjects are the topics of Chapters 3 and 4.

Playing the *performance* is the fifth and final level. Here the behavior is drawn from the real or anticipated audience. This is the *theatrical* level of acting, whereby the actor creates and *projects* a dramatized human being. This is the subject of Chapter 5, and it is summarized, in conjunction with the preceding chapters, in Chapter 6.

If the actor's situation is properly coalesced – if it is dramatically and theatrically aligned before the actual "acting" begins – then that situation will demand the most unique, appropriate, and theatrical forms of interaction, characterization, style, and performance. By finding the mechanisms for aligning the dramatic and theatrical levels with the human one, acting becomes organically integrated; and character, style, and performance become mutually aligned spines of the action rather than add-ons or detractions.

This alignment is therefore a mental one; a way of looking at things, a structuring of the actor's consciousness. Whether the actor makes her alignment consciously or spontaneously, of course, depends on the actor, and it may depend on the play as well. When talking about their craft, many actors of previous generations acknowledged that they simply acted spontaneously – as the mood struck them. Film actor John Wayne described his acting theory as "I read what's in the script and then I go out there and deliver my lines." But he did manage to align his targets and interact reciprocally with them. "I don't call myself an actor," Wayne concluded, "I'm a reactor."[2] Actors working on the stage, and tackling more subtle roles, however, or attempting to attain more difficult styles or characterizations, will probably wish to pursue these acting alignments more consciously and purposefully.

The acting controversy

For a great many years, acting has been discussed as some sort of battle between two contradictory notions: the actor's "internal belief in her role," and her "external performance technique." Schools have arisen to claim that acting is predominantly one or the other. Different schools have tried to combine the two in some sort of package, often an awkward one, calling for a lot of Scotch tape. "You must live the life of your character, but you must also be heard in the back row," is the familiar packaging, with numerous variations. Clearly, belief in one's character and proficient technique on the stage are both involved in successful acting, but if actors can approach these as complementary rather than contradictory forces, the package need not be so awkward, and a synthesized and integrated art of acting may develop. This, indeed, is the goal of this book.

For the fact is that both "internal belief" and "external technique" are fundamental and interwoven aspects not merely of stage acting, but of the basic processes of living and communicating. They can, of course, be separated for reasons of analysis, and it is clearly to the advantage of the behavioral scientist or the dramatic theoretician to do so, given their protocols of dissection, designation, and theoretical investigation. But the actor's goals are quite different from these. The actor's ultimate task is neither to dissect nor analyze, but rather to put together, to enliven, and to create a sense of life in a whole and fulfilling theatrical experience. To the actor, it is not the separation of belief and technique that is at issue, but their marriage.

In this book we will not, therefore, be concerned with dividing the actor's separate tasks into their various components, but with integrating these components into their most perfect possible alignment. In doing this, we will take, not the critical or theoretical perspective of the objective observer, but rather the perspective of the actor herself. We will take, that is, a subjective approach. We will approach acting from the inside, not the outside, but in so doing we will try to suggest ways in which the actor can direct her inner consciousness into a highly useful, productive, creative, artistic, and, above all, performative instrument. A real instrument, that can be used in a real world.

Let us begin.

Acting is real

"The beginning and end of the business [of acting] from the author's point of view is the art of making the audience believe that real things are happening to real people."
Irish/British playwright George Bernard Shaw[3]

4

Acting takes place in "plays," and is called "playing." These words connote deception and non-seriousness, and usually lead beginners to think that acting is wholly different from "real" behavior. It is not. There are, of course, many differences between acting on stage and behaving in life, but the differences are not exactly those between "reality" and "unreality" or between "honesty" and "dishonesty."

In the first place, reality is not a very simple concept to define. Certainly we can agree that reality includes trees, birds, rocks, the human skeleton, and the sky; but what place in reality do dreams, feelings, numbers, love, or despair occupy? They are real if only because we feel they are real; their realness, though subjective, is as influential in our "real" decisions as hard and fast tangible reality.

One of the basic questions about acting, however, has to do with whether or not an actor's feelings are or should be "real," or "honest." When looked at from the subjective aspect of reality, this question only gives rise to thousands more. "Real to whom?" "Honest to whom?" "To the actor?" "To the audience?" And even these questions are undermined when we start to question the "reality" or "honesty" of some of our own feelings. While, to be sure, we are often overcome by wholly spontaneous waves of emotion, there are also many times when we are vague and unsure about our feelings. We go to a funeral and wonder if we are weeping because we are sad, or because other people expect us to. We laugh at a comedy, and wonder if we are laughing at the joke, or to encourage the actors, or to convince others in the audience that we understand the point of the humor. We smile at someone and wonder if we "really" mean that we're happy, or simply wishing to make a show of fondness, or are even getting out of a sticky situation gracefully. To say that an actor should be "real" or "honest" is all well and good, but it is not clear that by saying it we are in fact saying anything of substance.

Findings in what has become known as cognitive dissonance – which could be interpreted as "fooling one's own brain" – have changed our understanding of psychological reality sufficiently during the past fifty years to make these studies of significant importance to understanding the "act of acting."

The basic principle of cognitive dissonance is that we come to believe in what we find ourselves doing, regardless of the reasons we first started doing it. In the most critical first experiment, conducted by Leon Festinger in 1957, Festinger administered a very tedious examination to a group of volunteers, and then requested the volunteers "help" him by telling new volunteers that the test had been "fun to take." As compensation, Festinger had paid some of the original volunteers a fee of $20 (a large sum of money at the time); others, however, he paid only $1. At a later date, he asked the original volunteers if they had enjoyed taking the exam. Most of those who had received the $20 fee told the truth and said "No," but most of those who had received $1 said "Yes." They simply could not believe they could have lied for a mere dollar, and so had come to believe in their lie. This is cognitive dissonance. It leads debaters who are randomly assigned a position to come to believe that the position is their own. It leads randomly hired lawyers, speechwriters, and advertisers to believe in their clients' claims.

A person who joins a political or religious group simply in order to meet people will usually come to believe in its cause. Thus what we "really" believe depends, in part, on what we find ourselves doing.

Actors, of course, have been asked by teachers and directors – notably Konstantin Stanislavsky, to "live the life of their characters on the stage." And often they certainly do come to "believe in" their parts. We are all familiar with this from newspapers and celebrity magazines. Romance on the set frequently leads to entanglements off. The celebrated affairs – and subsequent divorces and remarriages – of Richard Burton (Antony) and Elizabeth Taylor (Cleopatra), and of Brad Pitt (Mr. Smith) and Angelina Jolie (Mrs. Smith) are only the best known examples of situations not uncommon on film locations or the theatrical "roads" around the world. Likewise, history records brutish offstage behavior – including murders – by actors who often played villains, including the assassination of President Lincoln by actor John Wilkes Booth – who was the leading Richard III of his era.

But there is concrete scientific evidence for ordinary persons "living the lives of their characters" and thereby fooling their own brains as well. This was provided by Philip Zimbardo in his Stanford Prison Experiment of 1971. Professor Zimbardo had invited a random group of male students to participate in a mock prison exercise, for which he had constructed a full-scale model penitentiary in a campus laboratory building. Some of the students he arbitrarily designated as "guards," and others as "prisoners." Appropriate costumes were provided to each participant, "rules" were posted, and Zimbardo and his colleagues withdrew behind one-way windows. Two days into the projected week-long experiment, however, Zimbardo had to call the whole thing off. The "guards," it turned out, had started berating, assaulting, and even torturing their "prisoners." Their "prisoners," consequently, were falling into deep states of depression and nervous exhaustion. They were finding and exploiting scapegoats in their midst, and developing anxieties and psychosomatic twitches; one had a complete nervous breakdown while others forfeited their stipends and left the project. The interaction between "play" and psychological and physiological "reality" had simply become too intense. The "playing" of Zimbardo's "actors" had produced utterly "real" results. Professor Zimbardo concluded that "illusion had merged inextricably with reality," and that the "play" had become indistinguishable from the "real."

Seen from the outside, it is hard to understand the experiment's hypnotic effect on the participants' emotions. Why didn't the prisoners in Zimbardo's experiment simply lie on their cots? Why didn't they just remind themselves that "this is only a scientific experiment, and we'll be out of here in three days?" Within a "playing" context, however, one sees and thinks differently. A real, but different, universe exists. It is the universe of "play."

Consider a more common example of this universe of play: the "playing field" of sports or games. Like the theatre, the sporting competition is also a context for tightly structured performing, with fixed rules and regulations (its script), a

6

dimensioned playing field (its set), carefully selected teams of opponents (its cast), and goals for each participant (its objectives). The rules of sport, like the scripts of drama, are totally arbitrary. There is nothing intrinsic about three strikes that makes them constitute an "out" – it is only that the rule book so designates them – but the context becomes an insistent and definitive set of strictures. And the teams provide a further context: the San Francisco Giants are most likely not from San Francisco and are certainly not giants, but their home town crowds worship them as if they were both, passionately cheering their victories and grieving their losses. Within the context of "play," aficionados will believe in – and identify with – their heroes on the field. And these combats, played in artificially created, commercially presented, and intellectually meaningless sports, are seen as "real" human interactions – and are passionately followed all over the world.

"Acting is a lot like sports, and a lot of people don't get that. My focus is really acting, but jiu-jiitsu is a passion of mine. And there's a certain level of concentration in it that makes me a better actor."
    American actor-athlete Jonathan Lipnicki[4]

To the sports player and to his "fans," as to the Zimbardo "prisoner" and his "guard," the context is an absolute. During competition, the reality of the context is total; it is the whole universe. If a ballplayer strikes out, you can offer him no comfort by saying "It's only a game," for his look in response will be only astonishment: as if to say, "What world are you in?" Nor can you comfort him by suggesting, "Three strikes are an unreasonably unfair limitation: five at least should be allowed." To the ballplayer within the game, such remarks are nonsense: within his context the rules are absolute, and outsiders are suffered rudely, if at all. And since the rules are absolute, the energy within the context is wholly deployed in winning the game; it is not wasted on trying to change its regulations.

We can see from these examples that a fixed context surrounding an action does not fragment the passions, feelings, and intensity within it, it only heightens them. This is the brilliance of theatre. A highly structured context – and a play is one of the most highly structured there is, whether an improvised skit or a fully staged and scripted drama – acts as a crucible which intensifies everything within it, and which makes the reality of every moment, from the viewpoints of both the participant and the engaged observer, vivid and often overwhelming. Indeed, play experiences, whether in child's play, sports play, or theatrical play and film, are often the most remembered and most treasured moments of our lives. They become as "real" as life itself – they *are* life itself. They establish for us the models for what we think life's "peak experiences" should be but rarely are, and become the reference points upon which we measure our real-life feelings and behaviors.

Contemporary research has solidly augmented the significance of cognitive dissonance and the reality of the connection between our real and pretended behaviors. In 1992, psychologists Randy Larsen and Ed Diener found that mechanically making a sad face could be demonstrated to make a person actually sad, and that simply raising the corners of her lips could make a person happy – and could even, if done often enough, relieve her clinical depression. I myself have discovered that smiling mechanically while testing my blood pressure will give me a lower BP reading.

Shakespeare, of course, believed this – or at least had his character of Hamlet believe it, since Hamlet tells his mother to go to her husband's bed but not to have sex with him ever again. And how should she do this?

> [HAMLET:] Assume a virtue, if you have it not…
> Refrain tonight,
> And that shall lend a kind of easiness
> To the next abstinence: the next more easy,
> For use can almost change the stamp of nature.

Thus, in actors' terms, Hamlet proposes that his mother work "from the outside in" – pretend to be virtuous (in this case, celibate) and you will "almost" become so in "nature."

To suggest, therefore, that the actions (or acting) within a play are unreal or unnatural is to miss, quite entirely, the most striking aspect of the theatre, which is that insofar as acting is different from everyday reality, it is mostly different in the direction of being "more real" rather than "less real." Great theatre is, in fact, an investigation of what, in life, is intense, revealing, enlightening, evocative, joyous, and often hysterically funny. The theatrical context, whether it is composed of stage and scenery, street and trestles, or videotape and camera, is an arena for goals intensely pursued, battles vibrantly engaged, loves eagerly sought, and lives brilliantly lived. To separate acting from reality, therefore, is to diminish both.

Acting is action

It is axiomatic that acting is action. After all, these words – plus the word "act" as in "Act One" – all have the same root: the Latin *actus*, "to do." But we almost always first encounter a play by reading it. And therefore we may initially think of the play as a collection of words rather than a series of actions, of things characters say, not what characters do. Even in a play's production, the first rehearsal – though it may be preceded with warm-up exercises or improvisations – will ordinarily be a reading of the text. Of the words. There is nothing inherently wrong with this – indeed, it is generally unavoidable – but it does place an immediate emphasis on the play's language rather than its actions. And all too often that emphasis bleeds through to the actual performance.

Speech act theory, however, explains that words are themselves actions. The theory, given that name by J. L. Austin, in his 1962 book *How To Do Things With Words*, was considered radical in its time but is commonly accepted today, and taught and debated in academic departments of literature, if not in theatre schools. But its core notion is one of significant theatrical consequence, as it asserts that human speech is not primarily a matter of transmitting meanings but of provoking actions and behaviors.

In Austin's terminology, the vast majority of spoken language is "illocutionary," by which he means it is a "performative act," an "utterance with force, such as informing, ordering, warning, undertaking." It is not simply the transmission of facts that might be proven right or wrong, but efforts, however tiny, to change some part of the world. "Most utterances," Austin concludes, "at their base, are performative in nature. That is, the speaker is nearly always doing something by saying something."

Austin went on in detail to define several varieties of illocutionary acts with which we needn't concern ourselves here. The point is that he discovered what actors have known since the beginning of the theatre's history: that most talking in real life is not merely exercising our vocal folds, or explaining facts, or describing the universe. It is rather our effort to make a favorable impact on various people, both real and imaginary, who surround us. It is an action, not a recitation of memorized material. And the same must be true of talking on stage.

This may seem so obvious as to be meaningless, but let me use an example. One of the exercises I give actors, often in the first class or workshop I have with them, employs this sentence from a speech of Lady Macbeth after she receives the letter from her husband that makes her begin plotting the murder of King Duncan: "Come thick night, and pall thee in the dunnest smoke of hell." Lady Macbeth is asking "Night" to come down and cover itself in the blackest of all cloaks – figuratively, a "pall," the sort of black velour cloth that is placed over a corpse, or over a chalice in Catholic liturgy which will indicate that it has been desanctified. After the actors practice the sentence once or twice, I ask them why Lady Macbeth says the word "thick" in the phrase, "Come thick night..." Their answers are usually, "because night is dark, because night is unthinking, because you can't see through night, or because, coming after seven syllables in an iambic pentameter line, Shakespeare needed more three syllables to finish it. But these are all attempts at explaining the *semantic meaning* or *poetic scansion* of the line. They may explain why Shakespeare might have written it, but not why Lady Macbeth would say it. The reason she uses the word "thick" must be because she thinks this will somehow seduce "Night" into "coming." Lady Macbeth is therefore *doing* something, not just *saying* something. She is trying to attract "Night" (perhaps the actual "Spirit of Night" – as ten lines earlier she says, "Come, you spirits that tend on mortal thoughts…") to come down to her. Or perhaps it is the God or Goddess of Night that she speaks to. But in any case, she is speaking to what she at least hopes is a sentient – i.e. potentially hearing and reacting – "night." Thus her line is performative, not explicative. It seeks a very real result from an actual – or at least spiritual – "being."

And, we in the audience, while not particularly interested in the precise meaning of the word "thick" in this context, are passionately interested in why Lady Macbeth says it. We are watching a play, not merely listening to a playwright's language. If the acting is successful – and the line meaningful – it will only be so because we can see Lady Macbeth (and the actor playing her) in *action*. How can she convince Night to come? Does she seduce it? (him? her?) Does she sensually stick her tongue all the way between her teeth as she starts the *th* in thick at the beginning of the word, or boldly cut off the vowel in the *ck* that ends it? Does she try to make the word sound "icky" (i.e. repulsive), so that Night will know that she's evil enough to perpetrate the deed she is contemplating. Whatever tactics she uses, Lady Macbeth must try her hardest to invoke the spirit of "Night" to come down and cover her foul deeds. Indeed this could be a life or death issue, for if night doesn't cover them, she and her husband will probably get caught in their murderous act.

Lady Macbeth does not in fact succeed in hiding the crime she commits. Nor, for that matter does Macbeth, though he later begs, "Stars, hide your fires, let not night see my black and deep desires." But we in the audience want to see, and find believable, both of these characters trying desperately to drape their castle in total darkness with these words that come out of their mouths.

And this is the core of speech act theory. Begun by Austin in the 1960s, it was taken up by the highest level of literary theory when adopted (in a revised manner) by deconstructionist Jacques Derrida in the 1990s. But of course theatre people have known about it for 3,000 years. It's only a shame that they haven't used it more often.

Acting is interaction

"Acting" is a word we use to refer both to stage acting and to offstage behavior (as in "acting strangely," or "a heroic act"). As we have seen, there is no solid line of demarcation between stage acting and offstage acting.

And almost all of our waking actions are interactions. They are communications with the world around us. From rising in the morning to falling asleep at night, our wakeful life is filled with millions of subtle and not-so-subtle attempts to communicate with our fellow beings – and sometimes our pets or even wild animals. When we are in public, we often smile at others when they catch our eye, or shift our eyes quickly away if we want to avoid them. We walk and dress in certain ways, exchange words, frowns, and raised eyebrows; we snort, chuckle, nod, and feign indifference hundreds of times a day in order to convey some message to someone, or even to rehearse conveying some message to someone. Even when we are alone and unseen in our living quarters, or in bathrooms by ourselves shaving or putting on makeup, we are interacting *in our minds* with the people that will, in the future, possibly drop into our living quarters, or see us on the street. We are rehearsing things we might say to our friends, or our bosses, or our loved ones. We are reading things we hope to be able to share with others we will shortly be seeing. And what links virtually all these interactions is that, consciously or unconsciously, they are *purposeful*, intended to favorably influence, in some way or other, the attitudes and behaviors of others.

Purposes

To say that we have purposes is not to say that we are always – or even mostly, or even occasionally – exploitive, manipulative, or aggressive. It is only to say that we, as a species, generally behave in ways that we think will be helpful to ourselves. We have underlying purposes and intentions which are directed toward increasing our own well-being. Such purposes are usually unconscious, habitual, and entirely benign – the "stuff" of ordinary human relations. We smile to engage others to smile back at us, we "stroke" (as psychologist Eric Berne put it)[6] our friends with special words in order to be similarly stroked in return. "How you doin'?" "Fine, how're you?" These common communications, when written, appear as inquiries into the other's current health, but they're mostly not. They are "strokes" that say, each to the other, "I'm happy to see you and hope you are happy to see me – and will be happy to see me in future days." It is a way of firming up our connections with others – and sometimes making new friends. These are powerful purposes; indeed, sometimes the most important things we can do to have a good life.

In the way that we walk down the street or into a room, or speak, or smile, or glare, or sit in a chair, we attempt to communicate information about ourselves that will attract the kinds of attention we wish, and which will dissuade the kinds of attention we don't wish. In fact, as the "first axiom of communication theory" has it, when we are in public, "we cannot *not* communicate."[5] We cannot *not* have interpersonal goals, purposes, and intentions behind our daily behavior.

It was an emphasis on the purposes and intentions of human behavior that distinguished the first great theory of stage acting, that of the Russian master Konstantin Stanislavsky. Stanislavsky's approach to acting, both as a performer and artistic director of the Moscow Art Theatre, and as the author of seminal books on the acting process, was that stage acting rests on the actor's discovery of the intentions and purposes of his character, and his successful "playing" of those intentions. There is hardly an acting theory or an acting teacher today who does not, at least in part, accept this view. I accept it. It is fundamental.

But the subject of character intentions is treated, by Stanislavsky and others, as separate from the subject of actors and audience. This has led to the basic

Stanislavskian notion of "being real" and "being heard in the back row" as independent tasks. Would it not be better if these tasks could be fully integrated in such a way that the character's intentions and the actor's technical demands could be part of the same whole – indistinguishable as the actor performs? Developing such an integration should be the primary task of every actor.

The role of an audience

What has created the apparent difficulties for the actor in trying to "live the life of his character" is, of course, the apparently artificial presence of a theatre audience. The audience, which is the theatre's truest necessity, also creates its most perplexing set of paradoxes. Whether it is a live audience, as at a stage play, or a hypothesized future one, as for a film, interactions that appear as communications between two characters are, necessarily, communications contrived for the benefit of others. Obviously, it is necessary to find a way around this dilemma, or else everything played onstage will have to be conceded as false, deceptive, affected, and hypocritical. Many people, of course, have found it so since the theatre's beginnings: the Greeks, we must remember, named the first actors *hypokrites*.

The route is this: audiences do not exist solely in the theatre, they exist in life. And we perform for them in life. When a sixth-grade teacher raises her voice and says "Stop that, Jimmy!" she is interacting with Jimmy but also performing for the class, letting them know they will be punished if they do whatever Jimmy has been doing. When Marilyn Monroe sang "Happy Birthday, Mr. President" to President Kennedy in a super-sultry voice, she was not just wishing the president a happy birthday, she was letting the whole world know she was having an affair with him – or at least was hoping to have an affair with him.

But let us take a more subtle and everyday example. A company manager walks into a large office and, passing the receptionist's desk, smiles and says "Good morning." This is a simple interaction – Eric Berne's "stroke". But suppose the manager believes that the company president may overhear the remark. In that case, it is quite possible that the manager's real purpose is to show the president that she – the manager – is building company morale. The "good morning" is then both a direct interaction with the receptionist and an indirect interaction performed for the president. "Sincerity" and "honesty" become irrelevant: the communication is equally three-way whether or not the manager is genuinely fond of the receptionist, or whether or not she is genuinely trying to build morale, and, indeed, whether or not it is actually a good morning. It does not even matter if the president is actually within earshot – only that the manager believes that may be the case. The purposes of the manager's comment are then two-fold: it is an interaction with the receptionist and a performance for the president. And this is what acting on stage is as well.

Interaction and performance

Interaction and performance, then, are basic and interwoven levels of communication in life as well as on the stage or before the camera. Performing, far from being simply a profession for the trained and talented few, is a continual activity in which we daily, routinely, and all but inevitably engage. We speak to be heard, of course, but often to be overheard as well. A student may ask a bright question in class both to get the answer from the professor (an interaction) and to show the rest of the class how bright he is (a performance). A director may speak sharply to an actor both to reprove the actor (an interaction) and to show the rest of the cast that she means business (a performance). Most conversations between three people generally take the form of a series of duologues, or interactions between two of the participants who are simultaneously "performing" for a third. Sincerity, candor, honesty – these are not necessarily at issue in "performing." But neither, necessarily, are hypocrisy, artifice, or contrivance.

Nor do words even need to be exchanged. Suppose a young woman is seated at a lunch counter, and a man sits down next to her. She is silent and immobile; onlookers might think she is not communicating at all, but that is not accurate. What she is communicating is the very clear message, "I do not wish to converse with you." At this level, her communication is simply an interaction – if a silent one – with the man next to her. But suppose that she expects her boyfriend to join her, and that he might even be approaching the door behind her at this very moment. In that case her silence and immobility is not merely an interaction with the man next to her, it is a performance for the boyfriend who may or may not be present. Whether her lack of interest in the man next to her is sincere, feigned, or ambivalent does not alter the fact that her apparent inaction conveys a multiple communication: a simultaneous interaction with the man and a performance for her boyfriend – and, indeed, for all the other people at and behind the counter who may be curious as to what may be going on.

Plays, which are essentially composed of human interactions, also represent human "performances" in exactly this sense. In *Hamlet*, for example, when Ophelia converses with Hamlet while knowing that Polonius and Claudius are eavesdropping behind her, she is clearly engaging in an interaction (with Hamlet) and, simultaneously, a performance (to her father and the King). And characters sometimes "perform" to the same person with whom they are directly interacting: Amanda, in Tennessee Williams' *The Glass Menagerie*, pretends to drop a handkerchief so that she can then grandly stoop and pick it up in front of Laura – "a piece of acting" on her part, says Williams' stage direction. Thus the "actor" playing Amanda is "acting a character who is acting," or "giving a performance" to emphasize the importance of her action.

Of course plays have theatre audiences as well. Ophelia is performing for Polonius and Claudius, and Amanda for Laura, but both are also performing to a group of public observers sitting in the theatre's "house." This, naturally, adds new levels to the problems of acting, but they are not wholly separate ones.

13

Performing simultaneously to an onstage audience (the other characters) and performing to the audience "in the house" are not contradictory or antagonistic acts. They can be integrated, and for the finest actors, they are integrated.

The integrated actor

When she gets onstage, the actor faces a great many levels of awareness. She must interact and she must perform. She must relate in some way to a text, a theatre, an audience, scenery pieces, costumes, props, the demands of her director, the behavior of her fellow actors, and the actions of the stage crew. She must also deal with possible distractions: the awareness of potential critics that may be in the audience, of the state of her own career, and of the offstage relationships she maintains – or wishes to maintain – with her fellow performers. She must deal with the anxieties of stage fright, vocal tension, physical clumsiness, the terror of forgetting her lines, of drying up emotionally, and – worst of all – of letting her confidence sag. She must be spontaneous without thinking about being spontaneous, and without overtly appearing to try to be spontaneous. She must work within a fixed script, and yet make the words seem to emanate from her own mind and not some long-ago printed text. She must create the play's character, and yet be sufficiently personal and idiosyncratic to seem humanly alive. She must fit into the play's style without losing her sense of humanity. She must be credible and, in the best sense of the word, theatrical. These are, quite obviously, hard tasks, and the rest of this book is devoted to how they can be accomplished.

Of course there are many actors who can "pull together" the various demands of acting quite naturally and unconsciously. At least there are many who claim to. Certainly there are gifts which, at the very least, place individual actors at different starting points.

But the importance of "natural talent" and "born knacks" can be exaggerated. In the first place, it is quite appealing for successful actors to portray their art as a matter of native talent rather than developed craft; it makes them seem casual and effortless in their artistry. In the second place, the spontaneous talent that John Wayne suggested he possessed might also be the reason why he and actors like him were often limited to a small range, modest in subtlety or brilliance. Very few of today's leading actors succeed with such a narrow repertoire of skills, or show contempt for the artistry of acting. For most actors, success is achieved through study, struggle, preparation, infinite trial and error, training, discipline, experience and hard work.

Much of that work is on the actor's movement and on her speech. Such work is best performed with experienced teachers, sometimes with the help of a good book. Two such books (by experienced teachers) are in the Notes at the back of this one.[7]

But much of the work is on the actor's mind. That is the deeper subject of this book. It is the mind, in its conscious and unconscious workings, that initiates all our actions – and our acting. The mind controls the actor's concentration, her pursuit of intentions, her portrayal of character, her adoption of style, her performance within the theatrical context. It is the mind which integrates the actor's tasks, which integrates the actor herself. And it is the mind that generates the actor's, and thus the character's, *thinking*.

"Everything you do on the stage has to come from your mind."

American actor Jason Robards[8]

Thinking

When we watch an actor, we want to see her not just speaking and moving. We want to see her *thinking*.

There are two kinds of thinking that are important for every actor, however. There is preparatory thinking which the actor undertakes while working up her role, both in her study and in rehearsal. And then there is in-performance thinking; thinking on stage, thinking while acting. The two are quite different processes. Preparatory thinking can be, depending on the actor's own techniques, analytical, psychological, philosophical, literary, scholarly and/or theatrical – and a great deal else besides. In-performance thinking, however, can be none of these. In-performance thinking, like life, is spontaneous, free-wheeling, and creative, even in the most rigid of plays and dramatic styles and characterizations. It is forward-looking, purposeful, and bright-eyed. It is an exciting, often thrilling mental activity.

When there are fundamental problems in acting – problems such as self-consciousness, distraction, dropping out of character or out of style, listening to oneself, failures of projection, of understanding, of emotional responsiveness – these problems are caused by mixing these two forms of thinking. By the actor's trying to think about too many things at the same time – too many contradictory things, such as "How do I win this person over?" and "How will the critics judge my performance?" In order to combat this, many actors try "not to think," and acting coaches and directors the world over may instruct them "Don't think! Just do!" But human beings simply cannot *not* think – anymore than they can willfully not hear, or not feel pinpricks. The fact is that people think continuously, and actors are people. The problems of acting do not require that actors stop thinking,

15

but that they find out *what to think about.* Then the thinking can be fully aligned with the actor's actions – and the actor's acting.

If the actor's thinking is properly aligned, her tasks are integrated. She can perform single-mindedly and with total commitment in plays that are highly complex, with characters that are highly unique, and in styles that range from the most natural to the most abstract. Properly aligned thinking can release an actor into absolute spontaneity, and can reveal her personal wholeness. Finally, properly aligned thinking can provide the actor with her most effective and affecting instrument: acting power.

Acting power. It is the power to move, to dazzle, to entertain, to charm, to astonish, to frighten, to delight, and to engage an audience from the play's beginning to its end. Power is "strength," of course, but it is also wit, grace, depth, charm and openness. It is the basis of true relaxation. It is the title and quest of this book.

"Acting is a matter of becoming aware that you are thinking, of knowing what it is you are feeling, then of controlling it any way you want."

American actress Ann Bancroft[9]

1

OUT OF THE SELF

"People have said to me, from time to time, that they admire my 'technique.' These comments aren't always complimentary because so often what people mean by 'technique' is some sort of artificial or mechanical approach to a role. The best definition of technique I know is this: that means by which the actor can get the best out of himself. It's as simple and as broad as that – and as personal and private."

American actor Hume Cronyn[1]

It is utterly obvious that the actor is at the center of his or her character. The playwright may provide the words, the director the staging and the costume designer the apparel, but it is the actor who implements the role with her voice, body, phrasings, timings, inflections, modulations, movements, expressions, emotions, authority, appeal and charisma – among the hundred or more qualities that might show up in a favorable review of the production. And these all begin as characteristics of the actor, who will shape and filter them into the characteristics of the character she plays. Getting the "best of oneself" onto the stage, as Hume Cronyn wrote, is therefore the actor's fundamental job.

But what is the self? Is it how we are seen? Or how (and what) we see? Is it us as an independent, self-contained body, or as a living cog in the great machine of life? What most controls our behavior: our personalities or the situations that surround us?

In real life, these are not easy questions to answer. Philosophers have debated for centuries whether character shapes situation or situation determines character.

It is sort of a chicken-or-egg debate, but one with important real-world implications, certainly in the arenas of criminal justice and international diplomacy. Did the thief commit the crime because he is a bad person or because he grew up in impoverished surroundings? Did the country invade its neighbor because it had evil intentions, or because it was defending its borders against enemies? Are the gang members in *West Side Story* "depraved on account of they're deprived" or is it the other way around? Often the answers simply depend on what side you're on. Other people, we often think, do certain things because of the nature of their characters. We ourselves, however, do what we do because our situations require it!

For the actor, fortunately, there need be no debate. From the actor's viewpoint, it is situation, not character, which is dominant. This is true for a simple reason: all people, and therefore all characters in plays, think about their situations, and what they want from them, more than about their own personalities or characters.

An experiment in social psychology makes this particularly clear.[2] Professors Edward Jones and Richard Nisbett, in 1971, invited a number of subjects to "rate" various individuals according to a standard scale of character traits: strong-willed to lenient, aggressive to mild-mannered, stingy to generous, and so forth. The individuals they were asked to rate included their fathers, their friends, Walter Cronkite (a famous television anchorman of that era), and, last of all, themselves. The subjects were also permitted, if they wished, to make the response "depends on situation" for any particular pairing of person and trait. The results showed something very interesting: the subjects, to an extraordinary degree, used the "depends on situation" option only for themselves, while for their friends, their fathers, and Mr. Cronkite, they were able to find fixed character attributes. The professors concluded that the human being is peculiarly egocentric in this regard: that human beings believe that "personality traits are things *other* people have." Conversely, from our own perspectives, we find ourselves to be innately flexible, natural spirits whose behavior springs not from any rigid personality attribute, but which "depends on our situation." Other people are the "characters" in our lives. We, on the other hand, behave according to the situations in which we find ourselves. The name for this is egocentricity. We are at the center of our lives; everybody else, therefore, is somewhere on our periphery.*

And so we do not walk around in daily life simply concentrating on our "characters," or who we are. Rather, we concentrate on our situations, and who *other* people are, and how we can successfully work them into our goals?

Thus, for an actor to bring a character to life, she must act like the living person her character is to represent. And to do that, she must concentrate

---

* No one should confuse egocentricity with egotism, the latter of which implies one thinks only – and highly – of oneself. Egocentricity and egotism are discussed more deeply in Chapter 3.

primarily on her character's *situation*, not her character's *character*. Like the person she plays, the actor must look outward and forward, not inward and back.

In playing a character, one plays from the vantage of the character's egocentricity. You play the character from the character's point of view, not from your own, or what you might think is the audience's. If you play Iago, for example, you don't play that you are the villain that the audience sees, but that you are the aide to Othello who should have been promoted to lieutenant, but was instead passed over by some stupid pretty boy named Cassio. If you play Molière's Alceste, you don't play the misanthrope that the play's title calls him, you play an intensely honest man who is surrounded by vilely pretentious and obsequiously flattering liars! Indeed, you will think of yourself as the one person in the play who does not think of himself as a "character," but rather as a normal and very proper human being who is responding to this terrible situation around you. And by focusing fully on this situation you, you will let the audience and the other characters see who you truly are (a misanthrope), even if your own character never will.

So playing "characters," therefore, really means responding to the situations one's character *confronts*. Everything that follows in this book – including the chapter on "playing character," is based on this fundamental understanding of human egocentricity.

"You can't ... say to yourself, 'I am playing a villain.' [The characters] don't think they are, anymore than heroes think that they're heroes. They're just who they are and this is what they want. It's other people that put that label. So you can't judge the character you're playing, ever."

British actor Alan Rickman[3]

Situation and context

The situation of the play is generally considered the situation that exists among the play's characters. That situation, however, exists within a higher-level framework: the theatrical context. This context may be a theatre, with perhaps a proscenium, scenery, lights, text, and audience or some other sort of configuration; or it may be any other medium of performing or performance art. But how does an actor concentrate fully on her character's situation without coming into mental conflict with the unavoidable awareness that she must also be heard in the back row? This is perhaps the most basic concern of the actor, a problem that baffled Stanislavsky, who could only resolve it by contradicting his own precepts.*

It is utterly solvable, however. Consider the professional athlete – a baseball player, for example. His two worlds are quite distinct. His context is the world of baseball; where three strikes make an out, a ball over the fence constitutes a home run, a successful season means a renewed contract for next year, and a good rapport with the local fans means negotiating points towards a raise in pay. This information is all true, but the player cannot directly think about any of it while he is up at bat. He can only think of hitting the ball, wherever it crosses the plate within the strike zone. If he's thinking about his salary, or his wife in the stands, he will almost certainly strike out.

The ballplayer does this by the conscious effort of concentration. He is entirely focused on the immediate situational factors: the score, the inning, the signals from his coaches, the number of outs, the men on base, the pitcher (and how refreshed or tired he might be), the exact positions and subtle movements of the infielders and outfielders, and a dozen other factors. Plus there are a number of intangible factors that describe his situation: the feel of the air, the sense of morale (both in his teammates and the opposition), the dampness of the ground, and the apparent fatigue, drive, and strategies of the other players. The player's concentration on these situational aspects of the game is total, at least as total as is humanly possible. It is this *complete absorption into an artificial situation* which creates the immense excitement that draws tens of thousands into the stands for every game, and millions more to their television sets.

But the ballplayer will win his contextual goals as a by-product of his concentration on his situational ones. If his concentration is absolute, and his power and talents come to his aid, he will gain the avid following of the crowds that watch him and the owners that pay him – even when his team loses. If, however, he goes straight for the contextual rewards – if he continually "plays to the audience" – he will not only lower his batting average, he will be accused of grandstanding, publicity-seeking, and show-boating. Such players rarely last as professionals.

Situational involvement is the only way to suppress contextual awareness. This is one of the great ironies of consciousness: that it is impossible, on strict command, to *not* think of something. If we are told, "Do not think of a purple giraffe," we cannot not think of it, because we first have to think about

---

* The great post-Stanislavsky Russian director, Anatoly Efros, was stunned when he read, in Stanislavsky's plan for *Three Sisters*, "To rouse the public, briskly pick up the tone. This is very important." "Here it is: 'to rouse the public!'" reports the bewildered Efros. "And this is written by Stanislavsky!? I want to call this to the attention of those who doubt that Stanislavsky ever wrote – 'to rouse the public.'" Anatoly Efros, *Beyond Rehearsal*, translated by James Thomas, New York: Peter Lang, 2009, p. 85.

what we are not to think about. Psychologist Gregory Bateson called this a "double-bind," because it is a command that is impossible to follow.* A simple and clear example would be a sign that said, simply, "Don't read this sign!" "Relax!" is a common double-bind, because relaxing means not trying to do anything at all, but being *commanded* to relax requires a conscious effort – which is the opposite of relaxation. "Act your age," as a little contemplation makes clear, is a clever variation of it; to give in to this command, you must become a child again.

The only way to suppress contextual awareness is to fill the mind with something else. In concentrating on the past few sentences, the reader has forgotten the purple giraffe, although that could not have been done by forgetting alone. The mind can only deal with one thing at a time; the mind's eye must have a single focus.

This is not at all to say that the actor is unaware of contextual matters – that would be as undesirable as it is impossible – but only that the actor cannot concentrate on them in performance. In Chapter 5 we will see how contextual considerations of performativity, driven into deeper areas of the mind, come forth at the proper time to inspire performance to its highest potential. But this can happen only when the situation is fully realized and can be fully played. Even then, the actor's concentration, her conscious in-performance thinking, is strictly devoted to the successful outcome of her character's situation – that is, to *winning*.

Winning

Situations are not static, they are dynamic. All life is fluid and relative; even in the world of science, since Einstein and Heisenberg, we are given to understand that the concept of "a moment in time" is a useless one.

The situation of the ballplayer, as he comes to bat, is a mobile and dynamic integration of moods, feelings, perceptions, contingencies, and ideas. These are events – hypothesized, feared, expected, or intended – which come together in the player's mind. They would be absolutely chaotic if they were not organized into some sort of useful structure – and they are. That structure is winning. Winning – the lust for victory – is the mindset which determines the way the player sees his situation, and how he acts upon it. For the professional player there is no need to dwell on the focus on victory, which has been immortalized

---

* The double-bind theory was first proposed by Gregory Bateson and others in 1956. Bateson holds that the double-bind is pathogenic, and is one of the main causes of schizophrenia – as when a mother continually double-binds a child, forcing him or her into crooked and stultified ways of thinking. Shakespeare, however, was familiar with the concept, as we see from Claudius' remark, in *Hamlet*: "Like a man to double business bound, I stand in pause where I shall first begin, and both neglect" (III, iii, 42–44). See Bateson, *Steps to an Ecology of Mind*, New York: 1972, esp. pp. 201–278.

by the late football coach Vince Lombardi into the professional athlete's credo: "Winning isn't the most important thing. It's the only thing." It is the athlete's concentration on winning that structures both the athlete's absorption and the spectator's fascination; if the fans feel the game is fixed, or the boxer they are rooting for is not trying to win with all he's got, they boo ferociously.

Of course, with the professional athlete, the "win" is a quantitative victory, with the rules of the game awarding so many points for such and such behavior. Also in sports, one person's victory is usually another person's defeat; in these ways sports remain an imperfect metaphor for life, and for the actor in theatre or films. But the primary parallel remains: in acting as in sports, situations become dynamic only when a victory is sought, when the actor pursues winning, and pursues it with vigor, with all of his or her acting power.

Life is not a game, however, and the field of life has an infinite number of goals, not just one on each end – and an almost infinite number of players. Winning in life is not necessarily a competition against individual rivals or rival teams. It more normally means fulfilling one or more self-designated goals. These stem from the basic human instincts: survival, love, happiness, health, validation, respect. All human beings direct their actions, sometimes effectively and sometimes not, toward goals they draw from those general human instincts. The universal foundation of a credible and inspiring performance – and this holds true in any character, in any production, in any theatrical style – is the accurate and compelling rendition of a character who, like all human beings, is trying to achieve fulfillment, satisfaction, love, happiness. The character may not know exactly what these may be; she may be inarticulate, psychotic, perverse, misguided, or bizarre, but she is after something that represents, to her at least, a victory.

The character may not ever get her victory, of course. Lady Macbeth doesn't get night to cover herself in a pall, and her husband doesn't get the stars to hide their fires, but they both *try*. Victories are left to the playwright to determine, or sometimes the director; it may even be better to say that the audience will determine who won and who lost, or maybe that nobody will do so. In the final analysis, "victory" is an abstract and perhaps ultimately elusive concept. "Classifying people as successes or failures is looking at human nature from a narrow biased point of view," observed Chekhov. "Are you a success or not? Am I? What about Napoleon? And your servant Vassily?"[4] The actor cannot determine that her character shall win. All she can do, in enacting her character, is to *try* to win. And that is because the character, when seen as a real person, is trying to win.

"For when the One Great Scorer comes
To mark against your name,
He writes – not that you won or lost –
But how you played the Game."

American sports writer Grantland Rice

So "getting into a character's situation" is a dynamic and focused concentration, with the focus on the character's hoped-for victories both long-range and short-range. The actor, getting into the character's situation, focuses on improving it. Her ultimate job is not to analyze but to act, not to understand but to *win*. This is what people's lives are all about, what characters' lives are all about, and what the actors must portray. The actor who shows a character not trying to win in a life situation will be as successful with the public as a boxer who throws fights.

"You are the spokesman for your character, you put his case. Are you going to win or lose? There'll be no drama if you look like a loser at the outset."

British actor Clive Swift[5]

There are certainly cases in which this is not as obvious as it may seem. There are characters in the dramatic literature of all periods who seem confused and defeated by life, bored, disgusted, against happiness, against love, and generally nihilistic. Inexperienced actors frequently jump to weak, even nihilistic interpretations of characters, often because they are relatively easy and personally unthreatening to play. But the deeper, positive victories are there to be pursued. The deaf, dumb and blind Helen Keller (in *The Miracle Worker*) is, all the while, trying desperately to speak. The awkward, pathetic Solyony in Chekhov's *Three Sisters* is desperately trying to woo Irina, to whom he can barely talk. Laura, in *The Glass Menagerie,* desperately hopes to marry Jim

O'Connor – and to cover over her disappointment when he tells her he is already engaged – even though she is 99 per cent certain she will fail in both efforts, which she does. The most disillusioned character has deep longings for joy; the most anti-romantic one has a deep need for validation; and the most confused character has a passion for clarity. Hamlet's insistence on taking up arms against a sea of troubles instead of taking his own life is, in itself, a defining act of that dramatic character, and likewise of the actor playing that role – at least until the end of the play. The quest for victory is what gives characters their spine, their vigor, their challenge to the other characters in the drama, and their excitement for the playgoer. It gives them what George Bernard Shaw called their "life force" and what I call their acting power. So the job of the actor is to find just what kind of victory can be wished, what kind of situational improvement can be sought, what kind of winning can be pursued, and then to put all her forces together to achieve it – whether or not her "character" will come out victorious in the end.

Goals

"It's the actor's duty to find out the most exciting way a role should be played, then to play that role to the hilt. This could mean bits of business, it could be underplaying, it could be climbing up and down the walls, it could be chewing up the scenery, but if he doesn't give it hell, make his characterization as complete and compelling as possible, he isn't fulfilling his function as an actor."

American actor Jack Lemmon[6]

"It's a matter of deciding: What does he want? And then you behave accordingly. It's not a matter of finding out what he feels; it's a matter of finding out what he wants. If you figure that out correctly, the feelings will arrive – and the characterization."

Swedish actor Max von Sydow[7]

When discussed in regards to acting, a character's *goal* is simply what the character wants at any given moment. Other common terms for it are *objective*, *intention* and *want*, but *goal* is in fact the most useful term in the classroom or the rehearsal hall, first because it is short and concise, and second, like a goalpost, it can be *physically* imagined – as, for example, the target a football player sees as he charges towards a touchdown. It is an active, physical target, not a philosophical one.

The goal is not what the *actor* wants (which is normally to be great in the part, to get a better role in the next production, and other such career goals) but what the actor's *character* wants. And a character's goals are always situational. They are the specific things – love, success, validation, friendship, victory – that the character wants to win. Virtually all schools of thought about acting agree on this, and on these cardinal principles:

1 The actor must play goals, not attitudes or indications.
2 There is a hierarchy of goals, including big ones that exist throughout the play (super-goals), general long-range ones (regular goals), and small, moment-to-moment ones (sub-goals).
3 Goals are only positive. As the traditional maxim has it, "You cannot play a negative objective."

Principle One means that the actor must concentrate on improving her character's situation, rather than attitudinizing, posturing, or indicating to the audience that she is the character. The baseball player, for example, plays baseball; he does not try to look like a baseball player. Hamlet tries to get the support of his friends and the aid of the Players, to change his relationship with Ophelia and his mother, and to unseat his uncle and confuse Polonius; what he does *not* do is go around trying to look like a melancholy Dane.

Principle Two implies that some victories are more long-range and general than others. The need for love, for example, might dictate a drive for Romeo to wed Juliet, which might dictate a wish for him to gain the support of Friar Lawrence, which might then make him want to have the Friar marry them: The first is a super-goal, the last a sub-goal in this hierarchy, and there may be many graduated steps in between.

And Principle Three indicates that goals should all be phrased in their positive aspects – in terms of things the character wants to do, rather than things the character wants not to do. This is simply a matter of perspective. If you want to avoid the cold, your goal is to find warmth; both goals are correct, but only the latter can be played with focused power and intensity. Playing what you *want to get* is a lot more exciting, for both the actor and the audience watching her, than playing what you simply want to prevent.

Obstacles

Why doesn't your character achieve his or her goals right away? Obviously, because there are obstacles blocking your path. This is what makes drama dramatic. Without obstacles, there would be no drama, and therefore no play. Julius Caesar may, in real life, have said "*Veni, vidi, vici*" ("I came, I saw, I conquered"), but in Shakespeare's play he came, he saw, and he was assassinated.

You may feel, when you are alone at night meditating on your failures, that some obstacles are buried deeply within your own personality: You may worry that you are not smart enough, fast enough, big enough, rich enough, or pretty enough to win your goals. But you rarely think about these in broad daylight, when you're wide awake and your goals are right before your eyes. This is when you become, or try to become, a man or woman of action. This is where it is *other* people who are in your way – getting the jobs, getting the guys, getting the gals, getting ahead and, you are quite sure, having a lot more success and a lot more fun than you are. This is when melancholy meditation turns into strategizing and action. Conquering your obstacles and winning your passionately hoped-for victories consume your thoughts. Finding the ways to surmount the barriers which seem to stand between you and your future – and therefore between your character and *her* future – fills your mind. Your goal is then twofold: overcoming your obstacles and winning your goals. And so should this be for actors playing characters – if they are anything like you.

Many or most of a character's obstacles, of course, will be other characters. In the tragedies of ancient Greece, the principal characters were labeled the *protagonist* (main character) and one or more adversaries, called *antagonists*. In Sophocles' *Oedipus Rex*, for example, Oedipus is the protagonist (essentially the principal character) and Creon (his brother-in-law) and Tiresias (a prophet) are, at times, his antagonists. The antagonism between these characters becomes the crux of the play; the goals of each stand in the way of the other's hopes and dreams. In modern American plays and films, such paired roles continue: Blanche and Stanley in *A Streetcar Named Desire*, Willie and Biff in *Death of a Salesman*, and Roy Cohn and Ethel Rosenberg in *Angels in America*. Drama requires conflict, and while such focused protagonist/antagonist confrontations may be less common today than in the past, the antagonistic confrontations of characters on the stage is always what glues the audience to their seats.

Past, present and future

Achieving one's goals, though conceived in the past and pursued in the present, is aimed at the future. All three timeframes are in the mind of the character, and therefore must be in the mind of the actor playing that character as well. But the future is the most important. That is where victory – if it is to be achieved – lies. That's what we're looking towards, and that's what we think about the most.

Neuroscientist Rodolfo R. Llinás writes that there is a "sense of future inherent to sensorimotor images, the *pulling* toward the action to be performed. From the earliest dawning of biological evolution it was this governing, this leading, this pulling by predictive drive, *intention*, that brought sensory motor images – indeed the mind itself – to us in the first place."[8] It is in the future – the *pulling* toward the action – where the character's mind – and hence the actor's – must truly live.

In real life, however, the future is unknown. And here is where the actor must face her greatest conundrum: while the actor knows the character's future, her character does not. The actor who plays Hamlet knows before the play begins that Claudius has killed his father. He will know that Polonius will be hiding behind the arras in the third act, that Ophelia will kill herself in the fourth act, and that he himself will be poisoned to death in the fifth act. The *character* of Hamlet knows none of these things, however. Indeed he could barely imagine them ever happening. All Hamlet has is his *hopes*, which are constantly changing. Playing Hamlet's sheer ignorance of these coming events – when the actor playing the role has read and rehearsed them for weeks, and knows that most of the audience knows them as well – is one of the actor's most difficult, and unappreciated, assignments. For all the actor can play is his character's hopes, his doubts, and his fears.

"I doubt myself the way everybody else does. The thing I loved about doing Hummel [the title character in *The Training of Pavlo Hummel*] was this kid was inept at everything but he had this great hope. He had hope and I loved him for it. I loved to show that desire."

American actor Al Pacino[9]

The past

It is essential for actors, at least those in a relatively realistic and narrative drama, to determine the important elements of their characters' pasts: where they grew up, what sort of education they had, the basics of their romantic and professional histories, and the events that led up to the situation as of the time the play begins. Actors often call this their "backstory" – which they can discover through research and analysis of the script and perhaps historical sources, and through their imaginations. And often they will do this in concert with the director and each other. Macbeth and Lady Macbeth, for example, should come to some decision as to whether or not they have had children together so that they are thinking about the same topic when Lady Macbeth says "I have given suck, and know / How tender 'tis to love the babe that milks me." I am fully aware of the mocking question of "How Many Children Had Lady Macbeth?" that literary critic L.C. Knights posed in 1933[10] – Knights's answer being that the question is totally irrelevant to a fictional character – but actors playing these roles simply cannot be so blithe as to ignore it. "Performers do actually have to answer [that question] for themselves and their audiences," says Sian Thomas, who played Lady Macbeth in Dominic Cook's 2004 RSC production. "It is a subject that simply cannot be avoided or left unresolved by the two actors playing husband and wife," says Simon Russell Beale, who played opposite Emma Fielding in John Caird's 2005 London production.[11] Whatever Lady Macbeth means, Macbeth must be seen to understand what she's saying, since the two married characters must each be responding to the same event. It is likewise essential in *Much Ado About Nothing* for the actors playing the lovers Beatrice and Benedick to make some joint decisions about their backstory themselves – what their relationship had been before the play begins – even if they previously have had different interpretations of it, and, like the Macbeths, they will have to create this backstory because Shakespeare has provided only the most tantalizing wisps of clues.

But going into exhaustive details of a character's past, and writing long biographies of the characters one plays – as directors and acting teachers often proposed in earlier decades – does not seem to me a very important task. The play takes place in the present (even flashbacks are performed in the present), and it is aiming for the future. In real life, particularly during moments of high conflict as we see in dramatic stagings, we are almost never thinking of our pasts. Rather, we are immersed in the present and thinking entirely of our future: Will he hit me? Is she going to give in? Who is he in love with now? What is she trying to tell me?

And it is unclear – particularly in this post-Freudian age, as we will see in a moment – that understanding of our pasts gives us a great deal of help in finding the causes of our problems or the solutions to our futures. As Professor Paul Watzlawick reports, "the search for causes in the past is notoriously unreliable … The most appropriate strategy … is a search for pattern in the here and now rather than for symbolic meaning, past causes, or motivation."[12] Looking at her character's behavior from the here and now perspective, the actor can more easily isolate and focus the impetus of her character's actions.

The present

Most people, most of the time, live in the present – and so should actors. Plays are performed in the present, and take place in an imagined present. The word "now" appears in Shakespeare's plays nearly 3,000 times, 600 times more than the word "then," which refers to both the past *and* the future. It is therefore no surprise that "being in the moment" is the most common actor's desire in the current theatrical lexicon (replacing "being present," "being alive," "being in the now," or "being in the here and now" – the equivalent phrases in earlier backstage jargon). The present is simply where the action is.

And everything in the present, everything we are doing, is happening for the first time.

"When you are performing, it's never happened before. It's happening for the first time at that moment."

American actor Stacy Keach[13]

But what *is* the present? It is only an imaginary line that divides the past from the future. It is only a second – no, a millisecond – no, a microsecond – no, it is a *micromicromillimillisecond*! And not even that! When we say to someone, "Here we are!" by the time we say "are" our having said "Here" is already in the past – and an instant later so is the word "are." For as the ancient Greek philosopher Zeno discovered in one of his famous paradoxes, the "present" does not even exist. Speaking in less paradoxical and more common-life terms, the seventeenth-century French philosopher Renée Pascal noted that, "We almost never think of the present, and when we do, it is only to see what light it throws on our plans for the future." So now we must turn to the future, because that is what the character – and hence the actor – is actually facing when being "in the moment."[14]

The future

One of the reasons why directors and acting instructors may ask actors to write the biographies of their characters, and explore – and even make up – their character's past history, is to better understand the grounding of that character's motivations, ideas, and influences. And indeed, delving into a patient's past was the common practice of Freudian psychoanalysis throughout most of the twentieth century. Freud's technique was to have his patients (*analysands*) lie on a couch, their backs to him, and pour out their past lives in the hopes that he and they would find ways of resolving the problems that had led them to seek treatment. Such psychoanalytic treatments could last for years.

Psychoanalysis, however, lost much of its popularity even before the current century. Today, psychotherapists generally favor short-term cognitive/behavioral therapies, which spend little time searching through a patient's past and concentrate, rather, on helping patients learn and practice new skills that will help them cope with real-world situations. Such treatments, ordinarily, do not last more than a few weeks. And one of the central techniques of current psychotherapy is not to question patients on their pasts, but on their hopes and plans for the future.

This makes sense for actors as well. During a performance, the actor rarely thinks of the character's past and almost never, except in a rare soliloquy, concentrates on it. This is because people rarely concentrate – when they are around others at least – on analyzing their pasts. And for actors who are playing people, as most do most of the time, they have to be seen *thinking* as people – not as dramaturgs poring over the meanings of the play. The dramaturg's job – and it is an important one – is to analyze the characters and their problems, but the actor's job is to analyze how to *play* the character and try to *solve* his or her problems. The dramaturg sees the character from the outside; the actor *is* the character and is inside the character. The actor therefore doesn't see the character; she sees *what the character sees* – which is rarely herself. Indeed, the one thing humans can never see, without a mirror at least, is their own eyes – and what is going on behind them.

Motivations and goals

When I was in graduate school in the 1960s, the term *goal* was not used very much; indeed, I don't remember it being used at all. The going word at the time was *motivation*, particularly in what was known as Method Acting. "You must have a motivation," Method teachers told their students. "What's my motivation?" actors would ask their director.* Now the actor is more likely to say "What's my goal?" or "my intention" or "my objective." But what is the difference? Aren't motivations and goals the same things?

They are but they aren't. *Motivations* come from the past. *Intentions* and *goals* are envisioned in the future. They refer to the same sort of things, but from totally opposite perspectives.

Determinism and cybernetics

Motivation results from thinking deterministically. Determinism holds that every action (or "effect") is the result of a preceding action (or "cause"). There

---

* And if the director was anti-Method, he would simply answer "Your paycheck!" This exchange never happened in real life, of course; it is only the oldest backstage joke in the American theatre world.

is nothing wrong with cause-determined thinking. It is at the heart of Freud's psychology, Newton's physics, and Pasteur's medical microbiology. The Industrial Revolution could not have taken place without Newton's Second Law of Motion, and untold millions of lives have been saved by Pasteur's realization that germs cause disease. Newer thinking systems, however, taking into account twentieth-century physics, intracellular biology, information theory, post-Freudian psychology and cognitive science tend to replace many of our set, deterministic perspectives with future-oriented ones. We call future-oriented thinking *cybernetic*, from the Greek word for "good at steering." The term was coined by mathematician Norbert Weiner in 1948, when he realized that "teleological [goal-oriented] mechanisms" were far more critical than deterministic ones in advancing the then-nascent field of computer programming and technology.[15]

A quick example will make this clear. "Why did the chicken cross the road?" People fumble for an answer. They may then come up with something like "Because his mother made him." That's a deterministic conclusion, and it seems (and is) totally arbitrary – nobody can really tell if that's the reason or not. "To get to the other side!" we gleefully shout. That is the cybernetic answer. It is clearly correct. It is also simple: it is certainly what the chicken would give as his answer, if the chicken could talk.

It would have been easier to get the chicken's answer, however, to have asked not "Why did the chicken cross the road?" but *What* did the chicken cross the road *for?*" "Why?" demands an answer from the chicken's past; what made the chicken cross the road. "What for?" asks for an answer from the chicken's future: what did the chicken *want*. The deterministic question "Why?" assumes that there is some reason from the chicken's past that made him cross the road, but there is no evidence that this is the case. By asking the cybernetic question "What for?" the questioner is assuming *the chicken was thinking for itself*.

And, to drive this to a close, that's how we want actors to be. Thinking for themselves. Thinking about their potential futures. Thinking what they *want* – and how they can achieve it.

Freudian psychoanalysis seeks its answers from the patient's past, and trusts that the therapist will find them. Cognitive/behavioral therapies seek them from the patient's imagined future, and encourages the patient to find them. Both systems can be valuable. But actors are not patients. They are *actors*. And to be truly successful they must act, must be seen *thinking* their way through their characters' problems, and *imagining* the unlimited possibilities in their futures rather than worrying about the past lives that they can never change. Cybernetic thinking tends to be more accurate in complex systems (of which human thinking is surely the most labyrinthian), and it is far more useful in living, ongoing systems that cannot be fixed and frozen for analysis (as on a psychiatrist's couch – or an autopsy table) without severe alteration. The trend toward cognitive/behavioral therapies is a mark not only of changing thoughts about psychotherapy, but changing thoughts about thinking, and the use of the term "goal" (or "objective"

31

or "intention") in lieu of "motivation," and of "what for?" (instead of "why?") have now come to the fore in acting vocabularies.*

"I never know what my motivation is from one day to the next, so why should my character?"

American actress Sigourney Weaver[16]

The man and the bear

Let me simplify the importance of an actor approaching a role cybernetically (and actors need not know this term) instead of deterministically. A cybernetic approach focuses on feedback from the future rather than causes from the past. It is the best possible approach for the actor because it is the analysis that her character would make, and that we ourselves make minute by minute in our daily lives. Look at this illustration:

Most people asked to say what this shows would answer "It is a man running away from a bear." This is a normal deterministic explanation: The bear is the cause and its effect is to make the man run away. And because they are outsiders looking

---

* In many languages, such as French, Italian and Spanish, the English word "why" (respectively *pourquoi, perché* and *por que*) specifically means "what for?"

at the drawing, this is the most usual first-reaction description they would give to this scene.

The man running, however, would not be thinking this. He would be thinking, "How am I ever going to make it into this cabin?" "How am I going to open the door when I get there?" "What am I going to do if the door is locked?" At the moment of running for his life, the man is not thinking about what "caused" him to be where he is, or how the bear happened to be where the bear is. He is totally concentrating on how he can save himself. He is glancing at the terrain under his feet, hoping to avoid tripping over rocks or roots between him and the door. He is staring at the door knob, calculating which hand he will be reaching out to open it with. In short, he is planning his future – the next few seconds of it – and making contingency plans in case his first plans don't work ("If the door is locked, I'll climb on the roof!" "If the door falls off its hinges, I will use it as a weapon!"). The man, therefore, is lunging into his own future, and the actor playing that man must be lunging into that man's future as well.*

In another perspective, we might say that the man is being "pulled" by the door, just as he is being "pushed" by the bear. This is not literally the case, of course, but it is often the case in our minds. We feel "drawn" to a painting we admire, or to a cute baby or puppy dog walking down the sidewalk, or to a person on whom we are developing a romantic crush. We are pulled in various directions by new expectations of delight, joy, and excitement. And we are being pulled willingly.

We feel pushed much less often than pulled, but when we are pushed it is usually an awful feeling. We feel helpless, directionless – we have no target to look forward to. Being pushed basically consists of being said "no" to; we are forced to *not do* something, not do something we think we would enjoy doing. And being pushed from one direction without being pulled by another is truly horrific. Such depictions in plays – generally of torture or mental collapse – are rare and extremely brief. Ninety-nine per cent of the time, active people feel pulled, not pushed. And 99 per cent of the time, the actors that play people should feel so as well.

One of the greatest advantages of seeing action as being pulled rather than pushed is that pulling is a far more accurate process, as any child with a toy wagon knows. Accuracy in pushing depends on the interrelated assortment of many different vectors: in order to push a wagon (with freely rotating axles) it is necessary to push from at least two vantages with each force precisely counterbalancing the others. To pull the wagon, by contrast, requires only a single rope and no counterbalancing at all. In analyzing behavior in terms of the

---

* The "man running from bear" illustration and discussion is from the first edition of *Acting Power*. Rodolfo R. Llinás subsequently used a similar metaphor: "swimming away from a shark, you will try to get to shore and...probably not be thinking to yourself, 'Here I am swimming away from a shark.'" *I of the Vortex*, Cambridge: MIT Press, 2001, p. 23.

"pushing" of past motivational causes, we are forced to reckon with literally billions of incidents, traumas, memories, pushes, and shoves the flesh is heir to; this makes interpretation, in all but a handful of cases, mired in excess data. Being "pulled" by your character's goal, by contrast, allows your character to focus every one of her powers on her goal – and your own acting power as well.

It is vital for actors to make the reorientation from deterministic to cybernetic thinking, for it is the central mechanism by which an actor moves from *understanding* a character to *playing* the character and bringing the character to life. It is the process by which the actor enters into the character's mind, and sees with the character's eyes. Three key reminders will focus the actor's attention on this reorientation:

- Seek the *purposes* rather than the causes of your character's behavior.
- Do not ask "Why?" – ask "*What for?*"
- Look to your character's future; do not obsess about her past.

Why do we say "purposes?" It is occasionally comfortable in life to say that we have no purposes. Purposes often threaten others, and are confused with ambitions and schemes. It is certainly more pleasant to think of one's crying as "caused" by hurt feelings rather than "intended" to induce guilt. The child caught stealing a piece of candy will cry "Jimmy made me do it!" to imply he was "caused" to commit this misdemeanor instead of acknowledging that he "wanted" the candy, and thus gives a "why" response rather than a "what for." But the "what for" is the real inspiration for the deed, and the actor will always be better off by exploring, with frankness, the intentional and purposeful nature of her character's acts – even the most unconscious and seemingly innocent actions of sympathetic and innocent characters.

Feedback and the feedback loop

Feedback is the governing principle of cybernetic systems and of the actor-character's behavior when viewed cybernetically. Feedback, essentially, is information we seek to guide us in pursuit of our intentions. It is our radar. A common example of feedback in a cybernetic system is the thermostat on a heater; the heater goes on when feedback reveals the temperature is too low, and off when feedback reveals the opposite. A cybernetic system, therefore, is a *self-correcting* system rather than a continuously correct one. Space missiles are a great example of cybernetic self-correcting systems. When Jules Verne wrote *Rocket to the Moon* in the nineteenth century, his rockets, he assumed, could only reach their destinations by having been precisely aimed at their targets at lift-off. A billionth of a degree off in any direction, and the rocket would fly aimlessly into space. Modern missiles, however, are simply aimed upwards at lift-off; there, aloft, they begin to send and receive continuous feedback from their intended destinations, which allows them to revise their courses, second by second, and re-aim their trajectories so as to make an exact landing on the specified spot on the selected heavenly body. Once again, "pulling" an object from its intended target rather than pushing it from its point of departure is far more accurate.

The feedback loop becomes a cycle of information-exchange in any communication system, or any interaction. When two people talk, a simple feedback loop is engaged, in which both people are sending and receiving information to and from each other. Both of them, following their goals, seek the information which will guide them in improving bad situations – and in maintaining or improving good ones. A feedback loop is always engaged when people are conscious of each other's existence: Once again, one cannot not communicate. To remain "un-communicative" is itself a communication: it implies dislike, disapproval, or a variety of other similar feelings and informational bits. In the feedback of a common interaction – an ordinary conversation for example – literally thousands of signals are transmitted and received every minute. These include conscious verbal dialogue, conscious non-verbal signals (shrugs, winks, gestures), and the unconscious and autonomic behaviors of our physiology; behaviors of which we are all skilled observers and interpreters. We all know, for example, how to understand the way another person's breathing shifts when he or she is engaged with us in an affair (political, business, or romantic). We know how to read the hesitations, grimaces, nervous laughs, studious looks, eyebrow archings, flesh reddenings, eye moistenings, nostril flarings, and chin juttings of our friends, rivals, parents, and real or imagined lovers. Whether these behaviors are consciously or unconsciously generated may be a subject of controversy case-by-case; that they are all part of the feedback of information which makes us adjust our behavior toward the satisfaction of our intentions – and sometimes to adjust our intentions as well – is quite certain.

The actor who gets into her character's situation, therefore, gets into her character's feedback loop. Like the character she plays, she both sends and receives a great spectrum of information which guides her toward the fulfillment of her goals and super-goals. This is essentially what Stanislavsky meant by the actor "living the part," which could be perhaps more specifically described as "living the character's life," or experiencing the character's interactions. The mechanism for doing this may be called *making contact*. And this will be the primary subject of Chapter 2.

Summary of Chapter 1

In this chapter, we have looked at some fundamental principles of how an actor may approach a role. These include prioritizing situation over context, goals over motivations, and the future over the past. It suggests the actor focuses on winning victories, and pursuing the victories that will lead to them – whether or not the character wins them in the play. And it asks the actor to develop a cybernetic rather than a deterministic understanding of the character's actions and behavior.

What we have *not* done so far is specified how the actor might do this in working with other people – his or her fellow actors. This is the topic of the following chapter, which will include some "fantasy exercises"* that will help make this process bear practical results.

* See the Notes on page xvi.

2

INTO THE OTHER

Humans are social animals. Interactions with others are a major part of our waking lives from infancy on, and draw out our most powerful feelings. Babies left untended for hours on end in understaffed orphanages rarely develop vibrant lives. Solitary confinement, recent studies show, often leads to severe mental deterioration. "Can it be coincidental that almost all of our emotions make sense only in relation to other people?" asks famed neuroscientist V.S. Ramachandran, who goes on to say, "Pride, arrogance, vanity, ambition, love, fear, mercy, jealousy, anger, hubris, humility, pity, even self-pity – none of these would have any meaning in a social vacuum."[1]

Exercise: The fisherman

This is a one-minute exercise I sometimes use just to make a point. I ask actors to act the role of a fisherman. Virtually everybody who knows anything about fishing will know how to put an imaginary hook on an imaginary line, and, with a pole, cast the line into an imaginary river. But there they stop. The exercise is over, they think. But I say nothing. They look at me in discomfort. "Fish!" I say, a bit sternly. They look around at the others and get even more discomforted. "Catch the damn fish!" I say, this time quite sharply. Then they get it. They start to move their imaginary pole around a bit, try to sense the possibility of fish in the stream, and where they might be. They soon make imaginary tugs on their imaginary lines, when they feel imaginary nibbles. They now *want* to catch fish. Because that's what a fisherman does – he doesn't just want to throw bait into the water. The exercise immediately differentiates between playing the goal of catching fish rather than just demonstrating that the actor is supposedly a fisherman. The situation is lived, not merely shown. And the actor will be *interacting* with fish, albeit imaginary ones.

This fishing metaphor has a great many applications. We often think of certain things we say as "fishing" comments: that we are "fishing" for a compliment, for example. To an extent of which we are seldom aware, however, almost all of our communications "fish" for some sort of response. Many scene acting problems can be solved by the coach, or director, by simply asking the actor to play her scene, or line, as if she were "fishing for" something rather than "demonstrating" something. This prods the actor to employ the ever-present future goal – rather than past-determined motive – as the reason for the action taken.

And it prods the actor to interact – with a fish! Or with what she hopes may be a fish. She seeks feedback from the fish. She sends messages to the would-be fish and seeks for messages in return. She gets out of herself, and into the other. She is interacting. She is developing a relationship.

Plays and films are invariably about interactions and relationships. Even one-character plays contain interactions with others. In Jay Presson Allen's *Tru*, about Truman Capote, the solo performer of the title role talks directly to the audience, and also to others on the telephone. Samuel Beckett's *Krapp's Last Tape* portrays Krapp talking alternately into his tape recorder (for the benefit of his potential future listeners) and to the audience. Willy Russell's *Shirley Valentine* shows his title character speaking to an imagined "wall" which the playwright conveniently places in the audience. Even in Franz Xavier Kreutz' *Request Concert* – in which the solo character comes home to her apartment, cooks her dinner, uses the toilet, watches television, turns off the lights, and then commits suicide, all without speaking a word or being spoken to – there is interaction, although we do not see it until the play's end: she has been preparing her apartment and her suicide to convey a message to whomever discovers her body.

The interactions of human beings in life range from casual social strokes, as we discussed in the previous chapter, to more intense actions of debate, discussion, seduction, competition, and battle. They also include acts of investigation, discovery, and, above all, efforts to shape the thoughts and feelings of others. These are the interactions we commonly see performed in dramatic presentations. Most often, the interactions we see and in which we participate in our daily lives are not overtly intense, for in general we want people to like us, to feel comfortable with us, and to accept our presence and enjoy our company – even if we are simply nodding politely at a stranger on the street. But when conflicts arise, as they do in all plays, the "shaping of the thoughts of others" is what acting is mainly about. Other characters in the play, indeed, may be your character's major obstacles. You – and thus your character – will have to try to overcome them to win your goals. You will have to try to get around them, get past them, and even *beat* them. These efforts, more than anything, are what make drama exciting.

And there is no way to do this without making contact. Which you can do in any number of forms.

Oral contact

"Listen, listen, listen, really listen. You think you're listening,
but you really have to work at it."

British actress Vanessa Redgrave[2]

One of the first things actors are taught, often in high school drama classes, is "simply" to listen to the other actors. But that is not as simple as it sounds. After dozens of rehearsals and performances, with your fellow actors saying the same lines every time, you may have trouble really listening to them when you know your next line or action (or so you think) is a long way off.

If you can't do this, however, you will never be a great actor or even a good one. Just listening to what the other characters are saying – *as if you were hearing it for the first time* – is one of the most important things an actor must do.

Yet it is crucial that the actor do more than "just" listen. What is really important is not what the actor listens *to* but what she listens *for*. Listening, certainly in an even mildly contentious situation between two or more characters, is a focused activity. It has a purpose – which comes right out of your character's goals. You are of course listening to the content of the other character's remarks in order to see how you can make them helpful in fulfilling your goal. But you are not only listening to the other actor's words. You are also studying her inflections, her hesitations, her tone of voice, her searching for the right word, her confidence – or lack thereof. If these seem supportive you will wish to press your case more enthusiastically. If they seem antagonistic or disrespectful, you will probably be planning your withdrawal – or your counterattack – long before she has finished speaking.

Inflections of words often say more than the words themselves. Just saying someone's name can convey a lot of messages beneath the words. If you say, for example "Ellen" briskly, with a loud high pitch on the first syllable and a lower, quieter pitch on the second, as:

ELL- ↘

-len!

you will convey that you're excited to see Ellen, you like her, and if you have news to tell her, it will be good news.

But if you do the opposite, starting with a low your pitch on your first syllable and both raising and stressing it on the second, slowing down between them, like this:

you will convey a certain suspicion, as if you were surprised to see her here, or asking her something like "what's the matter?"

Worst of all, if you give the name a "dipped" inflection in the middle, starting at a high pitch and with a strong stress, then dropping the pitch, and slowly bringing it up again and drawing it out at the end, as:

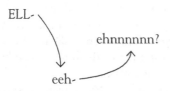

then you are signaling strong disapproval of whatever Ellen is doing: questioning her judgment and making clear that you want her to do something different next time.

These three wildly different messages are delivered unconsciously, but they are clearly *delivered*, and while they have no semantic content (presumably Ellen already knows her name), they have powerful *interactive* force. Indeed, relationships can flourish, survive or even end solely on the basis of such inflections between characters – in life or on the stage.

The point of contact between characters, and hence actors, is therefore not passive. And it does not end at the other character's skin. When you speak to people, your sound enters their ears and rebounds through their skulls; sometimes it vibrates in their bones, sometimes they can even feel it in their bellies. When you speak to a character, you try to *penetrate* her. If you succeed, the actor playing that character will actually *feel* the sound inside her. She will feel its vibrations – because, of course, sound is entirely composed of vibrations – and these are physical, not just mental. One of the hidden dimensions of speech act theory is simply that speech is a *physical* communication as well as a verbal one.

But maybe that character is (perhaps because of the playwright's or the director's intention) not listening to the actor speaking at all, but rather listening to the birds outside, or the music playing in the other room, or just the sounds in her own head. Each actor *tries* to penetrate the other characters, but he or she does not always succeed. At the beginning of Tennessee Williams' *Cat on a Hot Tin Roof*, Maggie is putting on makeup while giving a long speech to her husband Brick, behind her. But Brick, an alcoholic, is not listening to her at all – rather, he is listening for the "click" that comes into his head when he is sufficiently drunk to cut the sound of her voice out entirely. In Chekhov's *Three Sisters*, Vershinin and Tusenbach are trying to entertain a group of friends and family gathered in the sisters' home by talking – eloquently, they think – about the future of their country, when they suddenly realize that everyone else has fallen asleep. The actor must *try* to penetrate the others, but her character may not succeed.

Actors must then not merely passively contact their partners on stage; they must try, proactively, to penetrate them. But listening is simply one aspect of this contact. Seeing is another, and in most cases the more important one.

Eye contact

When I was a boy, I took boxing lessons. This was at a time when boxing was still a mainstream sport: colleges had boxing teams, and boys in my hometown of Washington, D.C. would hang around Goldie's Gym and learn how to make the left jab, the right cross, the uppercut, and, when they had more experience, Kid Gavilan's famous bolo punch.

What I learned from my boxing lessons, however, was not punching so much as *seeing*. I was taught to train my eyes fiercely on my opponent, to scan his every muscle and every twitch, and try to figure out the strategies that lay behind every shift of his head and target of his gaze. I was trained to make decisions by the millisecond: to "hit him when he blinks" and throw the right cross at just the moment his left hand started to droop. The most important muscles in boxing, I discovered, were not in the upper arms but in the eye sockets.

It is the same in acting. The eyes of the audience are merely receptive; they are taking in the play. The eyes of the actor, however, are active. They are taking in the other characters and deciding, on the spot, what they must *do* with their eyes. They do not use their eyes merely to passively see what's around them, but rather to *investigate* their situations and discover the best paths to achieve their goals. It is not a matter of looking *at* the other characters, but looking *for* clues inside the characters' brains. Actors must dig into each other's minds, trying to sense their opinions, discover their loyalties and weaknesses, and engage the support of neutral observers – even complete strangers – who may be in their presence. And the actor's subsequent actions are, in part, based on what they find in their search for clues.

"The closest thing to acting is bullfighting or boxing. It's a matter of adjusting to the other man's blows. You're so busy adjusting it's difficult to think of anything else."

Mexican/American actor Anthony Quinn[3]

For we only really see what we are looking *for*, not what we are looking at. This was brilliantly demonstrated in a famous 1999 experiment conducted by Christopher Charmis and Daniel Simons. These cognitive neuroscientists made a short film showing two teams – one in white shirts and the other in black ones – as they were passing basketballs back and forth. They then asked subjects they had engaged to watch the film to count how many passes were made by the white-shirted team. But the film also included a woman wearing a gorilla suit, who crossed the court, passing blithely through the players, then thumped her chest and walked off the court nine seconds after she first appeared. When the viewers were queried after viewing the film, they did reasonably well in counting the passes, but almost half of them *had no recollection of seeing a gorilla – or indeed, of seeing anything out of the ordinary*. This "invisible gorilla" experiment (which, at the time of writing you can view on YouTube) has been seen by millions. All are amazed by it, but the explanation is very simple. As psychologist Daniel Kahneman explains, humans have two completely different ways of thinking, one fast (which he calls "System 1"), which is basically reactive, and one slow ("System 2"), which requires focused cogitation. Kahneman finds that System 2 thinking focuses attention so much on our *purpose* for seeing that we may become oblivious to those things we would observe immediately if we were just casually gazing at them.[4]

So the actors' eyes, like those of the boxer, are not simply gazing or staring at the objects before them. They are searching for answers to specific questions they have, or victories they hope to achieve, for which these objects – they hope – will provide useful clues. The actor – just like the person in life – must employ both methods of seeing: the reactive method, as when a bear jumps out at you in the forest, and the cogitative, as you search for the cabin doorknob and try to anticipate exactly how you will open it. The actor's seeing, therefore, like her listening, is not passive. It is proactive, and proactive in quite different ways depending on the nature of the situation.

But actors use their eyes for more than just seeing. They also use them as weapons: tools that may help them intimidate, force, seduce, or persuade other characters into doing things they might otherwise not do. The boxer, to return to our model, does not use his eyes merely to perceive the incipient actions of his opponent. He also uses them to frighten. The darting glare of Rocky Graziano and the ferocious gaze of Rocky Marciano conveyed images of rock-hard strength associated with the champions' adopted names (both were actually named Rocco). The goofy, cockeyed smile of Muhammad Ali, by contrast, when he floated "like a butterfly" and mockingly circled his bedraggled opponents, dared them to step into a quick flurry of savage punches. Our eyes are therefore both perceptive and aggressive; they can threaten and they can seduce. They become tools that help us not merely see what lies before us, but to *change* that which we see.

When we look directly at another's eyes, we make what we call *eye contact*. In most of Europe and North America, this is a common – and often powerful –

component of social communication. We feel we are truly engaged with the person we are seeing, and can assess her sincerity and evaluate her emotional commitment to the words that are coming out of her mouth. Famous studies stress the importance of eye contact in job interviews, and experiments clearly reveal that applicants who engage in it are rated as "more alert, assertive, dependable, confident, responsible, and possessing greater initiative" than candidates who are seen as "looking down their noses" or acting "shifty-eyed."[5] It is wise, however, to realize in other parts of the world, direct eye contact is not always so valued. In many cultures, eye contact between persons of opposite sexes is normally avoided; in other cultures it is considered disrespectful to look directly at the eyes of those of a higher social rank. Persons in certain cultures may even worry about facing an "evil eye" which will cause them bad luck or even death, and single individuals everywhere may be reluctant or even afraid to look at others' eyes directly.

Nonetheless, making eye contact, or trying (against your culture's wish) to make eye contact, is absolutely crucial for dramatic interacting – except, of course, where the characters are blind, in which case their dramatic action would be to substitute their hearing, smelling, and feeling to discern what the other characters are seeing, doing, and thinking. What actors do with their eyes tells us who they are and what they want. As British director (and prominent acting theorist) Declan Donnellan puts it, "Acting is a question of what we see. For the actor, we are what we see."[6] When truly engaging with other characters in the play, therefore – i.e. when anticipating, judging, admiring, scaring, attracting, dismissing, and penetrating them – an actor's eyes, and the way she employs them, will tell us as much or more about her character as does her costume, makeup, accent, diction, movements, and, in many cases, even her words. For, as in life, the way we look at people may tell us about them, but it also tells them about *us*.

Human evolution has thankfully provided our species with eyes that are particularly easy to read and interpret, even from a distance, since our pupils are surrounded by an unusually large *sclera* – the whites of our eyes. "Humans wear the mark of their shared intentionality," explains developmental psychologist Michael Tomasello, by "a small but significant feature – the whites of their eyes, which are three times larger than those of any other primate, presumably to help others follow the direction of gaze. Indeed, chimps infer the direction of gaze by looking at another's head, but infants do so by watching the eyes."[7] So we are the rare creature that knows what other members of our tribe – even those moderately far away from us – are looking at. For an actor, that means that the audience will frequently be studying her eyes, and seeing what she is looking at. And thus the actors' eyes become the audience's window into her character's mind. "Big eyes" (meaning very visible and active ones) are, whether we like it or not, one of the factors directors and casting directors like to see when casting a play.

"It was clear from the moment Ms. [Christina] Ricci began
her audition that she would know how to handle the stage…
you could read those eyes from the back row of Radio City."
American director Daniel Sullivan[8]

Yet strangely, the most common problem we see among inexperienced actors is that they often tend to perform with glassy, vacant eyes, saying their lines with eyelids half-closed and a gaze focused on the floor or out into empty space. If they were boxers, they would be lying on the mat in the first ten seconds of the bout. If they were seeking a job, they would be shown the door. And when they are playing characters, the audience will have a hard time not falling asleep – for if the play's characters don't feel it necessary to look at what's happening around them, why should we? As Stanislavsky said, "Empty eyes are the mirror of an empty soul…It is important that an actor's eyes, his gaze, his glance, reflect the size, the depth of his creative mind."[9]

"Focus on them *[the other actors in the play]*! Don't worry
about yourself. If you focus on them you'll be fine."
*American playwright Frank Gilroy's advice to then-young
American actor Martin Sheen during rehearsals for his
Broadway debut in* The Subject Was Roses[10]

Eyes as tools

When I am asked to appraise an actor's performance the most important single thing I look at is her eyes. On whom or what are they focused? Whom or what are they trying to penetrate? What are they looking *for*? What are they hoping to find out? Of whom or what are they frightened?

But, equally crucial: what are her eyes trying to make the characters around them *feel* when they gaze at them? For eyes are not just receivers, they are *tools*.

And they are *powerful* tools: weapons that can kill, lures that can attract. Shakespeare, an actor before he became a playwright, gives us many examples of this. Hamlet describes his father's gaze as "an eye like Mars, to threaten and command." Henry V tells his troops at Agincourt to "Lend the eye a terrible aspect: let it pry through the portage of the head like the brass cannon." Iago entices Cassio to seek Desdemona's aid by telling him, "What an eye she has! Methinks it sounds a parley of provocation."

Here, in fact, are no fewer than 132 ways in which Shakespeare, in his plays, has his characters describe the eyes of other characters in the play they are in:

admiring eyes	dull eye	kind eyes	scornful eyes
adulterate eyes	duteous eyes	kingly eye	searching eyes
aged eyes	dying eyes	lack-luster eye	severe eyes
ambitious eye	eager eyes	leveled eyes	sightless eyes
angry eyes	eagle-sighted eye	liberal eye	sleeping eyes
assailing eyes	earnest eye	lock'd up eyes	soldier's eye
auspicious eye	empty eye	lover's eye	sore eyes
baby eyes	enthralled eyes	lustful eye	sorrow's eye
beauteous eye	expectant eyes	lustrous eyes	southward eye
best eyes	eyes sod in tears	mangling eye	sparkling eyes
bonny eye	fair eyes	manly eyes	steadfast eye
bright eyes	fairer eye	mean eyes	steadfast-gazing eye
burning eye	false eyes	medicinable eye	still-soliciting eye
charmed eye	fearful eye	melting eye	stranger eyes
charming eyes	fiery eyes	merriest eye	subdued eyes
cheerful eyes	firm eyes	mischief's eye	sun-beamed eyes
children's eyes	fluxive eyes	mistaking eyes	sun-bright eye
common eyes	fond eye	modest eyes	sunken eye
considerate eyes	fool's eyes	moist eyes	sweet eyes
constant eye	foolish eyes	old eyes	tender eye
cruel eye	fowler eye	old fond eyes	threatening eye
crystal eyes	friendly eye	opposed eyes	traitor eye
curious eye	full eye	outward eyes	true eyes
cursory eye	galled eyes	pale-dead eyes	unavoided eye
dainty eye	gentle eyes	pity-pleading eyes	unhallowed eyes
dangerous eyes	glutton eye	poet's eye	
dead-killing eye	good eyes	poor eyes	
deadly eye	goodly eyes	princely eyes	
death-darting eye	graver eye	prophet's eye	
deep-sunken eyes	hawking eye	purblind eye	
desiring eyes	heavenly eyes	rainy eyes	
discerning eye	hollow eye	raven's eye	
disliking eye	humbler eyes	red sparkling eyes	
divining eyes	hungry eyes	richest eyes	
doting eye	inferior eyes	rolling eyes	
dove's eyes	invited eyes	sad-set eyes	
dropping eye	inviting eye	savage eyes	

Most of us, when we describe someone's eyes, will only mention their color: "she has beautiful green eyes," or some such description. Shakespeare, however, only mentions eye color once in all his plays (Tybalt in *Romeo and Juliet* is described by Mercutio as having "hazel eyes"). While not interested in what his characters' eyes look like, Shakespeare is obsessed by what eyes *do*, and what they may forecast a character may do with them. For we use our eyes not just to see and penetrate, but to probe, to predict, to frighten, and to lure. And those who see us using our eyes in these fashions will be quick to characterize us accordingly – as Shakespeare did. The eyes of a character show the other actors on stage, and the audience in the seats beyond, just what she is searching for, and trying to achieve. The actor must focus her own eyes on her character's goals.

"When you watch Phil work, his entire constitution seems to change. He may look like Phil, but there's something different in his eyes. And that means he's reconstituted himself from within, willfully rearranging his molecules to become another human being."

> *American director Mike Nichols, referring to*
> *American actor Phillip Seymour Hoffman*[11]

When we penetrate other persons' eyes, we are penetrating their minds. Thus when characters are trying to capture one another's affections (as are Romeo and Juliet), or defeat one another in an argument (as are Cassius and Brutus), or persuade another character to reverse course (as Lady Macbeth does with her husband), the actors playing these roles, if they are to act convincingly, must be seen as *trying to get inside each other's brains*. When that happens, the actor is using her eyes exactly as a boxer does – to hunt out the other person's intentions, defenses, desires, and fears, and to find her path to victory in achieving her goals.

And, when an actor truly searches for something in another person, the audience will search along with her. And when she then seeks to motivate (threaten, entice) another character with her sharply focused gaze, the audience knows what she's doing and will root for her. But when her eyes are simply drifting into space, or focusing idly in the middle distance, her performance will lose the impetus, desire, and forward thrust that make drama dramatic.

Moreover, the intense, purposeful gaze of an actor does not stimulate merely the audience; it also stimulates the emotions (fear, attraction, excitement, anticipation) of the other actors on the stage. Linda Alper, a longtime actor at the Oregon Shakespeare Festival, remembers going nearly "insane with frustration" when performing a scene with an actor during a long summer season. "I felt he was never truly in the scenes with me. During one performance, however, everything changed: subtle cues were picked up and our scene really rocked. When we got offstage, I complimented him, and he told me that for the first time he was wearing his contact lenses on stage. I suggested he continue to do so in our remaining performances, but he decided not to, and our scenes never again approached the magical, subtle chemistry they had reached that evening."[12]

One of the sad things in rehearsals – particularly in amateur rehearsals where the cast members have other jobs or classes and can't devote their full time to the production – is that the actors often spend their first days or even weeks with their heads buried in their scripts. They may think they're acting, but they're not; they're only reciting their lines and going through the moves the director has given them. By the time the actors start making eye contact with each other, their patterns have already been set. They are acting by themselves, not with their colleagues. Actor Sherman Howard saw the reverse side of this situation when understudying veteran star Christopher Plummer as Drummond in the 2007 Broadway production of *Inherit the Wind*. "Just watching Plummer work on his role was a life-changing experience," Howard said. "He came in the first day knowing all his lines, and he used the rehearsal process to thoroughly explore each moment, eyeballing each actor he talked with on stage. It was authentic, alive, and deliciously real. He's masterful."[13] Whether actors should learn their lines before rehearsals begin or after the show is blocked is a frequently-debated issue in the field, but Plummer's policy – which happens also to be my own – should at least be considered by every actor, and for Howard's stated reasons.

Why do inexperienced actors fail to look in the way boxers look: seeking ways to win their character's objectives, goals, and victories? Why do they spend so much time looking down at the floor or up at the ceiling? Perhaps they fear that looking purposefully at a fellow actor will make them forget their next line. Or because they're thinking of what their next line is rather than what they are trying to *do* with the words that are coming out of their mouths. Sometimes actors even close their eyes while speaking, with the notion that they are displaying the "action" of reflecting on their character's current situation, or summoning up some event in their personal lives to stimulate their emotions, as Stanislavsky (and certainly Lee Strasberg) proposed at various times under the rubrics of "affective memory" or "emotional recall." Such reveries on stage are rarely successful, however, and Stanislavsky more or less repudiated these notions in his later writings. If drama is to be dramatic, its characters must be seeking change in the characters they confront. Dramatic characters seek to attain goals, avoid catastrophes, and resolve conflicts *with and through other people*. Their eyes must be creative, searching, proactive. They must be *looking* and not just seeing, and looking *for* something: for solutions to what's troubling them, and for the subtle clues and tactics that can help them win their battles ahead – whether in war, in love, in ambition, or in debate. If they don't, the audience will lose interest in whether they succeed or fail in these tasks, and start studying the scenery instead.

Often this "refusal to look" is unconscious. I once directed a student actor who, while very handsome and well spoken, would literally close his eyes during the first word or two of every speech he gave. I pointed this out to him several times, but he adamantly denied doing it – until I trained a video camera on him and played back his performance. He was stunned, but still had difficulty kicking this obviously ingrained habit.

The physiology of seeing

Looking does not mean staring, however. Indeed, the fixed stare is as much an indication of lifelessness as the vacant stare, each implying that the character is dead or, worse, "dead behind the eyes." When we are actively looking at an object instead of just staring at it, our eyes are in constant motion as they scan the object under investigation. This is not a fluid process as, for instance, panning a movie camera. Rather, our eyes scan an object in a rapid sequence of jerky eyeball movements, which can shift our focus *several times a second* from one spot to another. These shifts, of which we are rarely consciously aware, are called *saccades*. Regulated by our unconsciously operating autonomic nervous system (or ANS), these lightning-fast eyeball movements can happen as frequently as every twenty milliseconds (that is to say, up to fifty times a second); they are, in fact, the fastest movements made by the human body. Collectively, saccades send a series of micro-images to our brains, which assemble them into the overall pattern that we think we see as a complete image. What we actually see, however, is a constantly changing and infinitely complex mosaic. Our eyes orchestrate a mental pointillism that continuously compiles thousands of tiny visual fragments into what is very like a Georges Seurat painting.

The reason saccades are necessary for human sight is simple: our eyes can focus only on a tiny point in the center of each retina. Called the *fovea,* this point is a dense concentration of those image receptors (rods and cones) that are uniquely able to distinguish details. If you focus steadily at a single word on a printed line of text, for example, you will immediately realize you can make out at most one word to its left and one word to its right. All the other words to the left or right, above or below the line, will be in your peripheral vision, blurred beyond readability until your nervous system autonomically initiates a saccade to capture them. Reading is therefore an action of jerkily shifting your focus from one tiny group of letters to another, several times a second. This process, known as *foveation,* is the main eye movement of our wakeful life. It takes place all the time, even in the rapid eye movement that occurs when we dream.

And there is yet another eye movement, equally unconscious, that partners with foveation: this is *convergence,* which causes us to refocus each *individual* eye relative to its partner when a saccade shifts our gaze to something that is either closer to or farther away from us. Also controlled autonomically, convergence is essential for us to retain the stereoscopic unity and three-dimensionality of the subject viewed. So when actors (or boxers) are truly engaged in searching for something, instead of just blankly staring at objects because they've been told by their coaches or directors to do so, their eyes are continuously, and autonomically, foveating and converging.

So why are these unconscious ocular activities, whose names are unknown to most of us, important to know about? Because the audience – and your acting partners – *can see you do them*. And when they see you *fail* to do them, they – even though they have never heard of the terms I've mentioned – will know you are faking the actions you are supposed to be doing.

When an actor's eyes are foveating and converging, she is therefore seen as being "in the moment" rather than passively looking where the director has told her to look. Such autonomic activities are not consciously learned. *They cannot be willed or faked*; no director can direct them and no actor can convincingly simulate them. They are instinctual; part of our evolutionary history – as almost all mammals foveate, just as we do. These natural, unconscious, mammalian movements of the eyes show that we are *alive*: that we are curious, energetic, eager to succeed and fearful of failure.

"Whoever has seen a great actor knows that he is not an animal to be stalked in its lair but a tiger leaping out on the spectator from the bush of mediocrity."
British drama critic James Agate[14]

How, not having learned these terms, do we recognize this physical phenomenon? Simply by experiencing and witnessing it every day of our lives from our very first weeks on earth. Just as the actors opposite you can tell immediately when you aren't foveating (though they won't call it that – they would say that your eyes "seem dead"), so too can a theatre or film audience. Stanislavsky's famous dictum that the actor must "live the character's life" thus requires foveating with your eyeballs as much as it demands blood pumping through your arteries. Indeed, acting requires the visible autonomic behaviors of all the play's characters if they are to be thought of as living creatures.

So how do you foveate, if it is unconscious? Simply by *looking intently for what you can find out about the other characters that will help you win your character's goals*. This is the basic reason why purposeful seeing, searching, and hunting down clues are what an audience must observe in the actor's eyes if her performance is to be credible and convincing.

One might think actors would be concerned about this, but that is rarely the case. Beginning actors often wonder what they should do with their hands, but rarely about what they should do with their eyes. Formal actor training in Western theatre rarely addresses eye focus or eye movement.* Indeed, prior to Stanislavsky there was almost no mention of actors' eyes in writings on acting, and while the great Russian master popularized "eye contact" between actors, he did so mainly as a staging technique that would override the traditional style of nineteenth-century star actors, who generally stood center stage and faced the audience instead of the other characters.

"Eye contact," however, is now a common lesson for beginning actors, specifically encouraging them to look directly into the eyes of their scene partners, and to study the unconscious breathing patterns, movements, grimaces, tics, and blushes of the characters. They try to see who and what the other characters are looking at, what they are reaching for, what they are trying to do with their hands, feet, postures, gestures, grimaces. This eye exploration is intense and proactive. It means looking for cues and clues, opportunities and dangers, overt and covert signifiers. When eye contact is continuous between two characters in a dangerous situation (and most truly dramatic situations are, or should be, considered dangerous), the eyes are every bit as important as the words. Imagine the famous "Queen's closet scene" in *Hamlet,* where Hamlet comes into his mother's bedchamber after confirming the King's guilt in murdering Hamlet's father. The stakes are life-or-death from beginning to end: Gertrude is terrified that Hamlet is about to kill her, while Hamlet, having just stopped himself from murdering the King, murders Polonius who is spying from behind the arras. The dialogue is filled with raging accusations, urgent interrogations, and a divine invocation ("by the rood"). The physical action, which includes the slaying of Polonius and (in most stagings) Hamlet throwing his mother on the bed and ripping a cameo picture from her neck, is relentlessly intense. And none of the characters believes for an instant that what they're *hearing* from the other is truthful! Thus if there *is* any truth for them to discover, they realize they can find it *only with their eyes.* Were this a real-life series of actions, neither Gertrude nor Hamlet would dare take their eyes off each other for a second. They dare not even blink – and nor should the actors playing them.

But how does an actor, not herself threatened with murder, stop from blinking? Our ANS helps us out here. Whenever you sneeze, your eyes close; it is simply impossible to keep them open. But if, just as you're just about to sneeze while driving down a winding two-lane highway, another car suddenly races towards you from the opposite direction, your ANS will automatically stifle

---

* Indian *kathakali* drama-dance students, however, are awakened at three in the morning to begin their daily eye exercises, which can last for hours each day.

that sneeze, along with the blink that would have accompanied it. Evolution has provided us with an unconscious mechanism that suppresses sneezing and blinking when we are genuinely terrified by an attacking force. This mechanism is the source of our phrase, "wide-eyed terror." If the actor blinks, we know she is not truly terrified.

So how do great actors create the terror that manipulates their ANS and suppresses eye blinks? Terror comes from not knowing what will happen next, but the actors in a performance, unlike their characters, *do* know what will happen next. Their best solution is a simple one: they engage their ANS by looking squarely in the eyes of the other *actor*. Not of the other *character*, because the character's lines – and future – have already been determined by the play's author, and his or her physical actions have already been staged by the director. But the other actor is thinking! And you don't know what he or she is thinking. So you look at the actor!

The old axiom for actors is to "believe in your character." My axiom is "believe in the other characters." To the actor playing Hamlet, the mind of Queen Gertrude simply does not exist; the "Queen Gertrude" as she exists in the script is purely fictional, and her actions were predetermined hundreds of years ago by a man named Shakespeare. But the mind of the *actor that plays* Gertrude is alive, sensate, searching, and a source of infinite mystery. And to that actor, the mind of the *actor playing Hamlet* is equally unknowable and mysterious. This will be true even if the actors have known each other all their lives, for while written characters are permanently predetermined, actors, being live human beings, are infinitely inscrutable and enigmatic. So the job of the actor in such a situation is to passionately explore the mystery behind his or her fellow actor's eyes.

"One of the most important keys to acting is curiosity... All people contain mystery, and when you act, you want to plumb that mystery until everything is known to you."
American actress Meryl Streep[15]

If the actors can plunge into the profound unknown of their fellow acting partners' minds, therefore, their own *autonomic* responses will be generated. Her eyes – like those of the boxer – will slow or even stop their blink rate for the duration of these critical moments. They will be foveating and converging autonomically. And the spectators will willingly suspend their disbelief if – as when watching a boxing match – they know they are seeing a genuine mental engagement between two actors – an engagment that takes place *at this moment* and for what appears to be – and in fact really is – the first time.

Indirect eye contact

Eye contact is not solely eye-to-eye, or course. It is also eye-to-body. The actor playing Gertrude will certainly look at actor-Hamlet's eyes, but also at his hands and the sword he holds in them, the raised arch of his eyebrows, and the baring of his teeth. She will be assessing his skin color (is his face reddening? turning pale?), his breathing (is he panting? gasping? holding his breath?), and the blood pulsing visibly in his neck. None of this requires conscious thinking; we have been reading these clues at least since kindergarten and probably much earlier ("What's making my mom so sad?" we asked ourselves when we were three years old). She will not always be looking at Hamlet, either; but at times will be darting her eyes to the arras, behind which she knows Polonius lurks, as well as back to Hamlet to make sure he doesn't see her looking at the arras, and she'll be glancing at the door to see if any servants outside have heard the argument they're having (particularly when she cries she will "set those to you that can speak"). Plus, she will be checking out any possible escape route she might take if Hamlet should actually raise his sword – while at the same time trying to hide the fact that she's planning such an escape. The only "seeing" that Gertrude will *not* be doing, most likely, is that which Hamlet has asked her to: She will not be using a metaphorical mirror to "see the inmost part" of herself.

Likewise, the actor-Hamlet is scouring the actress-Gertrude for reciprocal clues, and asking himself, "Is she blushing? Repentant? Frightened? Have I finally turned her mind against Claudius? Why are her eyes darting around the room? Why is she looking at the arras? How much loyalty does she have towards my father?" And his big, unasked question: "Did you have sex with my uncle before he murdered my father?"

Trying to find the answers to these questions while playing this scene can only be achieved through the actors' eyes. No character will get straight answers from the other in words alone. Each needs, like the suspicious Othello in another Shakespearean tragedy, "ocular proof."

The eyes are prime defensive and offensive weapons of the actor's character. They mirror the soul, yes, but they also reveal the characters' minds and propel the dramatists' actions. Because as Muhammad Ali said, quite famously:

> "Float like a butterfly.
> Sting like a bee.
> Your hands can't hit
> What your eyes can't see."

Exercise: The mirror

One of the first theatre-training games I experienced was the mirror exercise, and its impact on me at the time was phenomenal. I still think it is one of the greatest acting exercises ever created. It is an example of a pure feedback contact between two people, focusing on their eyes. It is quite simple, and I'm sure most of this book's readers know about it and indeed have probably done it. In the exercise, two actors face each other and mirror each other's movements. Neither is designated as leader; both simply watch and follow each other. "Thinking" need play no part in the mirror exercise, because the cybernetic principles work unconsciously; a leftward movement of one stimulates a rightward (mirroring) movement of the other; this all occurs at an instinctual level. In the purest sense, mirror exercises draw their structure unconsciously, and are naturally choreographed by the subtlest intentions and mindsets of the participants. Variations on the mirror exercise are manifold, and include:

- A mirror exercise accompanied by recorded or live music, or simply to randomly played piano chords. The music enters into the feedback loop and induces new directions in the movement.
- A vocal mirror: the addition of sounds and words, which must be acoustically mirrored (repeated) by the person opposite.
- Three- or four-way mirrors, or more: additional people in the exercise.
- A one-way mirror: with a real mirror.

The reason why mirror exercises are so effective, and so universally in use, is that they force a total situational concentration; a total concentration on the *other person* rather than the self, and a total concentration on the future (what is the other person about to do?) rather than on the past. These concentrations are strong enough to drive out all contextual awareness (such as the presence of an instructor or fellow class members), and therefore provide a powerful example of complete situational involvement. I left that initial hour-long session – during which I mirrored six different partners, male and female – a totally and permanently changed person. Indeed, I believe it was my initiation into just about every idea in this book.

Facing faces

The mirror exercise is also helpful to override the sadly overused tendency of an actor's "cheating out," by which actors facing each other on a proscenium stage in a line parallel to the front of the stage will each turn their face and torso – and invariably their downstage foot – diagonally halfway towards the audience. This old custom of theatre stagecraft is designed to allow the audience to see at least a good portion of each actor's face and overall frontal appearance at all times, and many directors (at least in school theatres) urge their actors to "cheat out" so they can be more fully seen and heard by the audience. The hoary custom has a long history: in 1803, the German playwright/director Johann Wolfgang von Goethe wrote in *Rules of Acting*, "It is mistaken naturalness for the actors to play to each other," and the practice of at least half-way facing the audience lasted throughout the entire romantic era and beyond.[16]

Unfortunately, however, "cheating out" is just what its name implies; it cheats the actor who does it, making her hold up a flag that says, "This is only a play; I don't really mean what I'm saying." Even if the actor's head is turned parallel to the footlights, and toward the actor she's speaking to, if her foot is half-facing the audience, it looks like she's got one foot out of the scene. In real life, of course, when people engage in direct, meaningful, and *purposeful* discourse (which is the general nature of dramatic dialogue), they face each other squarely whenever possible. The actor who cheats out, conversely, appears not as a character trying to win her goal by interacting with the actor opposite, but as an actor hoping that the audience will enjoy her performance. The audience may be happy to see the actor's face – but not if it means that she has stopped acting.

Good directors have no problems finding ways to stage scenes that will make the actors (and their eyes) visible to the audience at key moments, without "cheating." Nor is seeing the actors' faces throughout a production necessary; many productions in the current era are staged on thrust or arena stages where actors' faces can almost *never* be seen by the entire audience at the same time. There are many ways in which an actor's performance will reach out to an audience that will be discussed in later sections of this book, but "cheating out" is not one of them.

"Don't over cheat. It drives me crazy to see feet facing the audience and head facing the action."
            American director D. Scott Glasser[17]

Physical contact

Humans beings make direct physical contact in daily life too, of course, and so must the actors that play them. The physical contact in plays is often noted in the author's stage directions (e.g. "they fight," "they kiss"), but far more often they are suggested by a director or improvised in rehearsal by actors. Physical contact – even as innocent as a pat on the back or shaking hands – is always powerful on stage because it is a *felt* – not just shown –inter-penetration between actors. Unlike vocal penetration, physical contact contains no verbal or intellectual content, and is therefore a *sensual* intercourse, communicating feelings rather than specific ideas and building – or destroying – personal and emotional relationships. A handshake can be either firm, conveying trust, or weak, conveying uncertainty; or it can be a super-strong grip that conveys, "And don't you dare fail me on this!" A pat on the back conveys casual companionship; a punch on the arm friendly rivalry, and a soft graze of the fingertips on the back of another's neck is clearly an invitation to a romantic experience. These wordless physical contacts, rarely noted in stage directions, are often the turning points of a scene, or even a play. They will not only be noticed by the audience, they may be remembered when the words uttered in the play are long forgotten.

Physical touching literally bridges the actor and the character. Because it is sensual rather than intellectual, it touches not only skin but reaches deep into inchoate human emotions, firing off hundreds of biochemical and neurological responses that developed in human beings long before there was anything known as a theatre or even a language. It is therefore dangerous, both in life and on the stage – which is certainly a good thing on the stage, since the audience *wants* its plays to be dangerous.

Physical *combat*, of course, is, when well performed, always thrilling on stage, and since the sixteenth-century slaps, trip-ups, wrestling matches, fistfights, duels, stabbings, and full-stage battles both on land and sea (all of which are employed by Shakespeare) have been commonplace in the theatre – and are even more so now in films and television. But such staged combat can lead to broken bones if not professionally choreographed and supervised, and always requires the coaching and oversight of a trained (and, in some countries, a certified) combat director. *Romantic* physical contact may also prove dangerous as it may wrestle with actors' feelings, and with their moral values and upbringings, for while subtle caresses may not cause broken bones, they can lead to broken hearts and broken vows – marital or religious. Therefore, any sort of touching requires, if not a specialist's coaching, a certain sensitivity in approaching it. No actor wants to go through the example of the late Linda Boreman who, as "Linda Lovelace," played the leading role in the hard-core 1972 pornographic film *Deep Throat*, which became the first such film to be distributed and reviewed nationally and, as Boreman later acknowledged, all but ruined her life.

And therefore, physical contact of almost any kind on stage will almost always begin with a certain degree of *hesitation*. A real-life boxing match rarely begins with its two opponents charging full bore at each other on the opening bell and swinging ferociously at each other's heads. Instead, the boxers ordinarily begin by bouncing around (dancing, almost) while making tentative feints and jabs so they can sort out their opponent's strategy and develop their own. And few barroom fistfights simply start out of the blue; ordinarily it is a matter of raised voices, then swearing, then making fists, then pounding walls or tables, and only then breaking into a brawl.* Even thugs can be hesitant in starting confrontations that may cost them their lives.

Likewise, the caress that is an invitation to romance (as opposed to rape) is usually a mixture of boldness and timidity. Bold because it must suggest an encouraging response; timid because, if rebuffed, the inviter must be able to save face, and not seen to have been turned down. It is completely understandable why approaching romance is approaching danger: if it fails it can lead to humiliation; if it succeeds it can lead to unwanted commitment and a narrowing of options. First steps in romantic caressing are therefore usually *deniable* – as in Chekhov's *Three Sisters* when Vershinin, in the second act of the play, finally kisses Masha's hand, each being married to another and alone together for the first time. This kiss could be construed as either a sexual invitation or just a common formal gesture between these two upper-class nineteenth-century Russians. If Masha were to pull away, Vershinin could therefore act as if he had intended nothing other than a chaste appreciation of Masha's listening to the complaints he has just been making about his wife. But when Masha does not pull away ("What a noise in the stove!" is all she says), she is virtually inviting him to kiss her hand again. And within moments he does, and then tells her he loves her. There is no reason to think anyone approaching these dangers would be anything less than hesitant, at first, given the despair that a romance between them could (and indeed will) cause not only to them but to their kinfolk. And their awkward but completely believable hesitancy is what makes the scene – and its revolutionary playwright – world-famous.

Often these two physical contact situations – fighting and loving – combine as one. In the famous "wooing scene" between Kate and Petruchio in *The Taming of the Shrew*, for example, Shakespeare has specified (or at least implied) plenty of physical combat between the two: they grab, slap, spank, and trip up one another (and most directors add a lot more), and by the end of the scene Kate is limping. Yet, although neither is yet ready to acknowledge it, they are beginning to fall in love, as will be confirmed by the end of the play. For they love to fight. Theirs is a classic scene of alternately pulling at each other (falling in love) and pushing each other away (claiming independent authority), which is shown more through their physical interactions than by the words they so spiritedly exchange.

Yet none of this fighting would be of dramatic interest except for the fact that it is grounded in the character's vulnerabilities.

---

* A more elegant example of this build-to-battle is Touchstone's seven-step "retort courteous" speech in Shakespeare's *As You Like It,* V. iii.

Vulnerability

"One of the things I like about my profession, and that I find healthy, is that one constantly has to break oneself to pieces."

Swedish actress Liv Ullmann[18]

We are all vulnerable. Physically, we are vulnerable to disease, war, earthquakes, and accidents; emotionally we are vulnerable to rejection, embarrassment, discrimination, and bullying. Thus, contact of any sort, physical, vocal, or even visual (the evil eye, seriously feared in many cultures and nerve-wracking anywhere), can lead us into trouble. So while it might be thought that making contact is easy to do, since it usually begins with "mere" observation, it is often not. There is a reason for all the glassy stares and stiff acting we see in the student performer (and all too frequently in the professional): It is because nature has provided us with defenses against adversities. Stiffness makes us more formidable; glassy stares make us more impenetrable, labored breathing – with its portent of explosiveness – makes us more frightening. This has been true biologically for thousands of years, and it is hard to shake off now – particularly in the potentially threatening context of the theatre, with its audience, friends, critics, and employers, or of the soundstage, with its cameramen, lighting and sound technicians, directors, and producers hovering about. Directly concentrating on others, on the other hand, means reducing one's concentration on oneself – "dropping one's guard," we might say – and risks exposure to real or imagined vulnerabilities. For as British stage director Patrick Garland says, "All human beings surround themselves with layers of protection to prevent exposure, and yet actors are in part required and impelled to reveal themselves all the time."[19] One of the hardest things for an actor to learn, therefore, are the mechanisms for allowing her vulnerabilities to breathe, and to break down her emotional rigidities.

To the beginning actor, these rigidities are often, like cheating out, flags held up to say, "This character isn't me!" Nowhere is that flag more evident than in a heavily dramatic scene, where the character is seen to cry, scream, shout, and groan in despair. All too often the actor gives us, instead of her own despair, a grand, cruel, magnificent despair in imitation of a play or movie she has seen. In brief, while pretending to be in despair, the actor presents us with what she thinks of as magnificence, and what we actually see is not agony but (unfounded) exaltation. "Look at me! I'm the next Marlon Brando/Patti LuPone!" This is sham performance, and the audience, of course, sees right through it. Invulnerability is covered over by overacting – what the audience refers to as "ham acting."

What the actor must do is get down to an essential rawness in which her vulnerabilities need not be hidden. A sense of trust within the acting company, and a sensitive director and stage management team, can provide a productive environment for this rawness. Yet the actor herself must always be seeking techniques to develop her own freedom to fully expose the real desires, feelings and fears that arise during the character interactions she rehearses and performs on the stage.

"Laurence Olivier is a great actor partly because he shows us so much of himself in all his performances. Partly because he is unafraid to reveal those elements in his personality that most of us are trained to keep hidden. Men are taught from childhood to be ashamed of their femininity: Olivier exploits his brilliantly and therefore enables all of us to come to terms with a part of ourselves…"

British theatre critic Michael Billington[20]

A very simple and proven exercise can lead actors towards this on-stage and in-public vulnerability without being unduly threatening.

Exercise: I can be hurt by you

Two participants face each other, looking each other right in the eye. The first says to the second, "I can be hurt by you." The second responds to the first with the same sentence.

This "dialogue" is then repeated several times in succession, with the identical words and no others. The eye contact is maintained throughout, though the coach or teacher who had initiated the exercise may from time to time quietly interject, to the one about to speak, "Make her (or him) know you mean it."

The exercise is one of the most powerful devices for drastically deepening the situational involvement of actors in an intimate scene. When the instructor/coach ends it, there may be tears in one or both of the participants' eyes. The reason the exercise works so well, however, is not that the actors are "acting," but that each actor is saying something that is *absolutely true*. And everyone watching *knows* that it is true. For *everybody* has the power to hurt everybody else, and while those "hurts" may not be of equal degree, none of them is inconsiderable.

For we are all initially hopeful of the respect, admiration, friendship, and perhaps even the love of everybody we come across; thus every one of those persons has the latent power to hurt us by simply withholding (or, worse, openly rejecting) his or her interest, concern or affection. The exchange of sentences in the exercise is simply an exchange of known facts – but they are facts that are *almost never said in ordinary public discourse*. Quite the contrary, virtually all our daily and moment-to-moment public communications convey just the opposite: that we are powerful, invulnerable people who cannot be hurt by anyone! Our social conditioning has made us, when in public, at least try to appear practical rather than emotional, realistic rather than dreamy, knowing rather than naive, and enigmatic rather than wearing our hearts on our sleeve. A few bad life experiences, romantic failures, emotional rejections, losses and disillusionments – and our exteriors harden further yet. And this level of assurance, this bravado, is ordinarily quite acceptable in everyday life. Indeed, it is probably necessary in most of our daily experiences. But most plays and films – dramatic ones, at least – have climaxes that are not everyday experiences. And playing such scenes normally requires that we experience our own fears, worries and concerns. Such performances can touch our vulnerabilities at their cores.

The simple and pure conveyance of the "I can be hurt by you" message, therefore, lifts a huge burden from the actor's shoulders. It is a public admission of her most secret vulnerability, but once she has admitted it, and been seen to admit it, she has little left to fear, little left to hide. Then she is free to build a truer power base, one which derives from her own feelings about herself rather than a need to hide behind some artificial posturing in the name of characterization or stylization. The frank, shared confession of vulnerability is a first step toward acting with commanding power.

Expectation

Vulnerability liberates acting; expectation provides its driving force. Expectation is itself a powerful mover of the human spirit. Maxwell Maltz, in his 1960 bestseller *Psycho/Cybernetics*, shows how improving persons' expectations almost always leads to an improvement in their confidence, and eventually their fortunes; this also became the central premise of Rhonda Byrne's 2006 book and movie, *The Secret*, and its popular "law of attraction." But the value of positive expectation in leading to successful future ventures is not merely talk-show fare. In a series of celebrated experiments on classroom education in the 1960s, Robert Rosenthal and Lenore Jacobson tested groups of students and then told their teachers, in strict confidence, the names of those who had noticeably high IQ's. At the end of the year those students received better grades than their classmates, and had higher IQs as well – but the experimenters had in fact selected the names wholly at random! The students succeeded because their teachers thought they were going to be more successful and therefore treated them as being more promising, which led to the students fulfilling their expected "promise." The experimenters called this the "Pygmalion Effect,"[21] in which the mere expectation of success can – solely by itself – lead to actual success. Life is full of such examples: Sports figures and their coaches, for example, universally report that a "We're gonna win!" rally before a game gives their team a greater chance of actually winning the game. A musical comedy that gets a huge audience ovation after the opening number is more likely to become a great hit – which is why Stephen Sondheim put in a snazzy new opening number ("Comedy Tonight!") into his A *Funny Thing Happened on the Way to the Forum* during its poorly-received out-of-town previews. High expectation is usually a self-fulfilling prophecy, a service in its own behalf.

The great actor therefore attacks her situation not only with the hope, but *also with the expectation,* of winning her character's goals. This does not mean that she rationally expects to win them – any more than a person who buys a lottery ticket rationally expects to win the jackpot. But she *anticipates* winning. She dreams of winning, fantasizes her victory, and at some climactic moments even expects such triumphs – because her *character* has such hopes, anticipations and expectancies.

The actor's most difficult challenge in doing this, however, is that she has read and rehearsed her script beforehand and knows whether her character wins or loses at the end. And if her character is written to fail, the inexperienced actor, knowing this, may simply "play the result." This is absolutely lethal. In Tennessee Williams' *The Glass Menagerie,* Laura never wins the love of Jim O'Conner, whom she has secretly worshipped since high school, and she is virtually certain – at least in her rational mind – that she never will. But when she finally gets up the courage to speak to him, she begins to *fantasize* winning his love, and this fantasy soon becomes anticipation and finally expectation. It leads to a moment of sheer joy – without which, the poignancy, and indeed the tragedy, of the play (when it later turns out Jim is engaged to someone else) could never occur. It is Laura's *expectation of the near-impossible* that pulls us deeply into Williams's play, and it is the failure of Laura's – and the actor's – expectation to be realized that makes the play, and its solemn conclusion, unforgettable.

So actors should not simply look to the future; they should *lean into it.* They should fight to *win* – even when the play says they don't. Their concentrations should be active and positive – and their expectance of victory and persistence even after the inevitable reversals should propel them through their dramatic efforts. In a performance where all the play's characters are playing to win, and anticipating victories they may never achieve, the dramatic action will be dynamic and the acting powerful. In a production where the characters have simply given up by Act I (as in poorly conceived productions of Chekhov's major plays), the action will be perfunctory and the characters tedious; by Act IV the audience will be half-asleep. Whatever the final outcomes of the characters in a play, its actors should be "going for the gold" from beginning to end.

Relacom

So far we have been exploring aspects of interactions between two persons: particularly making contact, and the "push-pull" of vulnerability and expectations. Now it is time to look deeper into the process of human communication itself, and the fundamentals of communication theory as developed by, among others, Gregory Bateson and Paul Watzlawick beginning in 1951.

Bateson had been studying the programming of newly invented computing devices when he realized they needed to be fed two distinctly different kinds of information: first, as data that needed processing (numbers, for example) and second, as instructions on how to process this data (to add or subtract them, for example). The "how to" instructions then became a sort of *meta-communication* (Bateson's coinage) that provided a context for making the data useful. Thus, human to computer communication required two different but inseparable modes, occurring simultaneously. Communications theory has labeled these the *content* and *relationship* modes of communication.

Watzlawick, who went on to create the earlier-mentioned axiom that "one cannot not communicate,"[22] examined these two communication modes and realized they were equally required in our human life as well. On the first level, we transmit content, mainly through words; on the second, we proffer a *relationship* between ourselves and with whomever we are communicating, suggesting how the receiver of the content should process it. We proffer this relationship not through words, however, but through ordinary behavioral patterns: gestures, postures, tones of voice, and facial expressions being the dominant ones. If I say to someone, "I would like to talk to you," in a soft and cheery tone while smiling and casually sitting down on a sofa, it will be received in a completely different way than if I say it rising suddenly to my feet, frowning, raising my volume, clipping my consonants, and pointing to the person I'm addressing. The difference is like night and day.

The *relationship communication,* as with programming to a computer, is therefore an instruction as to how our words and other content are to be received. And it happens in virtually every verbal and even nonverbal exchange between human beings. For example, a college professor, in a lecture, says, "Shakespeare was born in 1564." That Shakespeare was born in that particular year is the *content* of the professor's message, but it is not the entire communication. That the professor stands while the class sits, that she appears unruffled, speaks in complete sentences, carries a briefcase, etc. – these all communicate messages too. They convey the *relationship message* that says, "The sentence I just spoke is factually correct, supported by scholarly evidence, and accepted by all authorities – of which I am one. And it is important that you know this when it comes time for the examination." The relationship communication directs how the content communication should be processed. If the professor had dressed herself in a clown suit, moved like a gorilla, and spoke like a baby, the content would surely be processed differently, and its impact on the class would be vastly altered.

Relationship communication (or what I will hereinafter shorten to the term "relacom") is the foundation of all communication – all conversation and all human interaction – because while relationship messages may be exchanged without a content counterpart (a smile, for example), content is utterly meaningless without establishing a relationship.

Relacom is not limited to persons speaking, however. In the same example, the professor's students will be sending relacom messages back to her: by the ways they may or may not nod at her remarks, chuckle at her witticisms, write down her summarizing epigrams, and smile encouragingly at her when she looks their way. Indeed, *at every moment* that we participate in human communications, we are seeking to further establish, clarify and perhaps change relationships. Moreover, we cannot *not* do this; remaining rigidly expressionless when spoken to can convey very powerful relacom to the person who sees you do so.

Relacom does not consist of statements, but invocations. One person cannot single-handedly define a relationship; she can only suggest how she would like it to be defined, implying it in such powerful terms that the other person or persons will accept her offers. And these relacom "suggestions" are mainly physical, not verbal. Psychology professor and communication expert Albert Meharabian estimates that "Fifty-five per cent of what you convey when you speak comes from your body language, thirty-eight per cent from your tone of voice, and a paltry seven per cent from the words you choose."[23] So when we listen to one another in life, we are not just listening for the words, or their specific semantic meanings; we are more commonly listening to the speaker's tone, his or her conveyance of attitude, interest, or affect, and the hidden meanings that may underlie his or her inflections, gestures, grimaces, and shifts in volume. These invocations are profoundly cybernetic – which is to say, future-oriented. And relacom is largely unconscious. We are not rationally analyzing other persons but rather "feeling them out."

"Acting doesn't have anything to do with listening to the words. We never really listen, in general conversation, to what another person is saying. We listen to what they mean. And what they mean is often quite apart from the words. When you see a scene between two actors that really comes off you can be damned sure they're not listening to each other – they're feeling what the other person is trying to get at."

American actor Jack Lemmon[24]

Relacom is a *continuous feedback loop* between communicators. As a continuous, ongoing event, it *continually redefines the relationships* communicators seek to achieve. Every person in life is engaged in relacom in active company with other people, and so every dramatic character should be seen as engaged in it at such times as well. Every character, like every human being, continually seeks to redefine, in a positive way, his or her relationship with those with whom they come into contact. The "I can be hurt by you" exercise becomes, after its first two lines, *solely* a relacom exchange, since the ensuing words do not change and so have no further content to deliver.

Responses to relacom

Responses to relacom invocations can take any of three basic forms: confirmations, rejections, or disconfirmations. The student who nods brightly at the professor's remarks obviously confirms the relationship the professor is trying to establish. So, in a more modest way, does the student who simply sits and listens. The student who makes scowling faces, however, or raises his hand in objection or creates a class disturbance, is expressing rejection. The harshest response to a relationship communication, however, is disconfirmation, as when a student is clearly texting a friend on his cellphone or handing notes to the girl next to him. The disconfirming response conveys the relacom message "I have no interest in this relationship – you simply do not exist for me." It is through the back and forth feedback of relacom invocations and their various responses – which themselves become relacom invocations – that human relationships grow, develop, change, and, in cases, decay.

Relacom is so wide-ranging as to be unavoidable in the study of acting, but theatrical parlance has yet to come up with a satisfactory term for it, and my own term has yet to enter the theatrical vocabulary. "Subtext," a word developed in the era of Stanislavsky and used extensively in American method acting, includes relationship communication, but it has a much broader meaning. Technically defined as that which is "under the text" or "between the lines," subtext is often explained as the "real" meaning of a line. Relacom, however, is often irrelevant to the lines. While it accompanies lines, it also accompanies gestures, movements, gazes, and sighs; it exists during complete silences, or when others are speaking. Therefore, I have little choice but to refer to it by Bateson's name, or by the coined (or "Cohened") term, "relacom." Perhaps you will too.

In summary, relacom:

a is the short form of Bateson's "relationship communication;"
b is the invocation of a relationship, not the announcement of one;
c is not necessarily communicated consciously, and in fact is usually unconscious;
d is a metacommunication: a format for communicating content;

63

e   exists whenever people are in conscious contact, even when there is no recognizable content exchanged between them;

f   is most usually nonverbal, and is often verbally undefinable.

Relacom is at the core of the most significant parts of most day-to-day interactions. If we study the tape recordings of ordinary conversations, we will find that most of them are trivial at the content level, but rich at the level of relacom. Apparent content questions like "How are you doing?" are, of course, not content questions at all, and no one expects a content answer. ("How am I doing *what?*" an Edward Albee character might say.) For many of our speeches are semantically meaningless, merely icebreakers for relationships: "Hey!" "Whatcha doin'?" "Nice day, isn't it?" "Looks like rain…" "Have a nice day!" What we are conveying is simply, "I'd like you to like me." As previously mentioned, psychiatrist Eric Berne calls these "stroking" communications, since their intended effect is not to share information but to induce a verbal caress akin to a mother's stroking of her infant. Berne goes on to show how predominant these stroking communications are in everyday life.[25] Psychologist Virginia Satir goes further, suggesting that "*all* messages, when viewed at their highest abstraction level, can be characterized as 'Validate me' messages."[26] Naturally such invocations of validation – or of love, respect, admiration, or trust – are rarely the conscious cause of our communications, but they are often, and maybe even always, an unconscious prompt. For the relationship mode of communication is not one we are normally aware of. The professor is probably not consciously trying to invoke respect, and the student is not consciously pulling for a good grade. These things happen, however, and they happen in life pretty much all the time; thus they must be seen to occur in any credible staging of life in a dramatic event. Relacom must occur onstage with the same subtlety and intensity it has in our own, real lives, for at least in the realistic theatre, it must be seen to exist in the "real" lives of fictitious characters.

Exercise: *The contentless scene*

The "Contentless Scene" is a relacom exercise that I invented and named in the first edition, and has since been used wherever acting is studied; a book of sixty such scenes was published in 2004 (Diane Timmerman's *Spare Scenes*), and many others have appeared in essays, websites, flashcards, class syllabi, and on YouTube. The point of such scenes is that they *have no content whatsoever* except at the relacom level.

Here is my first such scene. To experience it, memorize the dialogue with a partner, and then "perform" the dialogue as a scene that takes place in any *one* of the described situations:

THE DIALOGUE
A: Hi!
B: Hello.

A: What'd you do last night?
B: Oh, not much. How about you?
A: Oh, watched a little T.V.
B: Anything good?
A: Well, no. Not really.
B: See you later.
A: OK.

THE SITUATIONS

1   A casual pick up.
2   Husband and wife meeting the night after a trial separation.
3   Father and daughter at breakfast after she's been out late.
4   High school girls meeting after each suspects the other of dating a mutual boyfriend.
5   A rejection of friendship.
6   Lovers unable to meet except for a few moments.
7   Any of the above as a telephone call.
8   Any other situation suggested by the group.

The exercise may be performed by a large group, with A's serially pairing off with B's. When performed, it becomes clear that the content mode of the dialogue becomes insignificant and that the relacom becomes the "whole" scene – without anyone changing a word of the text. The exercise can also show how riveting a contentless scene may be when strong relacom is established by its performers.

A scene from Woyzeck[27]

Here's a close-to-contentless scene from Woyzeck, a nineteenth-century German play by Georg Büchner consisting of a large number of short scenes. Woyzeck is a soldier of the lowest rank, much abused by his officers and his girlfriend, whom he is thinking of killing. In this scene, reproduced in its entirety, Woyzeck buys a knife from a street peddler known only as "The Jew."

WOYZECK: The pistol's too much.
JEW: So, are you buying or not buying. Make up your mind.
WOYZECK: How much is the knife?
JEW: It's good and sharp. Going to cut your throat with it?
          Make up your mind. I'm giving it to you cheap as
          anybody. You can die cheap, but not for nothing.
WOYZECK: It'll cut more than bread...
JEW: Two groschen.
WOYZECK: Here! (Goes out.)
JEW: Here! Like it was nothing. And it's good money. The pig!

With a partner, choose and memorize the parts and play the scene, pantomiming the props of pistol, knife and groschen (German coins).

The scene clearly has content: Woyzeck is buying a knife with which he will kill his girlfriend and the mother of his child. But the characters and the setting are only barely sketched in: the scene can be played in countless ways. Performing it, both actors should try as hard as possible to *scope out the character they are playing opposite* in order to find out how much he or she is willing to pay for – or accept for – the knife. Each studies their partner's gaze (steady or shifty?), breathing (measured or rapid?), facial expressions (clenched jaw? pinched eyes? flared nostrils?), posture (slumped? erect? cocky?). Each looks for signs of anxiety beneath their partner's façade, aware that in difficult financial times – as they were in Germany when Büchner wrote the play – the difference between two and three groschen could mean life or death. And most important of all, each tries to negotiate their very best price for the knife! The Jew's last line, spoken after Woyzeck has left with the knife, could be delivered to a street passerby, or to the audience, or to God – or to an imaginary person so loudly that Woyzeck is unable *not* to hear it.

If there is a group of actors doing this, have half of them learn one part and the other half the other; then, paring each "Woyzeck" with a "Jew" have them play the scenes without rehearsing them. Then switch the pairings and have them play with a different partner. No one should talk *about* the scenes, however, until the exercise is completely finished. Each actor should create his or her role wholly "from the inside" – and the actor opposite must not be told what that is. The job of each actor is to dig deeply into the actor opposite, establishing a continual feedback loop of intense relationship communication between them, and remembering, of course, that no matter how quietly this scene might be played, life or death hangs in its conclusion.

Relacom connections

In the previous chapter we looked at victories that characters, like persons in life, seek to win. We all have basic and biological drives toward survival, security, power, love, and validation. Most animals have these as well; these goals are innate and unthinking.

But we also have many specific goals, and achieving these almost always involves other people. Albert Einstein may have come up with his famous theories simply by digging them out of his brain, but somebody had to listen to him for them to get published and distributed. Sometimes we need the help of others, and sometimes we need others to get out of our way. During our lives, we will need at times to acquire allies, to win over or defeat rivals and opponents, and to impress important people who don't (yet) agree with us or even know who we are. It is *from, with, and for other people* that almost all of our life-victories must be won. We do not act in the abstract, we act in the context of our world, and for the most part that context is human. Humans, like it or not, are social creatures.

And thus most if not all of the victories we expect will be gained, if they are, through our relationships with other people.

In relacom, we try to favorably redefine our relationship with other persons in a specific way. As we are egocentric beings (see Chapter 1), we tend to characterize others in our lives as having a functional relationship to ourselves. When I refer to Lorna Cohen as "my wife," for example, I am defining an individual person as a function of "me" rather than as an entity in her own right. In general, we tend to think of other people, at least privately, as "my lover," "my friend," "my enemy," "my colleague," "my roommate," and so on. We define them in terms of the relationship they have with us. (Let's not feel too badly about this: they do the same thing with us.) Socially, treating other people as functions of ourselves may seem reprehensible; psychologically, however, it is ingrained, since it develops in earliest infancy. Specialists in infant psychology have clearly demonstrated that the child's first impression of reality is wholly self-centered; the infant believes that his mother, for example, is simply a part of him, and that she does not even possess a separate existence. Indeed, the infant's first intellectual task is to distinguish himself from his mother; to discover her as a separate person living a separate life. And this task is *never entirely completed*, not at the deepest levels at least; all adult life, it is possible to say, is in part an effort to come to terms with the separateness of others.

Our relationship communications, therefore, are innately self-centered. They are also, at the deepest levels of psychological reality and human intercourse, self-aggrandizing. We not only see people as being functions of ourselves, we seek to redefine that function favorably to ourselves. To the infant, the mother is not thought of as a mother, for that notion would be incomprehensible to a child. To the infant the mother may be at first, if the infant could use words, "my nurse," and "my pillow." Later she will be "my cradler," "my playmate," and eventually, when harsh words begin to be learned, "my enemy."

In our actual life, our relationships are redefined over time. "My colleague" may become "my boss" or "my underling." "My friend" may become "my lover," then "my husband," then "my ex." "My friend" can become "my enemy" – "my idol" can become "my nemesis." We have some control over these changes, but so do the other persons we're speaking of. *Negotiating* these relationships, therefore, is part of our everyday life – even though, in most normal lives, there may be very little to negotiate. But dramatic situations, we must remember, are ordinarily not about normal lives. And in truly dramatic productions, raised voices, sudden gestures, contorted expressions, floods of tears, and passionate, romantic embraces become the norm, not the rare occurrence.

Relacom in drama

Relacom consists of pursuing the character's goals as the actor defines and imagines them. Merging the playwright's dialogue, the director's staging and her own personal psyche and theatrical gifts, the actor plunges into relationship communication with all her fellow-actors to realize the goals she seeks. Whether she will get them or not is the playwright's decision: her decision is simply to try.

Some dramatic scenes are virtually all relacom: the dialogue between Hamlet and Polonius about a cloud, for example:

POLONIUS: My lord, the Queen would speak with you, and presently.
HAMLET: Do you see yonder cloud that's almost in shape of a camel?
POLONIUS: By th' mass, and 'tis like a camel indeed.
HAMLET: Methinks it is like a weasel.
POLONIUS: It is back'd like a weasel.
HAMLET: Or like a whale.
POLONIUS: Very like a whale.
HAMLET: Then will I come to my mother by-and-by…

This scene has absolutely nothing to do with clouds, camels, weasels or whales. Its content is limited to the first and last lines in which Polonius tells Hamlet his mother wants to speak to him, and Hamlet says he will come to her. Everything in between is pure relacom: Hamlet and Polonius verbally sparring with each other to scope out each other's thoughts and attitudes and establish a priority of power within the Court. For this is indeed a power struggle: Polonius is both Lord Chancellor of Denmark and King Claudius's closest ally, but Hamlet is of royal birth and, technically at least, heir to the Danish throne. Who gets to order whom? Before responding to Polonius' passing on his mother's request, therefore, Hamlet humiliates the fatuous lord by forcing him to respond serially to his deliberately silly and contradictory statements and, only then, says that he will do what the lord has told him. This is face-saving relacom, having nothing to do with the content of the communication, and everything to do with the redefining of the power balance between the two men. Here is a far more complex – and dangerous – dialogue from Othello:

IAGO: My noble lord—
OTHELLO: What dost thou say, Iago?
IAGO: Did Michael Cassio, when you woo'd my lady,
            Know of your love?
OTHELLO: He did, from first to last: why dost thou ask?
IAGO: But for a satisfaction of my thought;
            No further harm.
OTHELLO: Why of thy thought, Iago?
IAGO: I did not think he had been acquainted with her.
OTHELLO: O, yes; and went between us very oft.
IAGO: Indeed!
OTHELLO: Indeed! ay, indeed: discern'st thou aught in that?
            Is he not honest?
IAGO: Honest, my lord?

OTHELLO: Honest? ay, honest.
IAGO: My lord, for aught I know.
OTHELLO: What dost thou think?
IAGO: Think, my lord?
OTHELLO: Think, my lord?
>By heaven, he echoes me,
>As if there were some monster in his thought
>Too hideous to be shown. Thou dost mean something.

Read literally, and only for content, the scene is meaningless: Iago is asking questions, and Othello doing his best to answer them. No line literally suggests there is anything about which Othello should be concerned. But the relacom implicit in the lines – and played by the actors – gets deeply into him, and soon Othello will be saying "yet there's more in this," then "What dost thou mean?" and eventually, "O misery" and "O blood! Blood! Blood!" Iago, who has been relegated to serving as Othello's "ancient" (ensign), has by the end of the scene become his virtual commander, fulfilling his prediction that Othello, his general, "will as tenderly be led by the nose as asses are." Here, pure relacom – tone of voice, gaze, proximity, winces, waggles of the head, "I dunno" gestures and the like – rather than logic or verbal discussion or argument has, in two minutes or so, utterly reversed the power relationship between the two characters.

Does this mean people are always manipulating each other? That we are all grasping, climbing, plotting, or designing people, with "designs" on the lives of others and fantasies about them? No, not at all. The vast majority of relacom during our waking hours consists, for most people, of seeking to maintain and if anything improve the amiable relationships we enjoy with our friends, families, colleagues, neighbors and acquaintances. But plays are rarely about strictly amiable relationships. In exploring and defining the goals sought by her character in dramatic relationships, which are generally laced with conflict, danger, and potential betrayal, the actor must on occasion allow reckless abandon to overcome restraint, and ferocity to overcome sensible argument, since consistent timidity in approaching critical situations, unless specifically called for in the script, can only lead to insipid performances.

Reckless abandon? Ferocity? Don't worry; these are relative terms. For Laura to dance with Jim O'Connor near the end of *The Glass Menagerie* is an act of reckless abandon. She has abandoned her shyness, at least for a few moments of joy. When the deaf and dumb Helen Keller says "wa-wa" ("water") towards the end of *The Miracle Worker*, it is an act of ferocity: She has struggled so hard to overcome the provocations of her teacher that she has, for the first time in her life, managed to utter her first word.

Actors must be brave. We are all, of course, socially conditioned to abhor naked ambition, or at least of admitting to it, and we are reluctant to have others picture us as grasping individuals. But that is what we often are, and so are characters in plays. We must not shrink from proactively pursuing our characters' plans, hopes, and fantasies. The drive for winning our goals should be penetrating, incisive, potent, and subtle. It should involve unique and idiosyncratic fantasies, unexpected and theatrical ambitions. The relacom between actors should dig and it should reveal. Probably nothing so regularly typifies deadly theatre as the actors who insist – usually passionately – that their characters wanted nothing but modest goals, pleasantly pursued. On the contrary, most plays, and the lives of most of the characters in them, are replete with lures of success, lusts for adventure, hopes of a happy life – and perhaps an afterlife to supersede it. To ignore this is to opt, in dramatic performances, for a genteel and quite un-lifelike banality.

Relacom between actors

How do you actually play relacom? Since it is mostly comprised of unconscious behavior, it cannot be consciously choreographed. Fortunately, the theatre provides the perfect and complete mechanism for playing relacom: the actor plays it *with the other actors*. While we must be dubious about any single statement claimed to be "the secret of acting," there is some reason to think that if there were a secret, that would be it.

At the level of relacom, actor and character have merged. They are indistinguishable from each other. You are not falling in love with Juliet, you are falling in love with the "Ellen" who plays Juliet. It is not Othello you are leading by the nose, it is some guy named Derrick. It is Ellen's eyes Romeo will be looking into, it is Derrick's trembling lip and sweaty palms that Iago is tracking. Relacom is *biological* communication, and characters are nothing but words on paper until there is a biological actor speaking them.

Almost all of us are outwardly polite, pleasant, well-socialized beings, but there is hardly a one of us that does not harbor dreams of glory, sexual fantasies, or genuinely murderous impulses – and usually all three – from time to time. These are the actor's greatest tools. When Romeo looks into Juliet's eyes, rehearsal after rehearsal and performance after performance, he is trying to seduce Ellen, not Juliet, because "Juliet" has only words – no eyes, no breasts, no lips. But Ellen has eyes, breasts, lips, and hormones, along with sexual "buttons" that he is only too eager to push. So this Romeo is trying to woo her with – along with Shakespeare's words and the costume shop's apparel – absolutely everything he's got inside him. And she is doing the same with her classmate Harry who's playing Romeo.

And when Iago tries to lead Othello to disaster, he is studying Derrick's lips and palms and everything else that can sharpen the knife he is slowly whittling into Derrick's brain.

This is why acting is acting. It is also why acting is also hard, because acting engages not only your conscious control of body and voice but the unconscious portions of your human organism – your autonomic nervous system, above all, along with the sweat glands, emotions, tear ducts, and thousands of hidden processes that are under its control. These shape your heard intonations and resonances, your observed gestures and movements, and even your heartbeats and your respiration. They are all part of your relacom – and your partner's relacom.

Playing relacom is also hard because it is scary. Beginning actors, in particular, are often embarrassed, or downright afraid, of allowing their lusts, fantasies, or dreams to drive them "over the edge" in an acting class or student performance. And they may have a very good reason not to go over the edge in certain cases – my own classes are governed by a written and distributed "protocol" that specifies a few physical things that cannot be done, such as parts of the body that cannot be touched, weapons that cannot be used, and fights and falls that will have to be carefully coached and rehearsed. But *mentally*, relacom must be open to anything on the stage – as it is open to anything every moment of our "real" lives. For while none of us likes being thought of as having the dreams of glory, sexual fantasies or murderous impulses that our unconscious minds harbor from time to time, we know (or should know) that these are normal human musings – often, at least in some fashion, from the age of two. If we do not put these in our bag of "actor tools," we will never be able to act the roles that make theatre a dazzling event.

Relacom, however, while something in which actors engage all the time, is also something they must never talk about. If an actor discusses his or her relacom with an acting partner, or the two of them discuss the relacom of a scene they are rehearsing, it then becomes content communication, not relacom. It becomes conscious and mental, not unconscious and biological. Relacom is something to be lived, not revealed. It is, in fact, an actor's secret. It is *your* secret. And it should remain your secret! No one needs to know your sexual fantasies or murderous impulses. And you would be probably reluctant to let them loose in your mind if you were aware that others around you knew what you are thinking. For playing relacom necessarily means playing out your *private* fantasies. From actress-Ellen's vantage, actor-Harry is the Romeo she sees. Actress-Ellen is aware that "she" embodies two persons: the Ellen she is and the Juliet she plays. But the body across from her is only one person: one body and one voice. She has never lived inside that body or that mind, so they are all one to her. She is performing, then, to the person, to the body and to the voice, not to an abstract name. "What's in a name?" she might well ask, for names are irrelevant to relacom. Relacom takes place between real human bodies, real human beings, not "names," or "identities," or even "characters." Believe in that person! Win her or him over.

Do people worry about being over-identified with their characters? Yes, sometimes. All actors are concerned about being reduced to "types," and some fear their stage or film personalities may be confused with their real-life ones. But while it may be better for an actor to turn down a role that she cannot play with confidence than to perform it while holding a figurative flag in the air that proclaims "This character is not me," it is better yet for the actor to plunge into

"The process is believe: Believe the other person; believe in
your own capacity to believe your own emotional reactions
– or even lack of them – just believe that it's real."

American actor Harrison Ford[28]

the life of the character she is offered. To the actor, nothing should be unimagi-
nable; nothing should be at least *mentally* unplayable. What the actor does in
her private life is, of course, her own business; what she allows herself to
fantasize in the theatre is the theatre's business. An actor who is mentally
inhibited from playing relacom which, in life, is repugnant to her, is an actor
whose range will be critically limited, both emotionally and behaviorally.
Actors should have a vast mental freedom, for the greatest theatre comes from
the enlarged imaginations of the actors free enough to indulge – at least
mentally – in life's extremities.

"An actor must interpret life, and in order to do so he must
be willing to accept all experiences that life can offer."

American actor Marlon Brando[29]

"The better I get as an actress, the freer I feel. Actresses have
to exhibit themselves, to hang themselves up on a
clothesline. Onstage, you often find that you're free to do
what you can't do in real life…In my own life, I was brought
up to be well-mannered, no matter where I was or what I was
doing…Onstage, I found…I was free to reveal exactly what
I felt."

American actress Jane Fonda[30]

Emotion

Playing relacom with another actor brings out the actor's own emotions. This is vital because we have to feel that these are the actors' own emotions when we see them played out on the stage or screen. Such emotions – such real emotions – are essential if stage actions are to be seen as dramatic, and to compel our rapt attention. As cognitive psychologist Keith Oatley says, succinctly, "Emotions give life its urgency."[31] And that is why actors and directors treasure them on the stage or before the camera.

Doing a role...means living through all of the emotions that it brings with it. I know it's make-believe, but if you're going to create a dark moment, you can't create it just because you imagine it. You've got to live it. And if you live it, it costs you."

American actor Mandy Patinkin[32]

But how do actors show *real* emotion on stage, performance after performance, when they are "just acting"? And do they really need to show *real* emotion? Can't they just fake it? These have been the major questions addressed about acting since ancient times. Back then, the answer to the second question – do actors need to show real emotion? – was simple. It was (and this may surprise you) a resounding "Yes, they certainly do!"

Ion, the famous rhapsode (solo performer of rhapsodic stories) of ancient Athens, explained to Socrates, "When I tell my tale of woe, my eyes fill with tears. And when I speak of horrors, my heart throbs and my hair stands on end." These are certainly symptoms of real emotion – even though Ion adds that he also finds time to look down at the audience to make sure they're reacting properly. The notion of "real emotion" lasted through the entire classic period. The Roman poet Horace, in his *Ars Poetica*, told actors who recited his works, "*Si vis me flere, dolendum est primum ipsi tibi,*" or "To make me cry, you must first feel grief yourself," and this phrase soon became the great Horatian maxim for subsequent actors. The Roman orator Quintilian even described a method for performers to truly feel grief as opposed to just simulating it: they could create, he said, "Fantastic... daydreams...whereby things absent are presented to our imagination with such extreme vividness that they seem actually to be before our very eyes." Quiltilian, therefore, imagined the death of his own wife and children when he orated a tragic poem. The Roman actor Polus took imagination a step further: When playing the role of Electra, in mourning for her brother Orestes whom she believed had died, it is said that Polus brought the real ashes of his own cremated son on stage with him, and then "embraced them as if they were those of Orestes."[33] This use of what Stanislavsky was later to call "the magic if," we are told, "filled the whole place not with the appearance and imitation of sorrow but with genuine grief and unfeigned lamentation." Real emotion on stage was only seriously challenged (principally by Denis Diderot, in his "Paradox of Acting,"[34] and Goethe in his essays on German classicism) during the Age of Enlightenment. It came roaring back, however, in the Age of Realism, particularly with the early twentieth-century teachings (and stagings) of André Antoine in Paris, Konstantin Stanislavsky in Moscow and, in New York, the Austro-Hungarian émigré, Lee Strasberg. "Strasberg was a fanatic on the subject of true emotion," said Harold Clurman, his co-partner in the founding of the Group Theatre, which revolutionized American acting in the 1930s. "Everything was secondary to it," Clurman went on. "He sought it with the patience of an inquisitor, he was outraged by trick substitutes.... Here was something new to most of the actors, something basic, something almost holy. It was revelation in the theatre."[35] So actors today, particularly in America, are usually committed – and often obsessed – with creating truth, honesty, integrity, and "real emotion" on the stage and screen. But it is not entirely clear how "real" these "real emotions" really are!

We have learned a great deal about emotion since the time of Stanislavsky and Strasberg, and particularly since the first edition of this book appeared. We have not only realized that emotion comes from our brains (in earlier centuries it was thought to come from the "humors" in various organs in our lower quarters), we know pretty much what parts of those brains: chiefly the amygdala, an almond-shaped region right behind the eyes, and secondarily the anterior cingulate, a larger brain segment above it. The separate functions of these brain components are now beginning to be well understood, and many of the receptors and neurotransmitters that connect them with parts of the body and other parts of the brain have been identified as well. Neuroscientists are also identifying, for the first time, the major link between emotion and action, and thus the mind and the body. This link is the insula, a pair of prune-shaped portions of the brain that, in concert, provide "the wellspring of social emotions, things like lust and disgust, pride and humiliation, guilt and atonement." Within the insula are the Von Economo Neurons – or VENS – which, we are told, "are in the catbird seat for turning feelings and emotions into actions and intentions." Tampering with the insula and interrupting the VENS has proven successful in ending addictions, which has landed these subjects on the front pages of newspapers in recent years. But they are also critical in connecting the two main areas of acting, actions and emotions, though this has warranted far less scientific examination.[36]

Brain mechanics are maddeningly complex. Perhaps the most important new studies on the complexity of human emotion are those of Portuguese neuroscientist Antonio Damasio, beginning with his landmark *Descartes' Error: Emotion,*

Reason, and the Human Brain published in 1994. Damasio divides emotions into two major categories: primary ones, (those "the squirrel feels when the eagle flies overhead"), emanating from the amygdala and anterior cingulate, and secondary (considered) ones, which "involve a conscious contemplation of the primary ones," and emanate from the prefrontal sensual cortices. "Emotion is the combination of a mental evaluative process, simple or complex, with dispositional responses [i.e. personality traits] to that process," Damasio concludes.[37]

Primary and secondary emotions are quite different, however. Not only do they emanate from different parts of the brain, they come to us at different times, and we experience them in radically different ways. Our primary emotions aren't really emotions at all – not in the common sense. When the eagle flies overhead, we must assume the squirrel's brain is not pumping out emotions but plans – "How the hell do I ditch this eagle?" When the man in the previous chapter is running from the bear and towards the cabin, he is not really "feeling fear" as much as he is thinking "How do I get into that cabin?" Indeed, his mind is so pre-occupied with figuring out his next step that there is simply no room in it to bring up feelings at all. The man's response to the bear's charge is a *reaction*, with an emphasis on the two final syllables of that word, rather than an emotion. The emotion will come only later, when the man is safe inside the cabin, when it will come over him like a flood.

Damasio did not discover this. William James did, in 1884, creating (in a completely different fashion) the "bear in the forest" analogy I have illustrated in Chapter 1. James basically reverses "see the bear, get frightened and run" with "see the bear, run away, and then get frightened at what just happened."[38] When we speak about emotion in our own lives, therefore, we are really thinking about what Damasio terms *considered* emotions, which are secondary to our primary reactive ones. Thus we rarely if ever consider primary emotions as "feelings" – we are much too committed to follow up on them: to save ourselves from situations that make us afraid and to plunge into situations that attract us through romantic desire, only afterwards reflecting, "Boy, was I scared!" or "Wow, I think I'm falling in love!" So emotion comes in radically different forms.

Damasio has also noticed that two completely different muscles are required to make a genuine smile. When comparing stroke victims, he found that those whose left brain hemisphere had been destroyed would smile crookedly if told to smile, but would smile normally if simply responding to something amusing. Those whose right brain was impaired, however, would do just the reverse! These discoveries shows that one part of our brain operates a muscle (the orbicularis oculi if you are taking notes) that responds only to *genuine* emotion, while another part (operating the zygomatic major) responds only to *willed* emotion. "The willed smile will always be a bit crooked," Damasio concludes, adding that "the career of actors and politicians hinges on this simple, annoying disposition of neurophysiology."[39]

But that doesn't mean there can't be some will power beneath "genuine" smiling. Modern neuroscientific experiments have also discovered that humans can experience genuine emotion when they *simulate* certain expressions. "Emotional feelings and/or behaviors are tempered by *facial feedback*," three neuroscientists report in *Emotional Contagion,* and humans can "feel the specific emotions (love, joy, anger, fear, or sadness) *consistent with the facial expressions they adopt.*"[40] While this might at first thought seem absurd, I think it is obvious. If, out of pure habit and good manners, we smile at a waitress who comes to take our order, it makes us happy to be smiling, and our smile will probably provoke *her* to smile, which will make us happier yet. The researchers go on to say that "if subjects are made to look angry, for example, they feel angry...An actor playing King Lear, for example, would himself become angry as he enacted his part – cursing Fate, shaking his fists, and thundering at the heavens."[41] Who of us that have directed this play (as I have three times) has not noticed this, at least in rehearsals?

Emotion, therefore, is a highly complex mental activity. It has many sources, each working in collaboration with the others. Fake smiles may become genuine; fake anger can cause our real blood pressure to rise. How then should emotions enter into the playing of a part? The great French actor Jean Louis Barrault had a sublime analogy for it: Barrault compared emotion to the sweat of a long-distance runner. If the runner is really trying to win the race, Barrault says, sweat will form on her brow. But if the runner is trying to merely *sweat* while running, she will probably neither sweat nor win the race. The sweat comes only from *trying as hard as you can to win the race*, not from "trying to sweat."* It is noteworthy that Stanislavsky, late in life, developed a "theory of physical actions" which switched from prioritizing emotion to prioritizing action in the actor's work. Even Lee Strasberg's classes, when I audited them at the Actors' Studio in the early 1960s, usually emphasized action more than emotion, although his writings never reflected this.

The actor's drive toward trying as hard as she can to win victories, particularly through relacom, will draw forth her own emotion as surely as the drive toward the finish line draws forth the half-miler's sweat. (Indeed, really trying to win relacom victories on the stage, even without running or physical exertion, often leaves actors drenched with perspiration. Haven't we all seen that in the rehearsal hall?) Emotion, like perspiration, must be drawn out from under the skin. It cannot simply be pushed out at one's will.

Thus, actors must be seen arousing emotion, but not be seen *trying* to arouse it. How do they do this? The problem of creating emotion both honestly and

---

* The complete line is worthy of citation: "The actor lives uniquely in the present; he is continually jumping from one present to the next. In the course of these successive presents he executes a series of actions which deposit upon him a sort of sweat which is nothing else but the state of emotion. This sweat is to his acting what juice is to fruit. But once he starts perceiving and taking cognizance of his state of emotion, the sweat evaporates forthwith, the emotion disappears and the acting dries up." Jean-Louis Barrault's quote is from his *Reflections on the Theatre,* translated by Barbara Wall. London: Rockliff, 1951, p. 126.

idiosyncratically does not end simply by understanding Barrault's analogy; understanding emotion and creating it are two different things. Every actor, however, at one time or another will face the stage direction "she breaks into tears and sobs helplessly." Without a satisfactory mechanism to turn on one's own tear duct systems, the actor is forced to rely on fakery or gimmickry. Real emotions are indeed important because they are unique to the individual actor who feels them, and are idiosyncratic to the actor's personality. Therefore, they contain the actor's unique "breath of life." Sean Penn's emotions are his and no one else's; anyone trying to imitate them will almost certainly look foolish. Moreover, real emotions stimulate and catalyze the body's real autonomic systems, and lead to the otherwise consciously uncontrollable endocrine reactions: increased heartbeat and blood pressure, dilation of the pupils and bronchi, adrenalin and sugar release in the bloodstream, contraction of the spleen, and so forth. These are signs that the audience members, if they are not doctors, will not be able to identify by name, but will certainly understand as what the character is going through. We in the audience are not medical experts, but we are people experts. We have been analyzing other people since we saw them on the playground in elementary school.

So let us take a look at the classic "illustration" of emotion on stage. That would be tears. Real tears.

Tears

The most common example of visible real emotion is crying real tears. It is often critical in acting – and even in getting into a play. In auditions, says longtime casting director Gary Shaffer, "The person who cries real tears gets the job."

But what are "real" tears? Real tears are generally assumed to be those we cannot consciously control, and there is no question that they sometimes (if not most times) are. A baby cries moments after it is born – the baby has certainly not "learned" how to cry; this behavior is simply instinctual. But we all have had the experience, during our childhoods at least, of having tears well up in our eyes, and then *deciding whether or not to let them flow*. We may then "decide to cry" – in order, say, to make our mother feel guilty that she has so hurt our feelings, or make our older brother feel sorry for us. *This is relacom*. Many of us have cried simply to relieve tension – what is sometimes known as "having a good cry" – or to stop an argument that we no longer wish to pursue. So there are times we have practical *reasons* to not hold back our tears, and therefore reasons to cry "real" ones. For they are certainly real tears, and they will literally moisten a handkerchief or two.

No one has written more, or more succinctly, about crying on stage than – surprise! – William Shakespeare. The words "weep" and "tears" appear more than 600 times in his plays, almost always in reference to someone sobbing in front of someone else on the stage. Othello, for example, weeps when he confronts Desdemona ("Am I the motive of these tears, my Lord?" she asks him). Menenius sobs before Coriolanus ("Thy tears are saltier than a younger man's," Coriolanus tells him). Romeo wails wildly in the Friar's cell ("There on the ground, with his own tears made drunk" complains the Friar angrily to the Nurse, pointing him out). Often the sobbing is fully in public: Claudio has "wash'd" Hero's foulness "with tears" in front of the whole wedding party in *Much Ado About Nothing*. Enobarbus weeps openly amidst Antony's brigade of also-sobbing soldiers ("Look, they weep, And I, an ass, am onion-eyed") in *Antony and Cleopatra*. In *Hamlet*, Polonius even stops a play because the actor playing a "Player" is seen to cry when performing a dramatic speech ("Look where he has not turned his color, and has tears in's eyes. Prithee, no more!" says Polonius). As I have demonstrated more fully elsewhere,* actors clearly cried real tears in Shakespeare's plays (they had to be real ones; the Globe theatre audiences were only a few feet away, watching the play in full daylight).

But Shakespeare also refers to faked tears. In *The Comedy of Errors*, Adriana says she will "weep what's left away, and weeping die;" but then changes her mind, saying "No longer will I be a fool, / To put the finger in the eye and weep." Obviously, digital massage can bring about tears. So can alcohol: Falstaff, improvising the "role" of King Henry at the Boar's Head, orders an attendant to "Give me a cup of sack to make my eyes look red, that it may be thought I have wept." And in the induction of *The Taming of the Shrew*, Bartholomew's Lord asks him to perform a woman's role in the play-within-the-play, suggesting that the lad employ a time-tested technique to bring copious teardrops right on cue:

> [LORD:] And if the boy have not a woman's gift
> To rain a shower of commanded tears,
> An onion will do well for such a shift,
> Which, in a napkin being close convey'd
> Shall in despite enforce a watery eye.

But these characters – Adriana, Falstaff and Bartholomew – though played by professional actors, were not *playing* professional actors. And professional actors don't use fingers, wine or onions to create their tears – or their "real" emotions.

So tears flowing on stage – and emotions expressed on stage – must be real, but their "realness" will also contain a component, and often a strong component, of the character's (and hence the actor's) will. This is nothing more than an extrapolation of Damasio's primary and secondary emotions that emanate from separate areas of the human brain, and the *Emotional Contagion* coauthors' explanation that our "real" emotions are "tempered by [our own] facial feedback."

---

* "Be Your Tears Wet: Tears (And Acting) in Shakespeare," *Journal of Dramatic Theory and Criticism*, Winter 1996.

The character (and hence the actor) thus has options as to how she can temper – or *use* – her innate emotion. The engagement of the body's physiology is an adjunct of emotional involvement, which cannot be fully faked. In the close-up acting of films, of course, the physiological behavior of the actor can be quite directly observed. Ian McKellen admiringly quotes Michael Caine as saying, "when the camera is close you don't have to act – all you have to do is think."[42] These are both British-trained actors and expert specialists in acting technique, but their most fundamental method is to let their mere thinking do the heavy lifting of their (at least filmed) performances. Even in stage performances, however, the audience is quite aware of major physiological processes going on before their eyes. In a celebrated example, I (and the rest of the audience) observed the superb American actor Hume Cronyn's face break into a fiery red blush, vivid from the back of the house, for more than thirty seconds during a climactic moment in Noel Coward's *A Song at Twilight*. The moment occurred when Cronyn's character, alone on stage at the end of the play, re-read for the first time in years a past letter from a former homosexual lover. When asked about his "technique," Cronyn reported that it was simply to let himself become deeply involved in the situation, releasing the emotions which naturally flowed from that involvement.*

When the actor tries to simply *push* emotion, or *play* emotion, it almost always fails. An actor who tries to "show fear" only "shows showing," which is showing-off. Actors should never "play emotions;" they should play to win goals that will draw emotions out of them. Pushing emotion makes the actor self-conscious. It appears indulgent; we see the actor emoting because she wants to, not because she has to. One of the first mechanisms developed by Stanislavsky was what he called "emotional recall" or "affective memory," in which the actor recalled a situation in her own life in order to stimulate an emotional display during the course of her performance. Stanislavsky eventually dropped the procedure, but many actors continue to attempt it. They shouldn't. While it might prove occasionally helpful in emergency situations,† it essentially removes the actor from the play, its situations, its interactions, and its relacom. It makes the actor self-conscious, thinking about her own life and career (her real-life context) and not about winning her character's goals. Whereas playing within the situation, using both text and relacom to win her goals, elicits the actor's primary and secondary emotions so natural to humans.

But scientists' findings, and actors' experiences and metaphors, are not all we have to help us deliver this on the stage.

---

* George Bernard Shaw similarly witnessed the actress Eleanora Duse blush vividly onstage while performing in a romantic German play in the 1890s. "I could detect no trick in it: it seemed to me a perfectly genuine effect of the dramatic imagination," Shaw wrote. *Our Theatres in the Nineties*, 1931, p. 162.

† TV actor Clarence Gilyard Jr. once told me he used it only when he would come back to the set from lunch and find he had to do his "final take" of a highly emotional scene in the next ten seconds.

Playing the opposite

"Playing the opposite" – a term not at all unique to this book, and an acting axiom that has been used for decades – is based on the fundamental push-pull of every character. It is an outgrowth of the innate ambivalence in human beings: that in critical situations we all want to be both adventurous and safe. We all want to go far but not too far; to plunge deep but not too deep.

To play the opposite, the actor contemplates all the physiological symptoms associated with the emotional state the script dictates her to play; then tries to consciously suppress them! If the script asks her to sob helplessly, for example, she tries *not* to cry. She tries as hard as she can to "breathe normally." She tries to *stop* the churning of her stomach, the perspiration welling up under her arms, perhaps the feeling of looseness in her bowels. But of course she already *is* breathing normally, and her stomach, armpits and bowels are just as they were beforehand. *Trying to make her body "normal"* when in fact it *is* normal, however, will trigger all the body's natural defense mechanisms that come into play when these irregularities do appear. And the actor will thereby be "fooled" into actually experiencing the imagined ailments she is trying to "really" overcome.

An example from my own life: driving home on a broad and empty street late at night after a rehearsal, I swerved to avoid hitting a squirrel crossing the road. Flashing red and blue lights quickly appeared behind me – and I was pulled over by a police officer. "Walk this line," he told me, pointing to a stripe on the side of the road. I had drunk no alcohol whatever that day or evening, but I found "walking the line" almost impossible to do without staggering. My body was simply, and unconsciously, "trying too hard" to do something that, were I not facing potential arrest, I could have done perfectly and without any hesitation. I was trying so hard "not to fail" that I almost failed – as an actor trying hard "not to cry" will start to cry.

This is a variation of Gregory Bateson's "double-bind" theory as discussed in the first chapter. Fooling one's own body "works" because our body is familiar with suppressing the manifestations of emotion; finding those suppressive functions at work, the "body" comes up with the emotion to justify it! Deterministic stimulus-response theories find this difficult to explain, but it is a very simple outgrowth of cybernetic and feedback-oriented systems. Playing the opposite draws emotion from the actor through real, personal, and situational means, for it is nothing more than engaging in the character's own behavior. It is the actor herself who tries to suppress emotional displays which threaten her posture of invulnerability. When she engages in this, when she tries to tighten her own (and her character's) bowels, breathe normally, and stop the sweat she feels beading under her armpits, she is simply doing what her character would be doing, and her emotions will be forthcoming as a reaction to her character's intentions, not as a direct and conscious result of them.

"When you start to rehearse with other people something begins to happen. What it is exactly I don't know, and don't even want to know. I'm all for mystery there. Most of what happens as you develop your part is unconscious, most of it is underwater...you get taken over by some force outside yourself. Something happens."

American actress Kim Stanley[43]

Exercises: Playing the opposite

Here are a few simple exercises in playing the opposite:

- Play a drunkard by trying to walk a straight line with absolute precision. (A classic example, slightly different from my own. The drunkard is identifiable not because he cannot walk a straight line, but because he tries so hard to suppress his fear of being unable to do so.)
- Play a son grieving for his mother's death by trying to laugh at a joke told by your well-meaning but insensitive uncle.
- Play a wife who is fearful of dying from cancer by bravely giving your husband instructions on having the house cleaned before you return from the hospital after surgery.
- Play a love-torn fiancé by coldly describing your lover's desertion of you for another.
- Deny that you hate someone.

In all of these exercises, you need not "protest too much;" simply "enough" will do. Concentrate simply on doing the exercise rather than making the exercise work. The exercise cannot be "pushed" or it becomes exactly what it is intended to overcome. You cannot yourself judge if the exercise has worked (although you can certainly tell when it doesn't): better let an outside observer judge the exercise while you concentrate on doing it.

Tactics

Tactics are the means by which we win, or seek to win, our ideal futures. They are the conscious and unconscious strategies of relacom. It may seem at first glance offensive to discuss our behavior in terms of tactics. Most of us pride ourselves on behaving naturally and spontaneously, without any thought of tactically manipulating our environment, or other people. The idea that humans have tactics is particularly loathsome in most contemporary religious, moral, and social thinking, which holds spirituality as the virtual opposite of tactical plotting and planning. Added to this, knowledge of the tactical basis of our victories often takes much of the relish away from them; it is all the more pleasing to think that we have "won" something without having sullied ourselves by tactically "going for it." "Oh, I had absolutely no idea I could have won this Oscar!" burbles the film star that paid her professional publicist $50,000 to promote it. We all have built-in inhibitions against examining the tactics of our behavior, or even the tactics of our character's behavior.

These inhibitions are natural, and, of course, much of human behavior clearly is spontaneous and subconsciously generated. As mentioned earlier, the baby's cry as it leaves the womb is certainly not tactical; neither is the flinch we make when a needle is jabbed in our arm, or the laughter we emit when we see a brilliantly performed farce on the stage. The fact remains, however, that if we are candid enough to examine our behavior closely, we can see that most of it is tactically designed – consciously or unconsciously – as relacom that will aid us in achieving our most basic desires. Our flinch of pain tells the nurse to be gentler the next time she pokes us with a needle. Our genial laugh tells our seatmate that we get the joke, and encourages the actors to keep up their great performance. Even the baby, weeks or months later, will have discovered that his yelp of pain will bring someone to feed, cuddle, or entertain him. People employ tactics, characters that represent those people must be seen to use tactics, and actors who play those characters must play their tactics forthrightly. Tactics are therefore a necessary field for the actor to study, and to study closely.

Tactics may be lumped into two major categories: those that *threaten* and those that *induce*. The former are "I win, you lose" in nature. The latter, which are much more common in life, are aimed toward "win-win" situations: mutual satisfaction, mutual victories. Both tactical approaches can work, both can fail, and both can be used in a myriad of combinations. Together they create an actor's power and her electricity on stage, threat tactics being primarily responsible for the actor's fierceness and forcefulness, and induction tactics giving the actor her magnetism and charm.

Threats, of course, are dangerous tactics. They may incite others to threaten in return and, as when they lead to wars, end up in a lose-lose situation for everyone. But they are also at times essential. Yelling "Watch out!" to a child who is about to walk in the path of a streetcar may not be very charming, but – with the implicit threat of punishment if the child does not heed it – may prove absolutely necessary. When push almost comes to shove in any relationship – social, business, romantic or familial – a firm "No!" or "Stop that!" or "I can't!" is a weighty refusal that may have either good or bad consequences. Physical strength is not required for posing threats, and neither is intellectual supremacy; no one can be fiercer than a two-year-old – just ask any parent (or grandparent) who has one.

And "magnetism and charm" is not to be thought of in the debased sense of "charm school" posturing, but rather in the more evocative sense of each person's capacity to draw others into his or her confidence – as a snake charmer pleases himself, his snake, and his audience all at the same time. Unlike threats, magnetism and charm are infectious, and they are transmissible. They can lead to win-win situations. And in life, we use them whenever we can.

Nonetheless, *both* varieties of tactics are crucial, and actors must use both much of the time. We both try to "pull" (through induction) and "push" (through threatening) the people we deal critically with; particularly those whose help, or affection, or cooperation, we want and need. Actors need to play a wide range of relacom behaviors that lie within both these categories, including smiling, joking, pleading, winking, and whispering sweet nothings when inducing; and scowling, staring, shouting, brandishing fists, and rising to a great height when threatening. Great actors are masters of both categories: just think of your favorite actors and you will quickly recall such tactics displayed in their performances – often changing at lightning speed from one to the other. Inducing tactics show an actor's appeal and threatening tactics make her seem scary, and what great actor do you know that cannot, at different times, be *both* appealing and scary, usually in the same role?

Most tactics, of course, are unconscious and spontaneous. We may prepare ourselves for an encounter by thinking "I'm going to be firm with him," but we rarely think "I'm going to blow up at him." Your tactics during any interaction – onstage or off – may be aimed in advance, but they can only accelerate reciprocally, during the interaction itself. Try to win your goal, and try *as hard as you can*, and your tactics will rise to the occasion. You need not predict where it will take you, because for the most part your tactical trajectory will be the one you have been using for most of your life. It is part of your natural relacom, both in life and on the stage.

And actors should also remember that there is nothing necessarily malicious, unkind, or cynical about having or using tactics. Smiling to receive a smile is an inductive tactic, yes, but it is also a universal and usually spontaneous act of human kindness. We do not ordinarily smile in the privacy of our rooms; rather, we smile in order to create a climate that is desirable for us to inhabit. And threats can save lives and build coherent enterprises. Indeed, our personal survival depends on our ability to influence others; we cannot survive entirely on our own. Whether, then, the smile or frown we present in public is "genuine" or "fake" is an unnecessary question; it is almost always a mixture of the two, and can be tactically useful however it is expressed.

"People hearing about [Georgy Girl] would say, Oh, that's about a girl who has problems. Georgy Girl to me was a very different person, very ruthless. Most people saw her as a sweet softie. I don't think she was a softie at all. She was manipulating and very shrewd. People loved her, I think, because they recognized their own terrible faults and were glad to see them put up on the screen...I liked her for all that.

British actress Lynn Redgrave[44]

Tactics and expectations

Despite my insistence that there is nothing necessarily malicious about using tactics, and that we do it all the time in our own lives (without thinking of them as tactics), many young actors are still timid about performing them, perhaps because they do not wish to appear overly aggressive. Many actors hide behind the defensive statement "I don't want this scene to become just a shouting match." Well, I've seen a lot of shouting matches on major world stages, and most of them were absolutely thrilling. British director Declan Donnellan describes the situation of an actor limply playing the role of Macbeth in rehearsals when, angry with himself for forgetting his next line, he hollers to the stage manager, "Line, please!" and everybody in the room is suddenly riveted – for the first time in the rehearsal. "How can the stakes be higher in a rehearsal than in plotting the assassination of the Head of State? ...We fool ourselves that we are playing high stakes when we are not even remotely near where the situation demands," Donnellan concludes.[45]

Actors, being (at least traditionally) sensitive people, may be reluctant to express – and particularly exhibit – soaring tactics, either in fury or seductive appeal. Granted, there are sides of all of us we don't want everybody to see. But "everybody" does not (and cannot) include your fellow actors. When acting, you are interacting not only with actors, but with characters. And how you (and therefore your character) views these characters may release you to express the fury or passionate attraction that the play demands. So you must view them as persons that you (yes, you!) can affect, can persuade, can convince, can even defeat.

Consider this example from real life. On a morning some years ago, a frail lady schoolteacher in New York was taking her class of third-graders on the 7th Avenue subway to the Museum of Natural History. As the car was slowing to a stop at the 79th Street station, she stood up and loudly declared to her charges, "OK! Everybody out!" At which point, to her astonishment, the entire contingent of passengers – commuters, shoppers, and tourists – rose and meekly followed her and her third graders out of the subway car and onto the platform. The confident boldness of her three-word speech had given her a commanding authority over everyone hearing her, and they followed her lead as they would have followed a fire marshal's. Had she not had her students in the car, and was simply trying to get the other passengers to exit, it is doubtful that she would have been able to exert sufficient authority to have them even look up, much less rise to their feet. It is astonishing how much "power" is simply there for the taking. A tactical offense supported with *positive expectations of victory* will lead to the sort of take-charge attitude that would be necessary to achieve it. And this power resides in all of us. We just have to have the courage to use it.

Actors must not give in to shyness or fear, then, when employing their boldest tactics on others – certainly not in rehearsal. The actors on the other end of these tactics will not be dismayed at this, for in fact this will draw stronger performances from them as well – and most of them will realize this immediately. There is nothing wrong to have weapons – psychological, intellectual, physical, and emotional – at your disposal when you are acting a scene. There is only something wrong about not using them.

"An actor can't be a prude or a moralist. If he is, he shuts his eyes to the possibilities of feeling for or with another kind of human being."

American actor Melvyn Douglas[46]

Threat tactics

I'd like to give a few examples of the tactics people use, and actors should use, in everyday life.

Overpowering

Mere size, and the brandishing of size, is a threat tactic of high utility. Raising the volume of your voice has a frightening and sometimes a paralyzing effect. A whole host of predominantly male behaviors – huffing and puffing, setting the jaw, narrowing the eyebrows, curling the lip, flaring the nostrils, drawing up to one's full height – were in previous decades labeled "flexing" tactics by social scientists, who have claimed these may play a function in the control of women by men. Women (in America, at least) have, however, become much more inclined to use this tactic than they were when the first edition of this book was published. Much of this behavior is biological, and can be seen in animals: the roar of the lion, the caw of the crow, and the arching and hair-raising of the little kitten are all instinctual tactics to appear powerful – and they indeed *make* the animal more powerful.

Sharply observing

The investigative power is an intimidating and threatening force, and investigative agencies, regardless of constitutional restrictions that are placed upon them, quite frequently become bastions of might. Merely glaring at a person can be intimidating, and glaring while simultaneously taking notes even more so. The brilliant tactic of super-hippie Ken Kesey, whose itinerant bus crew was frequently subjected to police raids in the 1960s, was to counter the police by filming them when they entered his bus; the officers quickly panicked and went away. Since that time, the combination of cell-phone cameras and viral videos have proven threatening to high-ranking politicians, business leaders and even dictators, as well as to ordinary people, while traffic enforcement cameras have slowed down speeding drivers by the tens of thousands.

Lie detector tests, which depend on the subject's fear of exposure, can usually be defeated if the subject simply becomes an investigator himself, and simply observes his "investigator" for clues as to, for example, the investigator's family life. To be able to see without being seen (to be invisible), of course, is one of the great power fantasies of small children and not a few adults.*

Conclusiveness

A forceful person does not willingly prolong discussions; she seeks to conclude them to her benefit. Powerful speaking, then, requires conclusiveness: gestures, expressions, and tones that convey the tactical message "...and that is all there is to be said about it!" To be conclusive, an actor should say lines with the goal of ending an argument rather than continuing one – as if the line were the scene's curtain line. Conclusiveness seeks to compel silence, attention, respectfulness, and, finally, adherence. It is a powerful, and only subtly aggressive, tactic.

---

* Your author discovered this when he became trained and certified in lie detection during the 1970s, when conducting experiments on the relationship between stage acting and real-life lying.

"Attack" (Vocal)

I am using *attack* here in a specific sense: not as a military ploy but as a speech opener. Basically, the term denotes the technical need in speech and singing to give a strong emphasis on the first word – indeed, the first *syllable* – of a sentence or a song lyric. This, however, is as true in everyday life as in the theatre or opera house. If you are in the midst of a group of people chatting and you want to speak, you will have to "come in hard" with your first word in order for your second word to be heard. Indeed, your first task in speaking in such a group is, in or out of the theatre, to "claim the stage" – and the only way to do that is to shut everybody else up!

The actor's attack is, in fact, an echo of her character's tactic. For while a play arranges dialogue in the form of alternating speeches, in life one is not ordinarily handed the opening to speak – one must make it. Conversational analysts call this "turn-taking;" since in order to talk and be heard, one must first make everybody else listen (or at least agree not to speak at the same time). The actor must not assume that she has an unchallenged right to speak just because the playwright has given her a line to say, nor the unchallenged right to continue speaking just because she hasn't yet finished her scripted speech. She must earn the *right* to speak and to keep speaking. She must seize the floor, as it were; she must "take the stage" when on the stage.

At a formal public event, masters of ceremonies commonly clink on a glass or tap on the microphone to hush the crowd. In a group of two or three, persons with something they want to say may start off with a loud "Hey" as in "Hey, I was just thinking" where the word "hey" has no semantic value except to say "Shut up, everybody!" Or a complete non-word like "Ahhh..." may be used, as in "ahhhhhh, I'd like to say that..."). Grunting to gain access to the conversation was an early and useful (when not abused) technique of the Actor's Studio in their quest to duplicate the give-and-take of everyday life.

Preferably, however, the actor can attack her speeches strongly by declaring, in both manner and vocal tone, *situational intent* in the very first syllable. Playwrights, if they are good, will help out with this. A surprising statistic: More than 90 per cent of the first words of Shakespearean speeches are either one syllable words, which are easy to attack, or the names of the person addressed, which all but forces them to listen, or occasionally commands like "Listen," all of these being effective turn-takers in themselves.

Follow-through (Vocal)

On the back end of attack is the *follow-through*, an oft-given instruction spoken to beginning actors usually in its simplest (and least explanatory) form, "Don't drop the ends of your sentences!"

This is more than just a matter of acting "technique." What happens when an actor drifts off at the end of her sentences is usually that she is making a contextual, not a relacom, signal; she is letting the other actors know she is approaching the end of her written speech. When that happens, whatever tactics she was employing in her delivery of the speech will be set aside. "She doesn't care about actually getting what she says she wants," is what others will read from it. Like the fisherman in my exercise earlier, she thinks she has finished her speech when she has thrown her line into the water. In fact she has only finished it when she catches a fish!

Most frequently, at least in a play that has any meat to it, the end of the speech is where the character's *most significant* tactical communication resides. This is usually the *hook* of whatever invocation she is making. It is the implied or stated proposal, or question, that demands a relacom – if not a content – response from the person or persons to whom it is addressed. Speeches are not normally dropped; rather they are tendered, proposed. They beg for a response. The French often say *"n'est-ce pas?"* ("isn't that right?" or "don't you agree?") at the end of declarative statements. In English we might say "OK?" or "Ya' know?" More often, we convey the message nonverbally, such as putting out our hand, palm upward, as if inviting a response. But we convey it! Concluding a speech without seeking a response, and a *specific* response, robs the play of the heartbeat of intense, probing, dialogue; dialogue that will be at least interesting and at most thrilling to observers, including those both onstage and in the audience. When an actor's interest seems to flag at the end of a line, it is because the actor is bored with saying it (or happy to be finished saying it); if the line is meaningful to the character speaking it, however, the actor must make her final words the most *provocative* part of her speech.* They are her character's *last chance*, at least in this particular speech, to get what she wants.

Implying a hidden arsenal

Most actors, in my experience, are relatively gentle people. Few are, or ever become, thugs. And most of us – readers of this book – are probably not regularly engaged in violence, physical assaults, or other boldly aggressive tactics. I'm in this category myself, of course. But we lack some of the unconscious social training – or left it behind us somewhere around sixth grade – that will help us achieve a bit of thuggery when we might need it onstage. I have a suggestion for this. Put one hand in your pocket as though you were holding a loaded pistol in it. Then walk towards someone while using your other hand for something very casual, like snapping your fingers or rolling a couple of marbles in your palm. This very act will make you smile more, perhaps swagger more when you walk. You have a "secret weapon" and you know you could use it. Your body will seem to have

---

* My great friend Bill Needles, who spent more than fifty years acting with the Stratford (Ontario) Shakespeare Festival, said that actors who trailed off at the ends of their lines cuing his own were essentially "handing me a dead fish."

grown three inches – both to potential adversaries looking at you and to you yourself. Your voice will probably drop a half-pitch or two and your smile will become more of a smirk. You will find your inner thug.

Height

Height is another "weapon" for characters – and for the actors who play them. Most of us underestimate the implications of relative height. Of course, you cannot change your physical height, but you can certainly learn to "act tall" when the need arises. As an acting teacher, I often make "height adjustments" in scenes I work on with student actors, for the fact is that persons who have grown up shorter than their peers are (understandably) not experienced in dominating a room. For such an actor who is playing a commanding role – Henry V or Joan of Arc speaking to their troops, for example – I may ask them to stand on a platform or a chair, with their "soldiers" (the rest of the class) standing and sitting on the floor around them. Without giving any other instruction or explanation, the five-foot-two Henry or Joan suddenly becomes heroically emboldened. They speak with increased confidence and fire; they gradually become inspirational, even joyous. Indeed, some shorter actors tell me afterwards that they have become so used to physically "looking up" to people that finally talking "down" to them was a hugely empowering experience. They soon learn to carry this into their performances without having to be standing on a platform: they have an imaginary platform in their heads. Thus spake Napoleon.

There have, of course, been hundreds of actors five foot two and under who have become sheer dynamos in performance (Judy Garland, Danny DeVito, Holly Hunter, Mickey Rooney, Judi Dench, Ellen Page, and Lindsay Lohan among them). Obviously, their lack of stature has not held them back; perhaps something like hoisting them up on a platform, or putting an imaginary gun in their pocket, helped them do it?

Screaming

The scream conveys that the screamer is beyond rational control, and therefore beyond the restraints of reason. When added to the others, screaming is a very effective threat tactic, and it is used quite often in the theatre as well as elsewhere. It is obvious that Adolf Hitler perfected the tactical use of screaming, and was able to gain control of his generals, his armies, and of the German masses – including the intellectuals – by his supreme capability of seeming to totter on the brink of madness. Tantrums, recklessness, and gestures of indiscriminate violence can add to the tactical effect. And sometimes these behaviors are quite rationally employed. American President Richard Nixon has been quoted as saying, during the Vietnam War, "I want the North Vietnamese to believe that I've reached the point that I might do anything to stop the war. We'll just slip the word to them that for God's sake, you know Nixon is obsessed about communism. We can't restrain him when he's angry, and he has his hand on the nuclear button!" Nixon was many things, but he knew what he was doing; in fact, he called this his "madman strategy."[47] (That doesn't mean he was right. His strategy didn't work. But he tried, and that's all an actor can do – since, unlike a war, a play's end has been written before the play begins.)

Induction tactics

Above, I have provided a short list of threat tactics used in everyday life, in character interactions and in the actor's portrayal of character interactions. As has been suggested, they are essential in developing the force of an actor's performance. But threat tactics are only one of the two halves of the taxonomy. The other half is induction tactics, which create an actor's magnetism, and it is very important to look deeply into this as well, because induction is at the heart of romantic attraction – the most common theme in drama since, at least, the age of Shakespeare.

Induction creates a feedback loop of relacom and information which flows between people like the electricity which flows within a wiring circuit. When we speak of "electricity" between two people, it is a metaphor for the constant flow of emotional and intellectual vibrations that are mutually emanated, received, tasted, and returned between them. And electricity, in the form of electro-magnetism, has the power to attract. Indeed, while it can be generated by a chemical or atomic discharge, electricity is most commonly created by *induction*, in which an electrical circuit (a coil, actually) is rotated in a magnetic field. It is thus convenient, if not actually precise, to think of electrons as being *pulled* along by the magnetic force of induction – as contrasted to being pushed by the force of a discharge. And so the tactic of induction is really based on a human-to-human feedback that makes one character's goals another's as well. Induction is therefore the most powerful force we have to instill positive change in others.

By way of summary: Threat tactics are used in win-lose situations, or what game-theory specialists call "zero-sum games," meaning that for every point won, another player must have a point lost, and the "sum" of the players' scores is therefore zero. Induction tactics, by contrast, are the only ones capable of bringing about of mutual victories, or playing "non-zero-sum games." *Love* is the prime example of a goal which can be reached *only* through induction. You can force someone to marry you, have sex with you, and do your bidding in all sorts of ways, but you cannot force anyone to love you.

The basis for induction, and for its success, lies in the pronounced human tendency – if not the human instinct – toward social conformity. We are rarely aware of this tendency because adult life makes us far more conscious of our individuality than our shared social characteristics, but a little reflection reveals that in our day-to-day and daily routines we are far more similar to our fellows than we are different from them. This is a biological or socio-biological necessity. As a species, we seek security in numbers, in being one of many, in being part of a larger and stronger society than we can create on our own. In the long run, anthropologically, social conformity provides us with social protection, and we seek to insure that our uniqueness never becomes so eccentric as to ostracize us entirely from our fellows. Teenagers, entering adult society for the first time, acutely experience this instinct toward conformity. Whether we like it or not, or admit it or not, we are *joiners*.

And joining takes the form of imitation. If we see someone smiling, we tend to smile. If we are in an audience, and the audience applauds, we tend to applaud. If they laugh, we tend to laugh. If we are amidst glum faces at a funeral, we turn glum. We tend to dress, speak, and gesture as our fellows do – or certainly as those whom we would like to think of as our fellows do. We join a society, or a social class, by imitating the behavior of those already in it, and we have been doing this since kindergarten. To the extent that we do it with a group of people, it gives us a sense of social belonging, class status, and a group identity. To the extent that we do it with a single person, it becomes individual fusion, family, and love. It also becomes our escape from loneliness, isolation, and alienation. As such, it is one of the highest goals of humans; according to psychiatric analyst Erich Fromm, the fundamental goal of living is "the achievement of interpersonal union, of fusion with another person, in love." This is "joining" at its most powerful. Obviously the tactics which are based in this human tendency or instinct will be mighty indeed.

Induction tactics involve, primarily, *projecting onto the other person the same behavior you wish him or her to adopt*. The instinct for joining takes care of the rest, if nothing interferes. Smile and you will probably induce smiling in others. Put out a hand and someone will probably shake it with their own. Look serious and your friends will look serious in return. Talk quietly and those around you will lower their voices. A doctor's "bedside manner" is pure induction; by projecting a calm assurance, the doctor can usually induce her patient to be calm and assured.

More complex uses of induction involve the figurative "getting inside the skin" of other persons. In the induction of smiling, you virtually climb into their heads, and smile for them until they cannot help but smile in return. In this manner, induction becomes more like its sister, seduction. Stanislavsky had a marvelous sense of this. "Infect your partner,"[48] he suggested. "Infect the person you are concentrating on! Insinuate yourself into his very soul, and you will find yourself the more infected for doing so. And if you are infected, everyone else will be more infected." This is positive feedback, and it is thrilling both in life and on the stage.

Getting inside the skin means, above all, understanding other people and figuring out their mindsets and vulnerabilities. It means drawing others out, getting in synchronization with them, "walking in their moccasins," as the American Indian saying suggests. An actor who makes full use of her observation of others, and can project herself into other actors and infect them in Stanislavsky's sense, is an actor who has charm, magnetism, and most importantly, stage presence. Her stage power will stimulate intense audience interest. A few of the basic induction tactics that have universal utility are:

Confirming

Nodding, smiling, and under the breath "um-hmm"-ing is more prevalent in conversation than we usually think. These confirmations of another person's relacom can work like a magnet to draw her out and to draw her in a specific direction, much like the children's game of hot and cold where the "leader" says "you're getting warmer!" Nodding with someone indicates intellectual (content) agreement; smiling with someone conveys the impression that you share a sense of humor with her. Laughing at Joe's joke not only confirms it, but confirms Joe: it conveys not just "What you say is funny" but "Joe, I find you an amusing person."

Disarming

The handshake developed among medieval knights as a gesture that showed you were not reaching for your sword. Induction tactics involve the projection of visages of openness and harmlessness; the bowed head of the suppliant, the bended knee of the suitor, the helpless shrug of the negotiator, and the sloe-eyed look of the courtesan. The bows during the curtain call at the end of a play did not begin in order for the audience to applaud the actors, but for the actors to show their patron, often the king, that if he did not like their performance he was free to chop off their heads. Not only a disarming tactic, therefore, but a potentially decapitating one.

Lulling

Soothing by gentle sound or motion, lulling harmonizes with the body's alpha-wave systems and quiets the body's defense and attack systems. Lulling is useful for putting babies to sleep, as with lullabies, and to allay anxiety in adults. Soft music, euphonious sounds, and the "love hum" of people who make soft sounds when they kiss or caress are all lulling activities, which, however spontaneous, can have clear tactical results.

Amusing

Wit, joking, and engaging in humorous interplay are among the most wonderful induction tactics possible, since they connote a sharing of values (an agreement on what is funny) and a childlike playfulness in which union is both possible and desirable. Many of our most ordinary and clichéd "stroke" confirmations are based on something that was at least once whimsical: "How's it going?" "Can't complain." "Think the rain'll hurt the rhubarb?" Amusing tactics are also well accepted in theatre and film – and especially on television – since they are fundamental not only to farces and comedies, but increasingly to serious dramatic productions as well.

Inspiring

Although it is not easy to achieve, an inspiring appeal – a call to arms, an appeal to pursue a profound, greater-than-personal goal – sets apart not only the political leader but often the successful salesman, teacher, lover, or friend. That an inspirational tone may be tactical does not at all mean that it must be insincere; on the contrary, it is the sincerest of inspirational messages and tones that are almost always the most tactically effective. Expressions of *wonder* – at life, love, the theatre, the universe – and expressed commitments to values, ideals, causes, and people, can be used to inspire feelings in the hearts and minds of all who see and hear them. When, during the nightly bombing of London in World War II at a time when the war seemed to the English public to be all but lost, actor Laurence Olivier toured the countryside reciting the heroic and patriotic speeches of Shakespeare's *Henry V*; many English citizens at that time considered those recitals to have saved their country from capitulation.

Flattering

The word "flattery" originally meant a smoothing and gentle touch. While frankly deceitful flattery may be pernicious, flattery itself is an entirely benign and gentle act which simply means discovering the best parts of someone else and singling them out for a little praise. Flattery is rarely completely untruthful in any event. In Jean Giraudoux's marvelous play *The Apollo of Bellac*, the god Apollo advises Agnes to tell men that they are beautiful. "Even the ugly ones?" she asks. "All of them," he replies. "In the depth of their hearts, even the ugly ones know that they are beautiful." And when Agnes tells the ugly ones that they are beautiful, they become beautiful, much as students who are designated as high achievers become high achievers when they are treated as such. Flattery gives the recipient an expectation of improvement, and an identity to live up to. Agnes, in flattering men, liberates them.

Kneeling

Just as "standing tall" is a threatening tactic, kneeling is an inductive one. Kneeling is an act of submission; people may kneel (or bow, or curtsey, or bend a knee) before royalty, before God, before bishops – all to show their subservience to higher authorities. While St. Joan, in Shaw's play, might stand tall above her soldiers in the field, she will almost certainly kneel in supplication before the Inquisitor, bishop, and church officers at her trial in Rouen, and this change of her physical posture is a reversal of her tactical efforts from threatening to inducing those around her.

Frankness

Frankness is a special kind of flattery; it conveys the impression that the speaker means "you are my equal if not my superior, I have to level with you about this matter, you must be treated with importance." Creating the image of frankness is a high-priority task of politicians in America; no presidential candidate can afford not to cultivate it. Frankness is a confirmation of another's adulthood and intelligence.

Seduction

Seduction is the gold standard of relacom induction. As it is purely biological, it has deeply penetrating power; as it is crucial to romantic attraction, it is paramount, explicitly or implicitly, in the vast majority of plays ever written and performed to adult audiences.

In seduction, inducements are sexual. The mechanisms for stimulating sexual arousal are well reported in anthropological and sociological literature, and need not be detailed here except to say that seduction, as an inductive process, involves the projection of the physical self into the other – the imitating of the kind of physical behavior you want another person to adopt. Therefore seductive behavior usually takes the physical forms of the various mating rituals and body language that cue the winks, wriggles, gasps, croons, whispers, caresses, tickles, kisses, pinches, slaps – and the subtle movements of tongue, eyebrows, mouth, lips, hips, torso, eyes, thighs, pelvis, fingers, and feet which from time immemorial have catalyzed desire.

Playing such inductive tactics, then, requires the actor to take an active part in leading and guiding the attitudes and responses of the other actors. The magnetic actor is magnetic not because she makes eyes at the audience, but because she dazzles, delights, and infects the other actors with her presence, concerns, and her whole being. She makes them smile, she makes them laugh, she makes their bodies do strange things, she makes their juices flow – and that makes her juices flow. What goes on under the sheets, or under the clothing or inside the mouth, may (and probably should) be simulated, but that the actors should be *actively seducing* each other, if their characters are meant to be, is absolutely essential – at least until the curtain falls.

This, however, is part of the actor's job. Fine actors working inductively with each other develop rapport and ensemble. They develop a shared mutuality, which is a kind of love itself. It was Sir Laurence Olivier who said, "actors must understand each other, know each other, help each other, absolutely love each other: must, absolutely must."[49] This love comes out of the electricity of interaction in inductive feedback; it comes from acting with purpose and with tactical strategy.

Playing tactics

The tactics described here are part of the basis of moment-to-moment behavior in daily life. When they are thus used on stage they bring added life to the characters and give energy and power to the character interactions. But they must really be *used*, not just illustrated or outlined. If you are threatening a character, you try to frighten the actor playing her. And that means *really frighten* the actor playing her. If you're going to be an actor, you must act your part seriously. You must *really try to get what your character wants*. You are not there just to display the sort of thing the character might do in real life, you're there to *do* it. If you want to frighten her, then really frighten her! Make her tremble! Make her cry! Make her wet her pants!

And if you want her to fall in love with you, *make her* fall in love with you! Make her heart explode with passion! Make her leave her boyfriend! Make her leave her husband! Get into her deepest emotions! Re-calibrate her autonomic nervous system!

"Actors work on each other's emotions."
American actress Eileen Heckart[50]

Every actor should know the acting lesson that actor Robert De Niro gave his friend and director Martin Scorcese when they were on the set of the 1976 film, *Taxi Driver*. Scorcese, who was directing, had taken over a small part in the film when the original actor had an accident. He played a passenger riding in the back seat of a cab driven by De Niro, and he only had one line, which, referring to the taxi's meter, was "Put the flag down." After the first take, DeNiro, who had not looked back during the scene, said to Scorsese, "Listen, Marty, don't say 'Put the flag down.' *Make me* put the flag down!"[51] Scorsese spoke of this at the 2009 Kennedy Center Awards. "It was the best acting lesson I ever heard," he told the world, "'cause there's no line between reality and pretend." Well, it is the best acting lesson I have ever heard as well.

So I mean it when I say *make* her wet her pants and *make* her leave her husband. You don't have to worry. She won't do either. After all, she is an actor too, and she knows how this great art is supposed to work.

But try – try your hardest! And then try even harder! The consensus of pretenses which is a play permits you to do this; the need for brilliance and intensity in a theatrical or film performance *requires* that you do it.

And she will love that you try, because *this makes her performance better*. It will encourage *her* to try harder, to work harder, to care more. Acting, you must remember, is about trying, not succeeding. Succeeding is up to the playwright – trying is your job. What is essential is the genuineness of your attempt, and the strength and power you throw into it. As the great mile runner Roger Bannister reports, "Failure is as exciting to watch as success, provided the effort is absolutely genuine and complete."[52] And what applies here to the track applies equally well to the stage.

"I learned [from Peter Brook] that every aspect of the character has to be bigger than me. For example, let's say I'm playing anger. My anger has limits; my character's anger has to go beyond my limits. You have to stretch yourself beyond the everyday, beyond the suburban, and offer audiences something heroic and magnificent. It's not enough to be cute."

British actor Ben Kingsley[53]

As for the possibility of ensemble, the interplay of real people playing real tactics in a scripted "play" situation, far from threatening the ensemble, creates it. It is maximum sharing; the actors implicitly agree to believe in the reality of each other as characters, and by so doing they reveal their own personalities as they seek real victories, both personal and mutual.

Danger and the unknown

When asked if they enjoy acting, many young actors reply, "yes, if I know exactly what I'm doing." It may be foolish to take issue with such a lightly-asked and lightly-answered question, but it is worth considering that this attitude will make the actor both safe and sorry.

Confusion is the natural state of every human being. We exist in flux, in process, and neither our identities nor our personalities are fixed. Obscurity is at the heart of our actions: the obscurity of the unconscious, of our instincts, and of our carnality. Like Oedipus, we are drawn forward by a future that is as mysterious as it is compelling. The Greeks called it Fate, Elizabethans called it Fortune, existentialists call it The Absurd, and we call it our *target*. A target that is always beckoning, but also always stimulating confusion and uncertainty. At lucid moments we feel on the verge of grasping it; we are poised, expectant. These are the moments that psychologist Abraham Maslow calls "peak experiences." And although the grasp fails, the poise, the verge, the expectancy remains. This poise, this expectancy, this "playing at the edge," is the true dynamic of the actor. It is this flux, this confusion, that gives acting its excitement.

"I pretty much try to stay in a constant state of confusion just because of the expression it leaves on my face."
American actor Johnny Depp[54]

"There is always about a moment of fine acting a kind of fringe of wonder."
American playwright and drama critic Stark Young[55]

Friedrich Nietzsche said, "understanding precludes acting." He did not mean stage acting, but he might as well have. The merely good, "safe" actor contents herself with "understanding" her role objectively. That sort of understanding can be comprehensive and exact, but it stultifies rather than stimulates great acting because of its very objectivity. It is deadening because it means thinking of the character as a fixed object instead of as the living, breathing, fearing, desiring self; because it means "understanding" what the character cannot understand, that which is unknown and unknowable, in the future not the past, ultimately mysterious and subversive. The actor must face her character's unknown future; she must share her character's consequent danger, and she must risk being overwhelmed. She must let herself go, poised not only for a victory but on the edge of uncertainty, on the verge of out-of-control.

Example: The downhill skier

A downhill skier is, perhaps, a good analogue of an actor getting into a staged situation. His situational involvement in, say, an Olympic competition is intense, total. See him poised at the very moment between resting nervously on the hilltop and beginning his descent. His weight is forward; he is leaning into a future that he absolutely cannot control. He cannot stop himself at will. His precise course is unknown and dangerous; he must observe thousands of individual and discrete pieces of information at every moment – each rock, tree, hillock, patch of ice or powder, each crevice, each skier, each gust of wind. The finish line is his goal. He is induced both by gravity and by his will to win, and he adjusts his direction according to the feedback he receives from the snow, from the sounds of his skis, and from the cheering crowd. There is danger, and because of it there is exhilaration, both on his part, and on the part of those who are watching him. If he were mechanically glided down a track, there would be no interest in his race: the interest comes in the fact that he is *thinking* as well as skiing. He is creating his path. He is inventing and re-inventing his strategy. He is battling new obstacles at every turn. He is, at the moment we see him, the complete actor in a thrilling situation. He is an intensely theatrical figure.

Summary of Chapter 2

Tactics and the playing of relacom are the guts of interaction in life and on the stage. The actor who defines and seeks ideal futures, and who uses tactical relacom in their pursuit, is an actor who is visibly working. If she is going to perform the passion of Lear, the fervor of Juliet, the mirth of Arlecchino, or the sarcasm of Roy Cohn (in *Angels in America*), she cannot get away with mere shadows of passion, fervor, mirth, or sarcasm; she must give us their real presence. The actor must be seen to be seeing, thinking, planning, working, and acting. And she must be seen to be doing all these things not in the context of the theatre, but in the situation which she shares with her fellow actors on the stage. She must be continually redefining her relationship with them, and she must be seen, because of her positive and expectant communication of that relationship, or relacom, as striving for a better future. Only if this happens will the actor be able to create her own life on stage, and only if she can do that can she possibly create the life of a character other than herself.

But that is the topic of the next chapter.

3

PLAYING CHARACTER

"When I played a detective in Twilight Walk, I played him
as a human being who just happened to be a detective. Most
actors play detectives the way they've seen other actors play
detectives. I like to think I don't do that kind of imitation."
American actor Walter Matthau[1]

Much that passes for character acting among beginning actors is really a form of
character assassination.

There is an obvious reason why this is so. Having gradually evolved our own
personalities after many years of conditioning, we have a natural, unconscious
feeling that we are already the best "character" that we could possibly become,
and to play any character significantly different from ourselves is to "take a step
down." For this reason, young actors asked to play "character roles" often turn
immediately to stereotype and parody, particularly when asked to play a person of
the opposite sex, or with notably different sexual, racial, professional, generational,
or political orientations. They therefore *compete* with their characters instead of
playing them, and make clear their own superiority to the characters they only
pretend to represent – as if to demonstrate by winks and gestures, that "this
character isn't the real me!" The actor's "real" persona can be conveyed, if
necessary, in her program bio; it should not be implied by her performance.
Except, perhaps, in certain Brechtian-style productions,* actors must play their

---

* Productions staged with Bertolt Brecht's *verfremdungseffekt* or "distancing style" are discussed in
  Chapter 5.

characters as if they *are* those characters, rather than just imitating what they think they are.

And what exactly *is* a character? For no one is just "a" character. I, for instance, am a teacher to my students, a colleague to my fellow teachers, a husband to my wife, a father to my daughter, a grandfather to my grandson, and a neighbor to my neighbors. And I behave in different ways depending on what "role" I play among this varied cast of characters, all of whom are named Robert Cohen. The specific characters we exhibit depend on who we are with, to whom we are talking, and about whom we are thinking at any given time. We all think we know the "basic character" of most of the people surrounding us, but we have little idea of our own "basic" character, for we feel we can be anybody we want. We think of ourselves as just that – "ourselves." We already contain the various characters that we are able to play.

"The role exists inside you. It's not something you put on…
like a brilliant carapace. It's there, it's inside you, all the
time."

British actor Patrick Stewart[2]

Character egocentricity

Playing a character means playing the character from the character's point of view, not from your own. You may think Molière's Harpagon is a miser (as well you might; the title of Molière's play about him is *The Miser*), but Harpagon doesn't think he's a miser; he thinks he is an intelligent man who is smart enough to keep his avaricious neighbors from stealing his well-earned savings. And that – not "playing a miser" – is what should be going through the actor's mind when performing the role.

Playing a character requires adopting the character's egocentricity (literally, "self-centeredness" as discussed in Chapter 1) as well as his or her words and costumes. It requires seeing the world through your character's eyes and from your character's point of view. It requires thinking of yourself as a subject, not an object. It requires seeing yourself in the center of your environment – no matter what your role is in the play, or in the society depicted in the play. The so-called "spear carriers" standing around King Lear and his daughters in the first act of that play have no lines to speak and probably few actions to perform, but their minds – if good actors are playing them – are afire with observations and calculations about what is going on around them. They are analyzing Lear, his daughters, the earls and the suitors that come and go – and they are paying close attention to anything the King or earls or others may order them to do lest they be severely punished. And they will be making judgments about all of these people: "How could he do this?" "What does she mean by that?" etc. They cannot speak their thoughts while they are in the King's court (or on the Globe Theatre's stage), but boy, will they have stories to tell when they get home!

The one thing they will *not* be thinking, however, is: "I am a spear-carrier." They will play their part by watching everybody else play *their* parts.

And it is not surprising that we do this in life. While we normally have a general sense of "how we are seen" in the different worlds (our school, job, family, neighborhood, church) we live in, we never see ourselves with the clarity that others see us. We are too busy leading our lives to study them. Indeed, we never really see ourselves at all; eyes may be "the mirror of the soul," as the saying goes, but we can only see them indirectly, in a mirror, when they stare back at us in an unnaturally fixed gaze. (And mirrors did not even exist in the first 98,000 years of human history – the vast majority of Homo sapiens who have ever lived, therefore, were never able to see their own eyes at all.)

It is the *other* characters that the actor looks at and defines as "characters." Horatio doesn't see himself, but he has seen Hamlet over several years and has deduced that the Prince is a sensitive, noble, honorable, and brilliant young man who has been treated terribly by his evil uncle and his dismayingly confused mother. By the way he treats Hamlet, we in the audience will size up the character of Horatio. The actor playing Horatio does so, therefore, not so much by creating a character for himself, but mainly by characterizing his friend Hamlet and treating him accordingly. By doing this – by pursuing Horatio's goals and not thinking about Horatio's personality – he (the actor) will become the Horatio that Shakespeare wrote, and the one that we see and develop opinions about.

Egocentrism, we have to remember, has nothing to do with egotism. In fact, it is its absolute opposite. The *egotistical* person can think of nothing but herself; the *egocentric* person cannot think of herself at all – she can only see the world around her, being in its center.

The egocentric person lives, as it were, behind her own eyeballs. She is the only person she can *not* see. This begins in infancy. Child psychologist Jean Piaget explains that the child is "totally egocentric – meaning not that he thinks selfishly only about himself, but to the contrary, that he is incapable of thinking about himself.... The whole course of human development can be viewed as a continuing decline in egocentrism, until death or senility occurs."[3] It is precisely the childlike, self-centered perspective – a foundation of each character's personality – that an actor must find and explore in the quest for effective characterization.

We might recall the Jones and Nisbett experiments mentioned in Chapter 1, which showed that people tend to think of themselves as responding to situations, while thinking that only "other people" have fixed personalities: this one coarse, this one sultry; this one talkative, this one shy, and so forth. Such egocentric perspectives are mostly unthinking. They are part of our natural epistemological machinery, the mindsets we have derived from infancy. Well, characters in plays have the same egocentricity and the same self-centered epistemological machinery as we do. Characters do not think of themselves as characters any more than we do. They think of other people in the play as characters – while they, they think, are quite simply "themselves."

And so, the actor's performance as a "character" must be seen to emanate from a self-centered mind. The actor plays the situation as her own, and she plays her character as herself. But since she sees the other characters as, say, weird, heroic, tyrannical, pathetic, Danish, medieval, fantastical, invisible, divine, or whatever, she will adjust her normal behavior according to what she needs to do to satisfy *her* goals. She will make a *transformation*.

Subjective transformations

The transformation an actor makes in playing "character" is not a transformation of what she plays out of, but what she plays into.

In playing a character different from herself, as almost all characters are, the actor imaginatively transforms, not herself, but the events and the actor-characters in front of her. These transformations are contrived for dramatizing purposes. They are *subjective* transformations – transformations of what the character *sees* rather than what the character *is* – and because the evaluations we make of others are basically subjective, the actor will view them from her own perspective rather than a scientifically objectively one. The character will thus retain both the idiosyncratic uniqueness of the actor herself, and the intensity of her character's situational concentration and her consequential pursuits of victory. Characterization is thus drawn from the actor rather than pasted onto her, and can be played with urgency rather than mere caricature or parody. This can be made clearer by an example.

Example: Playing the paranoid

Imagine the task of playing the paranoid. To go about it objectively, you might research paranoid behavior in textbooks, or observe paranoid behaviors in a mental institution and then imitate the behavior you have researched or seen. This technique is objective because you retain your "objective" feelings and knowledge about paranoia as you yourself know it, and then mimic the paranoid manifestations as you have perceived in others.

The subjective method, however, which is infinitely superior, would ask you to research and discover not the paranoid's behavior but the paranoid's *vision*. This will let you, essentially, *become* a paranoid – at least temporarily. You would in this case not seek to transform yourself as a paranoid as seen by the world, but transform the world into how it would appear to you as a paranoid. Since paranoids think they see evil and danger lurking in the minds of others, you would, in your imagination, "see" all the other actor-characters as a vicious pack of would-be killers. Creating and responding to this imagined vision, you will need do nothing else to play the paranoid, for you will *be* a paranoid. Moreover, you will tap into your own vulnerabilities, and use them to play that paranoid for the duration of this mental transformation. You need not "try to be a paranoid" per se; you will just have to try keeping these monsters from pulling out weapons and killing you. You will have to study them intently, reading not only the movements of their hands but the shifting of their gazes and what they may be hiding under their jackets. You will then not be thinking about being a paranoid but be thinking *as* a paranoid; thinking only about those planning to attack you.

Subjective characterization demands the prior planting of certain imagined circumstances that will later govern the conscious and unconscious directions of a performance. It allows the actor, in the words of actor William Redfield, to "trap his unconscious," and even to "trap it on cue."[4] To do this means a certain amount of double thinking, to be sure, about character as well as about situation, but the thinking is on different levels and takes place at different times. The thinking about character ("I am a paranoid") takes place during the actor's homework. The thinking about circumstances ("these people are trying to kill me") takes place during the moment of performance. The character then becomes a melding of the person you are and the person the playwright has created.

"There are very successful mannerisms from certain parts that stick to your own personality. It may be a walk, it may be a way of listening to people, it may be a story, it may be a way of sizing a person up. You finally wind up as being half what you are yourself and half fragmentations of the characters that you play."

American actor Paul Newman[5]

Looking outward

The actor therefore is looking outward, not inward; forward, not backward. She is looking into the future: Where am I headed? She is pursuing goals: How can I get what I want? She is scouting out obstacles: What's in my way? She is dreaming up strategies: How can I overcome this? She is weighing contingencies: What shall I do if...?"

And finally, she is looking for her finish line, and plotting her best route to get there. But it is not going to be a straight line, for there be will many obstacles, and the finish line will keep changing. Here is an example of this process.

Example: The slalom skier

I have already offered the notion that an actor playing a situation resembles a downhill skier, racing to the finish line with total concentration and tactical absorption in the search for victory.

But the downhill race is only one event in a skiing competition; a more sophisticated race is the slalom, in which the skier must circumnavigate a series of flags in a preconceived order while still trying to reach the finish line in the fastest possible time. The slalom course is designed by a slalom designer to be difficult, and the skier, in negotiating the course, must trace a complex path that combines curves, sweeps, turns, and occasional straightaways. But the path is a graceful one, and makes the slalom a beautiful, as well as a thrilling, event for spectators to witness.

The elegance and beauty of the slalom race is achieved by the joint effort of the slalom designer and the skier, but the joint effort is not one of collaboration. Rather, it is a head-on confrontation. The slalom designer's flags are the skier's obstacles. The designer's goals are to create demanding challenges; the skier's goal is to surmount them. The slalom designer contrives the course in such a way as to elicit graceful turns and exciting contours; to have the skier leave, as it were, an elegant track in the snow. The skier, however, is not in the least interested in being graceful or elegant, or in leaving a beautiful track; she is only trying to get to the bottom of the hill as fast as she can without breaking the rules by going on the wrong side of the flags she circumvents.

Elegance, excitement, grace, and beauty are *unconscious by-products* of her race. Like the downhill skier, the slalom racer concentrates fully and solely on the obstacles and contingencies ahead, and on the processing of information in the mental calculus which will draw her toward the fastest path to the finish. Although her task is more complex, the slalom racer's pursuit of victory is no less single-minded, ferocious, and absolute than the downhill racer's.

Planting the character's flags

Characterization is approached in the way of the slalom race, by "planting flags" – which, in acting, are called obstacles. These "flags" are the obstacles the actor must circumvent or overcome as she pursues the ever-changing path – or paths – of her character's intended victory.

Most of the "flags" will be plot obstacles, planted by the playwright. Others will be physical obstacles, planted, perhaps, by the director and the scenery, costume, and even the prop designers. And some the actor will plant by herself during her preparation for the role. Then, during the performance, she plays *against* those flags; skirting around them, batting them down, *fighting* them and undermining them any way she can. This fight is what gives her character "character," and which lets her explore and display her intellectual, physical, and theatrical gifts. It is what makes her performance difficult and thus forceful, and gives the actor this book's title: Acting Power. For it is never enough for an actor to simply "play actions," the actor must *act actively*. She must take up arms against a sea of troubles, and must sweat for her living.

This doesn't mean she must be a brute, however. Let us look at an example.

Example: Descending a staircase

Imagine a character – let's say a wealthy, attractive, 45-year-old woman – descending a staircase while saying to her young son, who is among a few party guests below, "It is time, my darling, for you to go to bed." This is a very simple thing to do, and it delivers whatever plot point the playwright intended.

Now imagine that she is descending a spiral staircase, not a straight one. This is a bit of an obstacle, for the actor cannot descend quite as quickly or as easily – she might trip if she's looking at the son and not the steps – but the added effort has the advantage of showing off her costume and her lively gait to the party guests below.

Now imagine she is wearing high heels, a full-length gown and a diamond necklace. Now the obstacles are rather dangerous, for she might trip on the hem of her dress or find herself in the awkward position of having to hold it up with her hands as she descends – decidedly not the way she wants to show off herself or her attire. But her spiraling down does have the advantage of showing off her diamond necklace as she turns, allowing its multi-faceted reflections to sparkle brilliantly, reaching every corner of the room.

And now imagine that she is also carrying a full glass of champagne in her right hand, as she plans to lead a toast to the guests when she has reached the floor and her son has left the room. The difficulty level of her descent has now reached maximum levels – but, hey, she's making one hell of an entrance!

The spiral staircase, the long gown, high heels and diamond necklace, and the glass of champagne has made the descent quite difficult, but also breathtaking. We see the character in all her glory – and from virtually every side. She has turned her obstacles to her own advantage, and so we see her character's vitality, her playfulness, her bounciness, and her costume from all angles. And we see *her* – the actor inside the character – in vastly greater detail. For the character itself is generic – hundreds of actors may have played the role before – but the actor now playing it is unique, with her own looks, smiles, frowns and idiosyncrasies. If she had merely clunked her way down an ordinary set of stairs we would see little if anything unique in the few seconds of her descent, but by having to overcome these obstacles brilliantly, we are able to see an entire personality – and be utterly fascinated by her.

Obstacles make actors work harder to achieve their goals, but working harder brings out more of their individual gifts and talents. And an actor must have gifts to play this sequence: it takes bravery, a great deal of practice wearing ball gowns and high heels, an appreciative understanding of style and elegance, and probably some serious dance or movement training as well, to be able to just confidently sashay down a spiral staircase, holding – and not spilling – a glass of champagne. But who said acting isn't supposed to be hard work?

Characterization, in this sense, is not so much an actor "playing a character" as it is the audience *inferring* character from the actor's pursuit of her goals while responding to her situation. The character's goal in this example is to impress her guests with her wealth, her bonhomie, her physical gracefulness, her elegant clothes and magnificent jewelry, her love for her son, and possibly her hopes for a new romance for the handsome young man standing by the fireplace. She is not just "descending a staircase," she is entertaining, charming, dazzling, and flirting with her guests. All while trying not to trip while she does it. If she succeeds, it does not matter that the actor playing the role does not drink champagne and wears nothing but denim jeans, sneakers, and beads in her "real" life. The actor plays her part by tackling its obstacles. If, when she gets back to her dressing room and finds her gown drenched in sweat, so much the better.

The basic mechanics, then, for creating a character is to examine the world as your character sees it, and then play within – and at many times against – that world *as yourself*. You see the world as she does, you fear what she fears, and you want what she wants, so go after those "wants" with every skill at your command. Whether you remain "you" should not be of concern: you *are* you. You have unique qualities that will come through regardless of the character you play or the costume and makeup you wear. You are also capable of winning situational victories with your own powers, though these may not be powers that you use in your daily life. You retain the self-centeredness, the egocentricity, and the personality of all living beings. You can then bring that life into the character you play – a far more important task of the actor than presenting an objectified, well-dissected puppet or corpse.

"I know that whatever residue of experience I have is going to bleed through anyway. I don't even need to tap into it, it's going to come through."

American actress Laura Linney[6]

Physiological and psychological obstacles

Obstacles are not, of course, necessarily physical ones. Even more common are obstacles within the character being played. Some are physiological. Blindness (Suzy in *Wait Until Dark*), terminal cancer (Vivian in *Wit*), malformed limbs (Laura in *The Glass Menagerie*), ugliness (Cyrano in *Cyrano de Bergerac*), and a combination of deafness, muteness and blindness (Helen Keller in *The Miracle Worker*) give the actors that play these roles opportunities for heroic resistance to debilitating obstacles within the human body. Laura's shortened leg in *The Glass Menagerie* is a physiological obstacle that leads to a psychological one, as do, inevitably, those obstacles of the other characters mentioned here as well – and most humans who suffer them. And the poignancy and pathos of Laura's character stem from the conflict between her hoped-for victories and these psycho-physiological obstacles to them: her desire to dance confronting the physical malfunctioning of her legs, her desire to win Jim confronting her feelings of unworthiness. Such confrontations between goal and obstacle are usually at the very heart of most dramatic structures.

And some obstacles – perhaps most – are simply psychological. Hamlet, for example, vows in Act I, to revenge his father's murder, but he does not complete the deed until Act V; the nature of the obstacles which occasion this delay is a matter of choice and interpretation, but they are clearly internal, bouncing around in his fervid imagination, and these will determine not only what happens in Hamlet the person but in *Hamlet* the play.

Hamlet is a famous example of a principal character's inner psychological nemeses, but most plays involve such obstacles to the fulfillment of situational victories; this is what makes plays play. In *Death of a Salesman*, Willy Loman is offered a job by a kindly neighbor. If he took it, he would not have to commit suicide and there would be no death – but there would also be no conflict and no play. This powerful play depends on Willy's inner mental obstacles – excessive pride, perhaps – that prevent him from taking the easy (and non-dramatic) way out. If Romeo persisted in refusing to duel Tybalt, if Peter (in *The Zoo Story*) left his bench and went home, if Lady Macbeth didn't reverse her husband's declaration to "proceed no further in this business" (of killing Duncan), these dramas would simply cease to exist, because the characters' dramas would fail to be dramatic. The traditional dramatic structure of "boy meets girl, boy loses girl, boy gets girl" is worthless without the middle, muddling event.

It is the interpretation – the choosing, identifying, and planting – of these obstacles, together with the determination and specification of relacom victories, that will determine the "character" of the characters. Relacom victories, covered in the previous chapter, are frequently obvious, explicit in the script, and derived from the most basic of compelling instincts: survival, affection, security, validation. Obstacles are much murkier and lend themselves to complex and often varied interpretations.

Let's look more closely at the possibilities inherent in the example of a film role that anyone can now watch and explore on video, DVD or on the Internet.

Example: Benjamin

Dustin Hoffman's character of Benjamin in the now-classic 1967 Mike Nichols film, *The Graduate*, made the little-known actor a movie star. Benjamin is a young college graduate who is seduced by Mrs. Robinson, an older married woman played by Anne Bancroft. If Benjamin could have responded boldly and debonairly to Mrs. Robinson's first seductive remarks, there would have been no comedy to the film, and virtually no story either. So director Nichols and his team placed every imaginable obstacle in Benjamin's way, providing suspicious hotel clerks, overly friendly partygoers, a bleak hotel room, and an outrageously forward Mrs. Robinson. But beyond these physical and human obstacles were the ones that Hoffman himself created and played. These included his character's deep fear of sexual inadequacy, of being seen naked, and of being seen looking at an older woman's naked genital area. It was Hoffman's desperate, anguished playing through and around those psychological obstacles of his character that created the hilarity and poignancy of the role. In sum, and at the risk of a slight simplification: Hoffman's playing toward the relacom victory "I want you to be my lover" created his situation, while his planting and playing around the obstacles of feared sexual inadequacy created his character. And since both victory and obstacle could be "located" in the same specific area, Anne Bancroft's crotch, Hoffman's point of concentration was single-minded, direct and entire.

Playing against?

"Everything we portray on stage ought to be shown from two sides. When I smile, I must also show the grimace behind it, to depict the countermovement – the counter-emotion. Only... [when] no situation or character is obviously good or evil is it truly interesting to act."
Swedish actress Liv Ullmann[7]

As the excitement of the slalom racer derives from the confrontation between the skier and the slalom course, so the excitement of a theatrical performance derives from the confrontation of the character's hoped-for future and his or her obstacles, and the path the actor must take to try and achieve goals and elude such barriers. The confrontation provides the dialectical tension in a role, the inner conflict which is the mark of the human being in a dramatic situation.

In every case, whether the character's obstacles are physical impediments in the set, psychological anxieties, or physiological handicaps, they must be planted in advance, not during the moment of performance. Obstacles are not played, they are played against.

This means that the planting function and the playing function of acting are quite separate ones, and take place at separate times. Naturally the stage plants are, for the most part, imaginary; acting is more difficult, psychologically, than slalom racing. But the plants can be made, and made to stick, by the act of playing against them. Playing against an obstacle confirms the obstacle. Further exercises in this vein suggest a wide variety of character obstacles, physical and psychological, to play against.

Exercises: Playing against physical obstacles

The falling ceiling

The ceiling is being lowered down slowly on top of you. Struggle to push it back up. Lose the struggle; the ceiling is stronger than you.

The closing walls

The walls are slowly moving toward you by hydraulic pressure. Try to resist them. Fail. Like the falling ceiling, which you can do simultaneously, this is a standard exercise in mime. The act of pushing against the imaginary wall will "create the wall" in the mind of an observer.

Tug of war

With another actor, engage in a tug of war using an imaginary rope. Try to win, both of you.

Bucking the wind

Walk against an imaginary hurricane. Walk upstream on the bottom of an imaginary river (with imaginary diving equipment). Try to overcome the current's strength. Let yourself win. Let yourself fail.

Talk with your mouth full

Stuff your mouth with crumpled paper. Try to speak distinctly. Try to make someone understand that you require an ambulance immediately to save a dying child. Double the amount of crumpled paper and try it again. Do the same exercise with your mouth stuffed with imagined crumpled paper.

Hide your defect

Imagine you have a pronounced physical defect which inhibits movement. Try to move so that nobody will notice. Put a small stone under your foot in one shoe and try to walk so that nobody notices.

Hide your pain

Imagine enormous pain when you walk. Try to walk without showing it. Play, by this manner, a presidential candidate seriously in pain trying to hide the pain for political reasons. (This situation, which old-timers will recall with John F. Kennedy and George Wallace, is used as the climactic moment of the play *Sunrise at Campobello* when Franklin Roosevelt, recovering from polio, makes his first public, political appearance.)

Emphysema

Imagine that you have very little available lung capacity, and can breathe in and out only a half-pint of air per breath. Perform an improvisation unconnected with that condition, and try to breathe and act normally.

"I love obstacles because on the simplest level you have to achieve certain things as an actor because they're written, but then you try to put [obstacles] in the way to frustrate the character... A good example of this came in the introductory scene in *The Apartment*. Billy [Wilder, the director] had to show that he had all these people using the apartment, and he had them on the phone trying to juggle time. It was about five pages of necessary background to the plot. But Billy did a beautiful thing. He gave the guy a cold, and the scene worked because the poor son of a bitch had a temperature and a cold and was perfectly miserable, and the audience knew how goddamn lousy he felt and they loved the scene."

American actor Jack Lemmon[8]

Lose your bowel function

Imagine that you are afraid of losing your bowel functioning capability. Perform an improvisation unconnected with that condition, and try to act normally.

Be blind

Imagine that you have recently been blinded. With your eyes wide open, "try" to sense your position and the position of others. Perform an improvisation as a blind person, trying to hide from the others that you are blind.

Exercises: Playing against psychological obstacles

Fear of falling

Plant a dread of losing your balance, as after a long operation or confinement. Try to walk around the room without falling.

Fear of flying

Imagine that you are on an airplane which is experiencing extreme turbulence, and the flight attendants are panicking. Keep the person seated next to you from getting hysterical by explaining to her, untruthfully, that this is not a problem and you have been through these things many times.

Fear of death

Plant 20 ways you could die in the next five minutes, and perform an improvisation which attempts to defy those fears.

Fear of arousal

Plant a fear of being sexually aroused, and of being seen to be sexually aroused, by a person with whom you are about to perform an improvisation. Perform the improvisation.

Fear of becoming violent

Plant a great temptation to do violence on someone, and then fight that temptation during an otherwise unrelated improvisation.

Scripted scenes may be substituted for improvisations in any of the above exercises, which, when used as directorial suggestions during the rehearsals of plays, can be extremely effective devices for eliciting character and character behavior.

Choosing specific obstacles

The specificity of the posited obstacle is of vital importance; it creates the individuality of your character, making her unique and identifiable. It also lends itself to bold rather than timid characterizations. The exercises above tend toward the general, since they are not directed to any specific character but to the understanding of consciousness and "playing against." In creating characters that live in memory, it is necessary to create obstacles specifically.

Example: Three Hamlets

Let us return to *Hamlet* to discuss the specific playing possibilities of a single moment of high conflict: the moment when Hamlet, having come upon Claudius at prayer and drawn his sword on him, decides not to kill him at this particular moment. This is a crucial scene in *Hamlet*, and is particularly revealing of Hamlet's character and the nature of his thinking.

Hamlet "explains" the moment to us in soliloquy: he hesitates, and then spurns his initial reaction (which had been "now I'll do't") on the grounds that killing Claudius at prayer would send him to heaven, not hell, and would be an inappropriate revenge. Given the liberty of the theatre, however, we need not accept his explanation as complete, or even as correct. Hamlet is, after all, only a character in the play; he is not necessarily the best judge of his own behavior or motives, and he may have a great many reasons for persuading himself (or us) that such a rational motivation is the real one. It could easily be a rationalization for a much deeper dread.

The director and actor, therefore, have a variety of options in choosing how this scene will be played (what goals will be played for, what obstacles will be played against), and the choices they make will determine what kind of character we – the audience – will deduce that this Hamlet is. I'd like to suggest three specific obstacles that might vivify this crucial twenty seconds or so of one of Shakespeare's greatest plays.

Oedipal dread: Fear of drowning in Claudius's blood

This is a simple fantasy. Assume that your Hamlet is terrified of killing Claudius because, at the unconscious level, doing so would represent the acting-out of the tabooed Oedipal situation: a killing of the father-figure in order to take his place.* In Hamlet's case the Oedipal situation is intensified, because by killing Claudius, Hamlet would figuratively "become" his father (the unconscious goal of the Oedipal fixation) not only by name, which he already possesses, but by assuming his father's throne and title. But this is tabooed, and therefore Hamlet

---

* This is a classical Freudian analysis of Hamlet. See Ernest Jones, *Hamlet and Oedipus* (1954).

unconsciously dreads doing the deed. So *vivify* Hamlet's terror imagining that stabbing Claudius will cause a jet of blood to stream into your open mouth and, were you to go through with your plan, you would drown in Claudius's blood. Now *try to stab Claudius!* Are you able to do it? *You can almost taste his blood flooding your throat.* You find yourself paralyzed in a double-bind. And the harder you "try to stab" Claudius, the more you will gag and your body will tremble. So put up your sword and speak Hamlet's line. That it is a rationalization will at once be clear with no further effort on your part.

This is a highly emotional fantasy which can provoke a physiological reaction, and a characterization detailed and powerful down to the smallest bodily detail. And, while it is one of at least a thousand ways of playing this moment (two more will follow), it is a great deal more exciting for the audience than just deciding it is the wrong time to kill your uncle.

Fear of exposure: Fantasy of nakedness

This second possible interpretation derives from Hamlet's own "chiefly loved" speech which describes Pyrrhus's first attempts to kill "the unnerved father" Priam. The speech tells how

[HAMLET:](Pyrrhus's) sword, which was declining on the milky head
of reverend Priam, seemed I' th' air to stick.
So as a painted tyrant Pyrrhus stood,
And like a neutral to his will and matter
did nothing.

Imagine as Hamlet's fantasy – as Hamlet might well imagine it – that if you raise your sword to kill Claudius your arm will freeze like Pyrrhus's did. You will become paralyzed, "neutral," and exposed as merely a "painted tyrant."

Now vivify that terror with this fantasy: imagine that raising your sword will cause you to become suddenly naked and immobilized; your intentions (and genitals) totally exposed, yourself totally vulnerable to whatever torture or indignity that Claudius, turning and seeing all, may wish to inflict upon you.

Now try to raise your sword. *Again* you will be double-bound and probably physiologically paralyzed, and unable to go through with the deed. Do it with conviction and that paralysis, weird as it may seem to you when you read it, will seem both to you and those watching you physiologically accurate and psychologically engaging.

In both of these examples, the Hamlet that we see would be considered aberrational, possibly neurotic, even insane. To the actor, however, who has posited these fantasies in his mind, such behavior and its attendant physiological manifestations would be entirely logical and would follow from the very simple act of trying (and failing) to kill Claudius without drowning in his blood or freezing in his gaze. Hamlet's fantasies may well be considered neurotic, but the actor playing against them does so with the full force of his own logic and his "normality." It is just that the fantasies are, in the end, insurmountable and the sword cannot be swung. (Not at this time, anyway. By the end of the play, Hamlet says he has been "set naked" back in Denmark, and has no trouble swinging his sword at Claudius in the final scene.)

Fear of a Claudius-God alliance

This interpretation is Hamlet's: that his refusal to kill Claudius is a rational act since to do so while Claudius is praying may send the usurping King to heaven, not to hell. By itself, this is not a very convincing or dramatic rationale, but vivify it with this fantasy: Imagine that killing Claudius will send him immediately to God's dinner table. Imagine Claudius with God, Jesus, the Virgin Mary, and your mother and father sitting around the dinner table laughing and talking over a few glasses of ambrosia. If the fantasy makes you want to throw up, then it works in stimulating, again, a *physiological* and relacom underpinning of Hamlet's presumably intellectual "decision," and making his act – and his acting – visceral as well as cerebral.

As an exercise, learn Hamlet's speech in this scene (Hamlet III, iii, 73–95) and play it to an imaginary Claudius, and with a real or imaginary sword, planting each of these three obstacles. Then play it to a real Claudius. Create a fourth obstacle of your own invention, and play against that. Then ask an "audience" what kind of "character" your Hamlet was, in their opinion.

Choices

Planting obstacles *in the other characters* is then a pre-performance task for the actor to shape her performance. It closely resembles the planting of props on stage before the curtain goes up, but unlike props, which are normally established by the scenic and property designers, the actor is usually the person who will establish the mental obstacles that will uniquely define his or her own performance. And this requires making choices. The three suggested obstacles for Hamlet's decision not to kill Claudius might be suggested by a director, but much more often will be chosen by the actor playing Hamlet. And no one need – or even should – know that these mental obstacles exist apart from the actor himself. No one on stage or in the audience need think that Hamlet is choking on imaginary blood, or is humiliated by imaginary nakedness, but the actor's *reaction* to these imagined obstacles will be so unique and so alarming that everyone will realize that something very powerful is happening in Hamlet's mind. And that reaction will be unique to the actor who plays the role.

Bold choices bring out the actor's individuality. Most people – and actors offstage are like most people in this regard – behave in a relatively conforming manner in day-to-day life. Ask them to smile and they will present a fairly standard, everyday smile. Ask them to say "No!" in an everyday situation, and they will pretty much give the same stern vocal tone and physical demeanor of everyone else in the room. But ask them to kill a King whose blood will immediately spurt into their throat and choke them – and everyone will perform this in a manner different than any of the others. When performed spontaneously and seriously, these are the reactions to obstacles that will make audience members see deeply into the "real life" of the actor herself – and perhaps remember the moment for the rest of their lives. They are bold, rather than pedestrian, choices.

"Most actors' problems [are that] they haven't made a choice that has taken enough of their mental interest. They haven't made a vital enough choice; it's not up to a level that will engage their imagination and get them into pretending unselfconsciously."

American actor Jack Nicholson[9]

Reciprocal characterization

Specifically, then, the actor creates her characterization by characterizing others. It is a reciprocal process, for the way we see others determines how we approach them, think of them, and talk to them. And other people who see us doing this determine what sort of character *we* are.

We have seen an example of this already – Harpagon and the paranoid. The actor who plays a miser does not try to "play miserliness," she transforms other people into potential robbers and thieves. The actor playing a paranoid does not try to "play paranoia," she transforms the other actor-characters into would-be killers. Your characterization is an act of shaping *them*, not shaping yourself. You will do this automatically by the way you respond to what you now see them *as*. You will thus characterize yourself *reciprocally*, not directly.

Reciprocal characterization is directed outward rather than inward, and by projecting characteristics onto other people rather than playing them yourself. When the actor has characterized the other actor-characters in this fashion, her own behavior will be drawn from her as a response to these characterizing assumptions. In the case of the paranoid, the actor will give unpremeditated paranoid responses (typical of a true paranoid) by seeing these avaricious people trying to steal her money, rather than self-consciously imitating what she thinks a paranoid might be like.

This of course is true to life. As we recall from the Jones and Nisbett experiments described in Chapter 1, while people do not think of themselves as having fixed characterizations, they think of other people as being "characterized." The actor characterizes others as a result of own character's egocentricity; the way in which she characterizes them will direct the ways in which she will interact with them thereafter. Reciprocal characterization, then, is essentially a technique of characterization which is drawn from the way we behave in life's interactions. Like ourselves, our characters should see themselves as relatively neutral and normal observers responding to the behaviors of unusual, "different," and frequently peculiar and incomprehensible "other" people.

You can create a wide range of characterizations simply by responding to other characters through this reciprocal technique of characterizing them rather than yourself. For example:

Arrogance can be played by characterizing other people as fools, yokels, or weaklings.

Miserliness can be played by characterizing other people as greedy, grabby, and lurking.

Humility can be played by characterizing other people as powerful, brilliant, and knowing.

Bigotry can be played by characterizing other people of a suspected race or religion as being smelly, filthy, disease-ridden, immoral, and lascivious.

Apathy can be played by characterizing other people as insignificant, boring, having nothing to offer.

You can discover your inner **geniality** by making the reciprocal characterization that other people are lovable, funny, fun to be with, and fond of you.

You can create **confidence** by characterizing other people as admiring your qualities, approving your intentions, and supporting your actions.

And of course there are many other types of "characters," ranging through the entire spectrum of general and specific characterizations. In each case, the actor need only plant the characterizing assumption on the *other* actor-character; on his body, in the arch of her eyebrows, the glare of his eyes, the set of her jaw, the suppression of his fist, the restlessness of her leg. The plant should be on the physical person seen; not simply on the "actor" or the "character" as abstractions, but on the actual physiology across the table that will inspire reciprocal interaction and reciprocal characterization. In that event there need be no difference between the physiological manifestations of characterized paranoia and real-life paranoia, for both should be the same until the fall of the curtain wipes out the consensus of pretenses, and the plants, on which the "acted" characterization is dependent.

"Once you set the things you do and make them mean certain things, you then respond to the stimuli you yourself have set up. Then you feel. You might set it up as a combination of mind and feeling, but the feeling usually takes over."

American actress Maureen Stapleton[10]

"I don't act. I let others do the acting. I just talk to them."

American actress, Diana Ross

The "magic if" applied to the other

Reciprocal characterization has the enormous benefit of not reducing characterization to the level of "ordinary" human behavior, or to the "lowest common denominator" kind of characterization which was a well-noticed fault of the early American "method" actors and their stuttering Caesars, hem-and-hawing Hamlets, and everyday Ophelias. This tendency toward the humdrum derives from a misconstruction of Stanislavsky, and perhaps an ambiguity in Stanislavsky himself. Stanislavsky says, "Always play yourself onstage."[11] But playing yourself and playing *out of* yourself are two different things. Stanislavsky, naturally, understood that the self was the basis for acting, but that characterization also involved certain transformations. His key phrase for making the transformation was the "magic if," by which the actor suggests to himself "If I were in Othello's situation, what would I do?" Unfortunately, this is too frequently shortened, with a catastrophic and unintended loss of meaning, to "If I were Othello, what would I do?" This leads to objective, hindsight analyses of a fictional "Othello," and thus to imitative mimicry rather than situational involvement.

The "magic if" should be applied to the *other* actors, not to the self. The question the actor should ask is not "What if I were Othello?" but "What if she were really Desdemona?" He then can continue: "Is she trustworthy? What can I expect from her? Will she support me in public? What do I need to win her respect? Who are her friends? What does she really feel about black people? Why is she so nice to Cassio? How much does her father still control her? Does she know herself?" The answers that Derrick-Othello draws or plants onto Emily-Desdemona will really tell us – the audience – very little about Emily or

Desdemona. But they will tell us, during the course of the play, a great deal about Derrick-Othello.

Exercises in characterizing others

Perform a scene or improvisation with the following assumptions posited and fantasized onto the other participants in the exercise:

- They are stupid.
- They are dirty.
- They are evil.
- They are brilliant.
- They are gods.
- They are leaderless.
- They are lovable.
- They are ridiculous.
- They are devious.
- They are dangerous.
- They are beneath contempt.

Perform a scene or improvisation with one other person, making the following assumptions about that person:

- He (or she) is adorable.
- He is an undercover agent.
- He is a fascist.
- He is overly sentimental.
- He is too serious.
- He is smelly.
- He makes $500,000 a year.
- He wants your job, or wife, or boyfriend.
- He has killed a man.
- He has escaped from an asylum for the criminally insane.

Perform a scene or improvisation with one other person, transforming that person, in your mind:

- Into a rattlesnake.
- Into a sloth.
- Into a gorilla.
- Into a tree.
- Into a brick wall.
- Into Satan.

- Into God.
- Into a baby girl.
- Into your father.
- Into your worst enemy.
- Into a sex object.
- Into a diseased fingernail.
- Into vomit.

In all of these exercises, do not try to be anything but yourself. Just respond as if the other people were as described; make all the transformations on them rather than on yourself.

Past into future

Freudian psychology reports, axiomatically, that past experience dictates present behavior. Certain acute past experiences are called, by psychologists, "traumatic," and it is generally agreed that certain traumatic experiences can be said to cause current symptoms, even if the original experience is not consciously remembered. This is an absolute foundation of deterministic psychology, and actors who wish to explore the subtleties of their character have been urged, certainly since the time of Stanislavsky, to discover or fabricate their character's past life and experiences.

Cybernetic psychologies, however, focus on behavior as elicited by prospects of the future rather than causes from the past. The difference is one of perspective rather than correctness; while it is equally correct to say "water freezes at 32 degrees" and "ice liquefies at 32 degrees," we, living in warmer climates, are more likely to take the former perspective; the researchers on the South Pole are more likely to take the latter one. In the same way, the actor is more inclined to take a cybernetic and future-oriented perspective on behavior than a deterministic and past-caused one; this has the distinct advantage of allowing the actor to share her character's forward-looking thinking at the moment of action.

The distinction may be made clear by example. A man who, at five years old, had been attacked by a barking dog (the traumatic experience), can be seen to jerk violently as an adult (the symptom) when a dog crosses his path. This cause-and-effect analysis is made by us – the observers; we will say "the man jerked back because he was attacked by a dog when he was five." But the man himself does not, seeing the dog, think "That dog reminds me of the one I saw when I was a child!" Rather, he thinks "That dog is about to attack me!" At the moment of confrontation, the man is not thinking of the past, he is hypothesizing about the future. And an actor playing the man should do the same thing.

An actor, therefore, studies the past of her character only insofar as that past determines and shapes her cybernetic (future-oriented) thinking, particularly as it guides the fantasies, forecasts, hypotheses, and expectations that lie ahead of her. The actor-character will look to the future and act toward it. Obviously those characterizing contrivances which are dramatically useful to shape her characterization must be placed in front of her and not behind her. Detailed exegeses about a character's past history that do not reveal current thinking patterns often become a rather useless diversion of the actor's homework, and may lead only to blind alleys irrelevant to the play's dramatic trajectory.

The actor's homework, then, is concentrated on the task of developing the character's past into a spectrum of fantasies and expectations of the character's future. No doubt academic studies of psychology are useful to the actor, but so, unavoidably, are the actor's own well-earned understandings about human nature, gained through observation of life as well as reading novels, biographies, histories, and plays which encapsulate the observations of others.

Putting the past into the future involves, among other things, characterizing others. The man who had the traumatic experience with a dog may well characterize all dogs as dangerous. A woman who was gang raped as a teenager may very well characterize all men as beasts. Such generalized characterizations are wrong, of course, but they occur all the time, and often become embedded in a victim's thinking – but as unconscious prejudices, not as strictly rational thoughts.

The private audience

We have already seen that interaction becomes a performance when there is another person present to observe it. That "other person" becomes an "audience" to the interaction, and makes it communicational. In the presence of such an audience, one cannot not communicate; a performance is automatically, if unconsciously, engaged. Thus far we have only spoken of this audience as it consists of real people whose presence is entirely physical.

Some of our daily behavior, however, consists of interactions with an audience which is not physically present. This is the "private audience," which is composed of all the people, real and imaginary, living or dead, whom we carry about in our heads as witnesses to our daily behavior, and for whom, in an ulterior sense, we frequently perform. Our private audience includes all those people of whom we say "If only Harriet (or Dad, or Professor Sims) were here to see me now!" Parents, parent-figures, present and former teachers, siblings, lovers, relatives, friends and divinities all figure prominently in our private audiences; so does anyone whose respect or love we ever sought, successfully or unsuccessfully, and anyone to whom we have ever felt the need or desire to "prove" ourselves; to anyone, in short, whose opinion we reckon into considerations of our identity. The private audience is not real in the ordinary sense, and it is not present in the physical sense, but nobody can doubt its influence – sometimes even its control – over much of our daily behavior. Often we find ourselves playing for the satisfaction of our private audience instead of for the real and immediate one beside us. Often we phrase our remarks in a way calculated to gain the respect of a private audience member – and no one else. Sometimes we are restrained from certain behaviors because of the feeling that we are being watched by members of our private audience – the "parents of our imagination," perhaps – and sometimes that feeling persists long after the person in question is out of our lives altogether, perhaps long after they are dead. Although the private audience may not be "real," its effects are certainly real enough, and it must not be looked upon as a purely mystical concoction; it is a part of the actor's psyche and of the character's psyche, and it has real consequences for both.

We interact with our private audience in a variety of ways. There are some members of our private audience we wish to make proud of us; their presence at our victorious moments will serve to validate our victories. Then there are those people we wish to make envy us, people we wish to show up or surpass; our rivals, perhaps, or our enemies, detractors, critics, and deserters. Who has not felt the urge, on occasion, to "prove oneself" in one's own mind to a departed lover, an estranged adversary? And then there are those whose disapproval we seek to avoid, and whose presence only serves to make us guilty, remembering past sins, failures, and omissions. A preponderance of supportive people in our private audience tends to make us buoyant, optimistic, and happy to "perform." A preponderance of detractors, disapprovers, and guilt-purveyors tends to make us depressed, morbid, tense and pathologically irrational. While introspection can confirm the existence, and to an extent the influence, of our own private audience, psychological analysis is required to uncover the phenomenon in its greater and more pervasive complexity. Here are a few examples of the private audience in our daily lives:

- A young woman, accepting the proposal of marriage from a wealthy and handsome young man, a "good catch," gaily pictures in her mind her proud mother, her envious girlfriend, and her desolated former boyfriend with whom she recently quarreled. Later she will wonder why she accepted the proposal.
- An actor, receiving a big Broadway role, gloats at seeing in his mind the astonishment of former teachers and fellow students who have derided his ambition.
- A housewife, giving a dinner party, polishes the silver and crystal to the shine that would please her mother – who, however, died fifteen years ago.
- A professor gives a series of introductory lectures in a college course, but the lectures are too specialized for the freshman students. "I had the feeling," he later reports, "that the editorial board of the PMLA (a scholarly journal) was seated in the back row." This is a real story a colleague told me about; his imaginary and private audience had determined the nature of his lectures far more than his "real" audience.
- A secretary visibly tenses every time she makes a minor typing error, even though her employer has never rebuked her for these mistakes. "It just seems that Mom's looking over my shoulder when I work," she reports. This too is a real story, told to me by an administrative assistant in the office where I work.

Here are some cases in which the private audience is mentioned by characters in plays:

- Tom, in *The Glass Menagerie*, concludes the play with a speech describing his life following the play's events: "I left Saint Louis. I descended the steps of this fire escape for the last time and followed, from then on, in my father's footsteps...but I was pursued by something...Perhaps I am walking along a street at night...Then, all at once my sister touches my shoulder. I turn around... Oh, Laura, Laura, I tried to leave you behind me, but I am more faithful than I intended to be!" Tom's action is ruled by two members of his mental, private audience: his father, whose footsteps he pursues, and his sister, to whom he remains faithful. Tom's inability to "play to" both of these "non-present" characters simultaneously causes an emotional paralysis.

- Willy Loman, in *Death of a Salesman*, has actual dialogue with his brother Ben, whom he has not seen since he was three years old, and whom he "sees" now only in his imagination (although playwright Arthur Miller has allowed us to see Willy's imagination in this play, which was originally titled *The Inside of His Head*). Willy, whose only memory of his father is "a man with a big beard," has sought unsuccessfully to find, in his highly fantasized brother Ben, a father-figure who could validate his life. With Ben's failure to fill this function, Willy then recalls one Dave Singleman, a "salesman in the Parker House," who is also somewhat fantasized in Willy's recollection. Willy's final inability to find, and relate to, an effectively supportive private audience occasions his son's comment after Willy's suicide: "He never knew who he was." To fail to grasp one's private audience is to experience an empty and insecure identity.

- Linda, in *Death of a Salesman*, gives her final speech to her dead husband at his funeral, after she has asked the other attendees to give her a private moment with him. Her speech begins, "Forgive me, dear. I can't cry. I don't know what it is, but I can't cry. I don't understand it. Why did you ever do that? Help me, Willy. I can't cry..." But real tears certainly flooded the theatre by the end of Linda Edmond's performance of this speech in the play's 2012 Broadway revival.

The private audience and acting

The private audience ties into acting as a transformation between the actor and the character; it is one of the techniques of reciprocal characterization. The private audience of a character consists of all those people, living or dead, real or imaginary, for whom the character ultimately performs: those whose respect she desires, whose envy she wishes, whose disapproval she tries to avoid. The actor, in transforming into a character, creates and plants the character's private audience, and plays to it. She does not do this simply by naming off the "people" that populate her character's private audience, but by actively imagining them with human characteristics, both physical and emotional. Sometimes she will do this by substituting real people known to her, sometimes by imagining "people" in her own private audience that can be successfully, and appropriately, transferred to that of her character's. She then imagines these people as invisible witnesses to her behavior, judges to her actions, silent commentators to her deeds. She does not play to them directly; she simply plays knowing that they are there around her and in her – her ministering angels, her haunting spirits, the personified voices of her conscience and of her courage.

Example: Tom Wingfield

Let us return to Tom Wingfield, in *The Glass Menagerie*, as an example of a character with a complex and important private audience, which we have already seen in part. Tom knows the influence his father and sister hold over him in his mind, an influence that is no less strong for being irrational and unwise. But this is hardly the extent of his complete private audience. There is also his mother, more dominating than the other two, and the one we might imagine Tom more honestly speaking to at the end of the play when he asks Laura to blow out her candles. There is also his friend, Jim O'Conner, to whom Tom is probably not as indifferent as he outwardly pretends to be, and their boss, Mr. Mendoza, whose disapproval hurts Tom deeply, more than he lets Jim (or us) know. Then there is also "Malvolio the Magician," whom Tom assists one night in a vaudeville act (or so he says). Malvolio's influence would be no less great, however, if Tom had simply made up the story; real or imaginary, his image exerts an influence on Tom, which is all that counts. Then there are the even more shadowy figures; his co-workers at the shoe factory, the strangers on the street, the couples at the Paradise Dance Hall, the union officers at the merchant marines, and "the huge middle class of America...matriculating in a school for the blind," a generation with which Tom wishes to identify himself. Finally, there are four figures whose importance is inestimable, but who have no interactions with Tom (during the play) whatever. The first is Clark Gable, who for Tom epitomizes "all those glamorous people having adventures." The second is Shakespeare, whom Jim nicknames Tom after, and who Tom implicitly accepts as a role model. The third is the idealized "Christian adult" that Amanda continually holds up to Tom as the proper model for his behavior. And the fourth is the high school English teacher, never mentioned, who we must presume lies somewhere behind Tom's sneaking off to write poetry. We must realize that these many figures, only three of whom are seen in the play, filter through Tom's mind all the time: when he is out by himself on the balcony, when he is working at the shoe factory, when he is arguing with his mother, when he is joining the merchant marines, and when he is following his father's footsteps. The task for the actor is to identify and characterize this private audience, to plant and personify it, and then to play the play's action in an attempt to win his private audience's respect, to prove himself to his private audience, to avoid his private audience's disapproval, and, where necessary, to "show up" his private audience. The depth to which the actor can create and vivify Tom's varied private audience will be the measure of richness he can bring to his characterization.

Private audience and God

The presence of a character's private audience – while not present on the stage nor visible to the character – nonetheless hovers over her and inside her. Many times it has spiritual or even Godlike resonance. This includes not only the God to whom many characters pray ("O God! God! How weary, stale, flat, and unprofitable seem to me all the uses of this world!' says Hamlet). It is also the "voices" of Shaw's St. Joan, the good and bad angels of Marlowe's Dr. Faustus, and the Godot of Beckett's Vladimir and Estragon. It is, one way or another, the "God" of thousands of characters in countries around the world and in every religion that tolerates a theatre. Playing these characters means playing under the eyes of the character's God – whether or not the actor herself "has" or even imagines a God, or any other deity.

Characterizing a God is a reciprocal characterization when the character is understood to believe in – or even to consider the possibility of – a divine being that is aware of human behavior. For God-fearing characters, God becomes the supreme being of the character's private audience, and the actor playing that character – even though this is unspoken in the text – may be seeking the help of God (or of Jesus, Allah, Buddha, or any sainted figure) for aid, comfort, enlightenment or salvation throughout the duration of the play.

The characterizing, planting, and utilizing of a character's private audience creates some of drama's most powerful and intense characterizations. The more important and the more powerful the private audience, the more awesome the characterization might become. Private audiences that move into the divine or supernatural realms can be staggering; they are virtually required in dramas committed to ritual experience, and extremely exciting in dramas of deep spiritual, moral, or tragic import. How else can the actor even begin to play Antigone, or Orestes, or Sir Thomas More? The private audience is certainly a vital key to character, both in ourselves and in our characterizations.

Exercise: Private audiences

You cannot very well create a private audience for your character until you have discovered and analyzed your own. Think of all the people who come into your mind in various situations. Think, particularly, of your parents and parent-figures, of your past and present teachers, professors, coaches, best friends, lovers, brothers, sisters, roommates, and rivals. Think, if applicable, of your God or spiritual leader.

Do you think of someone special when you answer a question in class? When you write a paper? When you tell a joke? When you are in a first-class restaurant? When you drive a car? When you are in a romantic situation? Do you ever behave in a way directed toward that non-present person? Is that person's "presence" supportive? Is it harmful? Would you rather drive that person out of your mind? Are there times that you try but fail to drive them out of your mind?*

Discover, by analysis and creativity, a *dramatic character's* private audience. List:

- The other characters in the play known by him.
- Characters not in the play but mentioned by him.
- Unnamed characters known to be important in his past.
- People who might be presumed important in his past.
- The character's concept of God.

Rank these characters in order of their overall importance to you, and specify the situations in which each character might appear in your private audience. Then flesh out these "characters" in your own mind by visualizing them, imagining a conversation with them, putting words in their mouths, and so forth. Use people in your own private audience, if you wish, to embody people in your character's.

Exercise: *Play to a private audience*

Memorize a speech of a single character's, preferably a long speech that is particularly informative or characteristic. Recite the speech into a mirror, while imagining that the mirror image is not of you, but of an individual in your character's private audience. Repeat the speech, substituting another person in the private audience. Here are two initial character options:

Hamlet

Memorize Hamlet's soliloquy as he decides first to kill, and then not to kill, Claudius – as discussed in the previous chapter. Deliver the speech to an imaginary kneeling Claudius, or to another actor who will play the kneeling Claudius.

Then do the speech again, imagining the Ghost of Hamlet's father standing behind you, which Hamlet would almost certainly be doing.

Do it again imagining your *own* father standing behind you. Then with your own mother. With your own English or Philosophy professor, or your own priest,

---

* Most forms of psychodrama involve the patient's "acting out" of confrontation scenes (imaginary) between themselves and members of their private audience, with the idea that by making the patient aware of her private audience she will be free from its unconscious and often pathogenic control. Abreactive or cathartic therapies, which induce the patient to throw off the pathogenic control of the private audience (much as Aristotle said that tragedy should induce us to throw off pity and terror), employ such psychodramatic techniques.

pastor, imam, or rabbi. With your own God, if you "have" a God. And *make each of these people proud of you.*

Tom

Memorize Tom's last soliloquy in *The Glass Menagerie*. Deliver it as if to any of the people in his private audience, as developed in the example above. Deliver it to your father (as his father); your mother (as his mother); your English teacher (as his English teacher); your God (as his God).

Linda

Memorize Linda's speech from *Death of a Salesman*, the first part of which is cited above, to Willy who has just been buried in the ground before you. Then deliver it again, still directly to Willy, but knowing that your own son – or brother, or sister, or other family member – is standing behind you. Let them "overhear" your remarks to your late husband.

Any speech

Play any two-person scene, from any play, with one of the following people in your private audience:

- Jesus Christ
- Your greatest admirer
- Your idol
- Your favorite movie star
- Your worst enemy
- Your severest critic
- Someone you love
- Someone you want to love you

Since the person is not physically present, you cannot play directly for him or her; play entirely to your scene partner, but know that your private audience is hovering invisibly above you. Do nothing to indicate the existence of this private audience, and don't even tell your scene partner that you're doing it. This exercise cannot and should not be judged by anyone but you.

The character's thinking

In general, what we are pursuing in the study of characterization is this: the wholesale adoption, by the actor, of the character's *thinking* and of her *thinking processes*. This does not simply mean the character's thoughts; it means, in addition, the *way* a character thinks. This is the character's personal epistemological machinery, her mindsets and thinking channels. The transformation of actor into character cannot be complete without this adoption. When we, in the audience, see a character speaking we should also see the actor playing the character *thinking up what she says*. The character should not merely be saying the lines but *originating* them as she goes along. Edith Evans, the late and great British actress, reports that "by thinking you turn into the person, if you think it strongly enough." She continues "I think my (character's) thoughts when I'm playing a play that matters, because I am that woman all the time through."[12] The way the actor characterizes the other people in the play, the way she fantasizes, hypothesizes, and plans around them, the way she sees them as obstacles or (in some cases) friends; this summarizes essentially what the character thinks and how the character thinks. Dramatizing a character's situation and creating a "character" to deal with it must transform the actor's inner thinking as well as her outward behavior.

"The actor's task is not to think of words as part of a text, but of words as part of a person whom we believe actually minted them in the heat of the moment."

British director Peter Brook[13]

"I feel I am who I am playing…You must somehow be that man – not just the part that shows in the role, but the whole of the man, his whole mind…Oh God, yes, you have to feel it to do it. If you do it right, you do feel it. The suffering, the passion, the bitterness, you've got to feel them. And it takes something out of you and puts something in, as all emotional experiences do."

British actor Laurence Olivier[14]

Thinking, of course, involves a great many things that are rather difficult to pin down. It involves perceiving information from the outside world, and choosing what information to seek out and utilize. It means locating obstacles and planning paths through and around them. It means characterizing other people and trying to figure out what they might do for or against you in a whole host of situations. It means making hypotheses and plans in the pursuit of desired and expected victories. It means contingency thinking: "What do I do if …?" And it means continually playing out in one's mind a host of possible, moment-to-moment contingencies.

In a rather important phrase, Freud claimed that *Danken ist Porbearbeit* – literally, "Thinking is trial work." The eminent late psychiatrist Fritz Perls translates Freud's dictum more freely as "Thinking is rehearsing." [15]* Characters as well as people "rehearse," in their minds, the contingencies of possible future interactions. This is not rehearsing as it is commonly known in the theatre, which is rehearsing a given script. Life's rehearsing is against unknown obstacles and fantasized futures. The actor, of course, rehearses the events in the play that will happen, but the *character* that the actor plays rehearses in her mind the events that are *never* to happen. So the mind of Jane, playing Laura, races with thoughts of coming down the aisle to greet Jim O'Conner at the altar; Joe, playing Macbeth, strategizes his killing MacDuff; Ellen, playing Juliet, imagines having children with Romeo; and Tim, playing Arnolfe, is planning the guest list for his wedding with Agnes. These rehearsals are for actions that never (it turns out) take place, but they are the mechanisms with which the actor thinks his character's thoughts, dreams his character's dreams, and lives his character's life.

"In the creative state, life's an adventure. You love the exhilaration of every single moment. It's the opposite of what you see when you find actors…wanting to do things right or wanting to make a scene happen in a certain way. In the creative state you give all that up and embrace the free fall of not knowing what will happen next. You take off from the top of the hill and let yourself run down without control. It's a very exciting experience to work this way and a very exciting experience to watch people work this way."

American acting teacher, William Esper[16]

---

* Perls continues, "Part of the reason why Freud could not follow up on this idea was because rehearsing is related to the future, and Freud was concerned only with the past." Freud, of course, was a determinist, while Perls was a cyberneticist.

Exercises: Thinking the character's thoughts

The following series of exercises asks you to think the thoughts of any character chosen by you from a play that you know well; perhaps a play and character that you are presently working on or have recently worked on.

Rehearse, in your mind, the events surrounding your character's greatest possible victory. Who will be there? What will they say and do? What will they look like?

- Rehearse an imaginary victory dance.
- Rehearse, in your mind, the events which would accompany your character's totally fantasized (though practically impossible) victory.
- Rehearse your character's most humiliating defeat.
- Rehearse variations on your character's narrowly escaping that humiliating defeat.
- Rehearse your character's narrowly escaping the humiliating defeat and going on to achieve a sensational victory.

Think of each character to whom you relate in the play. From your own (character's) viewpoint, answer these questions about them:

- How would they react if you declared your love for them?
- How would they react if you tried to seduce them?
- How would they react in a natural crisis (such as a fire)?
- How would they react in an emotional crisis?
- What makes them nervous?
- What makes them frightened?
- What do they think about you?
- Do they care about you as much as they let on? Less?
- What do they feel about your race? Sex? Appearance?

Describe them in a few words. In one word.

Take a walk in your neighborhood, and notice what your character would notice. Hear what he would hear. In what ways does the character perceive information differently than you do? In what ways does the character want to perceive differently than you do? In what ways does the character fail to perceive what you do?

Write a letter to the editor of your local newspaper in character. Sign the letter with your character's name.

Tactical self-characterizing: masking

People do not characterize themselves to themselves, as we have seen, but they do try to characterize themselves to others, and to project an image of themselves for tactical purposes. Most of the tactics in the previous chapter would be carried out by a person's "trying to appear" one way or another to threaten or induce another party. This is *masking*, often unconscious but still deliberate. No matter how honest, spontaneous and transparent we may claim to be, we all share this trait – it is biological – of adopting, in T. S. Eliot's sublime phrase, a "face to meet the faces that you meet."[17] We talk and act a bit differently in bed than at work, or at a bar, or at a cocktail party, or at a PTA meeting. The idea of "just being yourself" is, quite frankly, a total abstraction, for we are many selves and we wear many masks.

We assume most of our ordinary daily expressions – our masks – for tactical purposes. The serious look of the student, the sly look of the rogue, the sober look of the politician, the "hale-fellow" look of the Rotary greeter, the tight grin of the M.C., the frown of the librarian, the smile of the bashful girl, the grimace of the schoolboy called on to answer a question, the wink of the lover, the chuckle of the sycophant, the wide-eyed indignation of the overcharged customer, the menacing sneer of the linebacker, the coy fake-innocence of a driver pulled over for a traffic violation – these all are adopted visages, calculated, usually unconsciously, to win some victory or other. Even expressions which we ordinarily think are spontaneous are frequently tactical. Letting go of tears, as we have seen, in an infant is a purely unconscious response to pain, but in an adult may be an unconscious response augmented by a willed decision to let the person who induced that pain regret having done so. At that moment, the crying becomes tactical – exhibited to induce sympathy, guilt, pain, relief, or reconciliation. Like the other masks above, it is donned to be observed, since you are "acting for" – and even "performing for" the benefit of somebody else.

Characters, therefore, act for each other. Just like the people in real life whom they represent, characters smile, laugh, cry, grimace, stare, wink, frown, glare, and smirk at each other to win situational victories through relacom. They may try to appear strong, wise, and knowing; or, conversely, they may try to appear naive, foolish, and helpless, but each of these strategies is for tactical reasons. When an actor dons a tactical mask, she is "acting for" the other actor-characters, not for the audience! She is not trying to pretend to be her character, but trying to enact her character's pretending.

This frequently reciprocates what we may think the character actually "is." The actor playing the shy man pretends to be debonair. But because he (or the writer or the director) has planted obstacles in his way, his pretending is going to fail. The audience will see through it: they see a *really* shy man pretending to be a debonair man, and they see the shy man beneath his pretence. I am using the pronoun "he" this time because, as you may have guessed, I am speaking of how Dustin Hoffman played Benjamin in *The Graduate* – as discussed earlier – with a tremendous effort to wear masks of sexual prowess and masculine savoir-faire that shattered to pieces every time that Anne Bancroft looked at him as she would a little plaything. The audience saw through the masks and "discovered" Benjamin's true character – the character that Hoffman was so obviously trying to "hide" behind his idiotic mask of unquenchable virility.

"Acting (and this is one difference between professional and amateur actors…) is not a matter of assuming a fixed role but of showing how the character acts – that is, how he moves in and out of his repertory of roles; how he changes his disguise to meet every moment of the play, responding to changes in his situation and in the characters around him, revealing one thing and hiding another. …I can't think of better advice for a young actor than to remember that in any part he plays he must be changing masks from moment to moment."

American acting theorist Michael Goldman[18]

Masking a character

The questions to ask with regard to masking a character are these: How does the character want to appear in general? How does she want to appear to the other characters in the play? To each other character? How does she want to appear to strangers? How does she want to appear to herself? How does she want *not* to appear in general? What appearances must she avoid at all times and at all costs? What appearances must she avoid with each particular character? I think we all know enough about our own behaviors that we think about these questions often, examining our own personalities – masks, we might say – and how others may see them.

Your answers to these questions will provide the shaping of your character's public behavior – what you try to hide with your mask, and what you try to show.

In the previous chapter we discussed tactics that come into play because they are generally useful. In developing characterization, however, we must study the tactics that our specific characters use. These are not necessarily rational; they are tactics we choose for subjective reasons, not objective ones, and we have no assurance they will actually work. The subjectivity of this tactical masking, of course, is the subjectivity of the specific character we play.

Most of our tactics come from the past. This is because for the most part we have learned them. The infant first cries by instinct, in response to discomfort, but eventually realizes that her flow of tears attracts persons who will alleviate her discomfort; soon she learns the tactic of shedding tears to attract caregivers.

But tactics, though derived from the past, must be adapted to the future. When the baby is about two, her caregivers realize that she – now a child – is only crying to attract their aid, and they begin to react with indifference. When the child eventually begins to understand what's going on, she replaces her crying with full-out tantrums, which cannot be met with indifference for very long. But soon, when the child is five, say, and her tantrums are punished by forced isolation, she learns how to sulk. Sulking, indeed, becomes the child's strongest trump card in her preteens, because it is the only real power she possesses at that time: the power to withhold her affection. To a guilty but still loving parent or grandparent (guilty, perhaps, for having overly punished the child's tantrums; loving because of sheer maternal/paternal instinct), this tactic is often successful, and as a result the nine-year-old often uses it well into adolescence. But that leads to yet a new problem; for sulking in adolescents, particularly when used as a tactic on anyone but their parents, is notably impotent and futile. And when used by adults, it will be seen as utterly absurd, making them look like the nine-year-olds they once were. Sulking, therefore, is a tactic learned in childhood because it proved successful at that time, but it becomes perilous when carried over into adulthood, by which time it has lost its effectiveness. One of the great sulking characters of all time, of course, is Hamlet, and his sulking does not work on Claudius, Gertrude, Polonius, or Laertes.

The actor can find in his or her character's past a great source of masking possibilities. How did Hamlet get his way with his mother? His father? With Polonius? With Ophelia? With his school friends? With the Court in general? With the Danish citizenry? What tactics did he use then, and which ones will he carry over now? What tactics did Amanda (in *The Glass Menagerie*) use when she was younger? What tactics does she use toward men, her "gentlemen callers?" How much of her handkerchief tactic (see p.13) described by Williams as "a piece of acting," derives from her past? Does the tactic really work the way she would like it to? How long will she persist in using it?

The masks that characters wear come from their situational tactics and the activities stimulated by their quests for victory. It is not a reflection of how the actor wants to be seen, but of how the *character* wants to be seen. The choice of masks stems partly from the character's conscious choice of tactics, and partly from his unconscious carrying over of tactics that worked for him in the past. The way these are blended determines the specific configuration of the mask, and the way the audience will see through to the "character" who wears it.

Tactical emotion

We have spoken of emotion in the previous chapter as comparable, in the Barrault metaphor, to the sweat of the runner, autonomically induced by the act of running. This is the primary emotion described by Antonio Damasio. It is a spontaneous reaction, and we have little if any control over it. But we do not "feel" it as much as we experience it. It prompts our immediate behavior, but we don't take the time to think about it; indeed, we don't feel that we *have* the time to think about it.

There is also, however, the secondary, or considered emotion. This often becomes part of a tactical mask.

We have already seen how, in life, crying may be stimulated autonomically but continued tactically. Even though the tactic may be futile, it may be pursued unconsciously as a carryover from the days when crying "worked." We have also seen how laughter can be feigned on occasions, or at least exaggerated from an originally spontaneous chuckle, as a way to show that we appreciate someone trying to amuse us, or want to let others know that we "get the joke," or at least that we like the fact that someone told us a joke. Actors who have performed in comedies are often dismayed at early rehearsal run-throughs when the few technicians who are seeing the show for the first time are all but silent during the run, and then surprised when the full house on opening night erupts in howls of laughter. Why didn't the technicians laugh? Simply because there weren't enough of them, and each felt awkward of becoming "the only one laughing." Laughter is contagious, because when anyone laughs, we all want to join in: but this is at least partly tactical, not wholly spontaneous, laughter.

And there are times, indeed, *many* times, when anger is tactically displayed – or at least "real" anger is exaggerated into a "performance" of anger – in everyday life. We use such performances to "re-characterize" ourselves. Parents often pretend to be angrier than they really are when they scold their children. Their goal is to scare their children into listening to them and (they hope) obeying them. Directors may show a pretence of anger in rehearsals when they feel actors are not paying proper attention. Often a director raising her voice a mere decibel will do the trick perfectly, not just to the person addressed, but everyone else in the room. Almost everyone in a supervisory position has learned to come up with a shift in volume, pitch, a raised eyebrow, or hand gesture that, they hope, reminds people "who's in charge."

Displaying emotion, and *meaning* to display emotions, each has a genuine function in human interactions. We often conciously display emotions to establish the way we want to be seen: as fiery, thoughtful, caring, goodhearted. We sometimes deliberately characterize ourselves in life, and characters characterize themselves on stage, by showing emotions. But are these our "real" emotions? Not always.

Of course, if onstage emotion is simply faked – "put on" and displayed by the actor as if it were makeup – the theatergoing audience will recognize it as artificial.

The theatre term for this fakery is *indicating* (short for "indicating emotion"), which is the opposite of feeling emotion. We have learned, however, from neuroscientists like Damasio (see Chapter 2), that emotions come from a variety of sources, and that smiles are controlled by different muscles (the orbicularis oculi and the zygomatic major) which themselves are controlled by different parts of the brain, and that completely different physiological sources stimulate both primary (instinctual) and secondary (considered, deliberate) emotions. Thus, what we casually call "emotion" is actually a compound of quite different mental signals and physical responses to those mental signals.

We have long heard (and the famed Russian director Anatoly Efros has confirmed) that Stanislavsky, when he disliked an actor's performance in rehearsal, would shout from the back of the theatre, "I don't believe you!"[19] I have always wondered, however, if any such actor ever turned to Stanislavsky and shouted back at him, "Well, I don't believe *you!*" Stanislavsky was saying, of course, that he did not believe the actor was "really" feeling the emotion he was expressing on the stage, but I seriously doubt that Stanislavsky was "really" feeling the anger he was expressing to that actor. Rather, he was creating the appearance of anger to let everyone else on the stage know that he would not stand for "fake" emotion. But my guess is that *Stanislavsky's* emotion was fake. For even though it conveyed his genuine belief, that an actor should "Live the life of the character on the stage," it was "performed" in an exaggeratedly angry manner to send a relacom message not just to the actor but to all other members of the cast that they had better follow his Stanislavsky System – or else!

Except in infants, pure uncontrolled emotion rarely exists, so the "genuineness" of emotion is not really at issue. Tactical displays of emotion occur all the time – because they are useful. The real (instinctual, primary) emotion behind the tactical display can be fully congruent with the physical display (a smiler can be genuinely amused), or it can be the opposite (a smiler can also be completely unamused but wanting to please the person trying to amuse her). Or, as is the case most of the time, the "real" emotion can be ambivalent, or even unknown. Tom, in *The Glass Menagerie*, for example, alternates between raging at his mother and making nice to her, but it would be quite shallow to assume that he simply rages when he is angry and turns gentle when he is forgiving. In fact, his feelings about his mother are obviously intermingled and confused; the playwright often shows him stammering, trying consciously to find the words that will express and clarify his feelings. Often Tom's displayed emotion is a "test" to see what kind of future relationship he and his mother might have if he were to behave in a different way.

In the cases where primary emotions are ambivalent, or confused and uncertain, a display of emotion may well provoke the actual emotion corresponding to that displayed. The principle of cognitive dissonance makes clear that we will tend to feel, or at least feel that we feel, emotions we initially only pretended to feel. Tom, while "acting out" his rage to his mother, may *actually* become enraged at her; thus the actor playing Tom, for his part, may actually become enraged at the actress playing Amanda. Both primary and secondary emotions can register in physiological tests; the autonomic nervous systems and endocrine systems function even though the displayed "emotion" began as something a character consciously and tactically chose to display.*

The lesson is this: while an actor rarely should "just" indicate emotion to the audience (the exception being when this is the whole point of the scene, in which the character is a complete hypocrite), she has many resources with which, as an actor-character, she can display emotions as part of the mask she adopts in her situational interactions. That display may induce her actual, physiological emotion. It may also induce an emotional response in the *other* actor – which will intensify the primary emotions of both of them. Which came first, the real or the displayed emotion? It really doesn't matter. The boxer trying to win the fight, like Barrault's long distance runner nearing the finish line, feels primary emotion. The slalom skier trying to beat the clock while going around the flags also feels primary emotion: Trying hard to win at anything difficult induces this immediate and reactive emotion. And facing off with someone who is trying hard to beat you induces even more emotion. And deliberately *displaying* your emotion in order to induce or threaten the person you are facing off creates *even more* emotion. Emotion builds on emotion. It thrives on its own feedback. Emotion is what makes thousands of spectators pour onto a football field and tear down the goal posts after a hard-fought football game, or explode in a street riot after a championship soccer match. These people can be described as swept away by their emotions – but they also *know what they are doing.* They're not really swept away, they are swept *into* the interpersonal events in which they are engaging. And that's true whether it's the Yankees and the Dodgers in the World Series or Masha and Vershinin in *The Three Sisters.*

Understanding that emotions are both spontaneous and tactical is obviously helpful to understand – and to counter – the problem first discussed in the previous chapter: crying on stage. It can also be used for laughing on stage, or any other seemingly spontaneous emotional outburst. Find the *tactical reason* for your character's display. Discover not "why" the character cries, but what she is crying *for*: what she hopes to achieve by letting her tears flow – or by holding her tears back. Find how the character *uses* crying, or *tries* to use crying, to solve her situational difficulties and achieve situational victories. Then play the crying (or the laughing) for all you can get. It will create a personal level to your character that costume and makeup can never do.

Actors have probably always known this principle. When Falstaff asks for "a cup of sack" so "that it may be thought I have wept" while performing the part of King Henry IV (see previous chapter), he is genuinely crying by the end of his "performance," acknowledging that, "now I do not speak to thee in drink, but in

---

* Nineteenth-century psychologists William James and Carl Lange independently proposed similar principles in what became known as the James-Lange theory – a notion that, while controversial, is still discussed in the literature of acting theory.

tears." Cognitive dissonance has done its magic: Falstaff's fake crying has turned genuine. "Perform the action, the feeling will follow," said William Ball,[20] who founded the San Francisco's Actors Conservatory Theatre in 1966, making the phrase his company's – and their professional actor training program's – core principle.

Actors, however, are often self-conscious and artistically "guilty" about displaying emotions they do not feel, or do not feel that they feel. Such self-consciousness or guilt is simply not necessary. In displaying emotions, both real and tactical and a mixture of both, actors are behaving exactly as their characters do; and they are "in character" as long as they are "in situation," and acting for the other actor-characters and not just for the audience.* Realizing this frees the actor from the self-consciousness of wondering about her feelings, a self-consciousness that people in life rarely if ever have, and which usually prevents spontaneous feelings altogether. Tom, for example, when he yells at his mother, cannot simultaneously be asking himself whether this is "real" rage or "fake" rage; so neither should the actor who is playing Tom.

Will real feeling follow, though? That depends on the play, the effectiveness of your tactics on the other actor-characters, and you, the actor. Perhaps your real feeling is not meant to follow; perhaps your character's display is only "a piece of acting," like Amanda's dropping the handkerchief. Primary emotion, and our self-awareness of such emotion, is an intangible; its existence cannot be quantified or particularized, and in most cases it remains a mysterious presence, or process, even to ourselves. Displayed emotion, on the other hand, is part of the tactical behavior in interpersonal interactions; it can be played in life and it can be acted by a player on stage, so long as it supports the overall drive of her character – and becomes a factor she hopes and believes will lead to winning her goals.

It may very well be sufficient to let it go at that. For as enchanting as the concept of "real emotion" may be, it remains determinedly intractable to pin down. Thinking about emotion virtually precludes emoting. The actor's and character's concentration must be on winning goals, on the other person, and on the situation. The rest will follow.

Properties and business

Characterization is not simply a matter of what's inside the character's mind, of course. It is in a large measure dependent on the play's style, as created by the playwright, and the production's style, as created by the director, designers, and the actors in rehearsal. These are the subjects of Chapter 5.

But a character's individuality comprises, in great measure, the multiple subtle and precise behaviors he or she exhibits, which combine to create, in the audience's mind, a sense of having observed a specific and individual personality.

---

* They are acting for the audience too, however. This is the subject of Chapter 6.

A character, in other words, who is a "character." Many of these behaviors arise spontaneously in the actor's performance, as we have seen, since they derive from the actor's own unconscious ways of behaving under various circumstances. And some of these behaviors will be specifically directed into each actor's performance by the director, or written in by the playwright. But a whole host of purely individual behaviors – and perhaps the most crucial of them – will be stimulated and evoked through the effective selection of appropriate *properties and stage business.*

The importance of props and business is twofold. Most obviously, they are useful in conveying direct and immediate information to the audience. A character wearing a certain type of spectacles, for example, will be identified by the audience as a pedant; a character who is chain-smoking will be identified as hypertense; a character drinking to excess will be identified as an addict, or as burdened by deep-seated anguish. Directors and playwrights often use props and business in this way, to create a shorthand and immediate characterization.*

But props and business can also give the actor keys to more subtle and well-rounded characterizations, because they create meanings for the actor as well as for the audience, and stimulate a whole range of unconsciously generated behaviors. These, too, will convey a specificity of the character, because the audience is not merely observing what business is done, but *how* it is done. The manner in which the actor responds to props, and implements stage business, creates the specific contours of her character, and the richness of her characterization.

Consider, for example, the wealth of character-specific details that are possible when an actor, while giving a speech, simultaneously mixes herself a martini, and at the conclusion of her speech drinks it. She must cross to the liquor cabinet (slowly? compulsively? nonchalantly? wobbling?), must pour fluids from two different bottles (carefully? sloppily? recklessly? craftily? looking at the glass? looking at the person she's talking to? looking at the bottle to see how much is left?). Does she take the time to recap the bottles? Does she offer other persons a drink as well? Does she tease other characters with such an offer? Does she brandish the bottle? Is she ashamed of drinking? Is she ashamed of the cheap brand of vermouth she is pouring? Do her hands tremble? Does she stir the drink or slosh it around? Does she omit the olive? Does she plop the olive in with greatly exaggerated pomp? Does she sip greedily? Nervously? Lustily? Defiantly? Desperately?

The possibilities are all but endless, and the answers to all these questions rarely if ever come from the play's text or the director's suggestions. But through such business the audience – and the other characters on the stage – will usually be finding out more about the individual nature of this particular character than in the words she speaks – or even the way she speaks them.

---

* They also use costume for these purposes, but that is to be discussed in Chapter 4.

Many playwrights are excellent at creating the kind of stage business that stimulates rich character performance. Chekhov's plays are notably detailed in behaviors: consider, for example, his initial stage description of Masha: "*Masha, in a black dress, with her hat on her knee, is reading a book,*" or Chebutykin: "*reading the newspaper as he comes in,*" and "*goes out hurriedly, combing his beard,*" or Solyony: "*Pulls a scent-bottle out of his pocket and sprinkles his chest and hands.*" So are many of the plays of Eugene O'Neill, Tennessee Williams, and George Bernard Shaw. Many directors, similarly, are very helpful in finding business and appropriate properties. Often, however, the actor is left to her own resources to develop business that will particularize and enrich her performance without detracting from its main line, or the main lines of the play. In these cases, the actor should explore the real behavior of other people for possibilities, and see if these can be incorporated into her performance. Remember, it is not the business itself that is of immediate concern to the actor, but the way the business is performed. Making a martini or opening an umbrella are very different activities, but the way in which the actor performs them can evoke – from the actor performing and the characters and audience watching – a highly specific sense of her "character's character."

"I have never worked with anyone else who knows how to use props the way that Geraldine (Page) can. She can change a handkerchief or a broom or a tablecloth into her inner landscape. She can let you know through these ordinary things her joy, unhappiness, longing, and also those undefinable and by no means ordinary mysteries hidden in all our lives."

Panamanian-American director José Quintero[21]

Exercise: Characterization through properties and stage business

For this exercise, take a single memorized speech of about 60 seconds from any play, and deliver it meaningfully and *without stopping* while surrounded by others who are watching you from all sides, all the while executing the following stage business:

- While mixing a martini, as in the above example, and taking a sip of it at the speech's end. Do the exercise without planning beforehand how you will mix it; let your behavior come as a response to your feelings and purposes in the scene. (But use water rather than the real thing!)

- While (a) opening an umbrella indoors, and then (b) realizing that the umbrella, opened, will not fit through the door, and then (c) closing the umbrella sufficiently to let it get through the door, and then (d) going out the door with the umbrella, and then, at the end of the speech (e) opening the umbrella and closing the door behind you.
- While taking off your outer garments and re-dressing yourself for some anticipated encounter.
- While setting the table for a dinner party.
- While trying to get comfortable in an underinflated inflatable chair, into which, during the speech, you accidentally drop and lose your purse or wallet.
- While sharpening a knife on a grindstone.
- While watching, and pretending not to watch, the sexual provocations of persons in the scene with you.

The character relishes life

"O wonderful, wonderful, most wonderful wonderful, and yet again wonderful, and after that, out of all whooping!"
Celia, in Shakespeare's As You Like It

We have, so far, discussed the character's intentions, her obstacles, her reciprocal characterizations, her past psychological history (giving rise to future projections), and the particular tactics and maskings she adopts to win her content and relacom victories. These all relate, one way or another, to the character's vision of the future. Now we must explore the character in her present – most particularly, the character as she takes her fleeting delights in those victories she does manage to achieve.

What is the particular thrill experienced by Hamlet, for example, when he sees his father – not in his mind's eye but in a ghostly apparition? How does he experience seeing his old friends Horatio and Marcellus? How does he relish his successful and "palpable" hits in the dueling scene with Laertes? His beautifully sarcastic farewell to Claudius? His bewildering of old Polonius? His convincing of Gertrude? Although the play is a tragedy, the particular joys of Hamlet are the apexes of his character, the peaks of his experience. In living through Hamlet's struggles, the actor must also live (and enliven) Hamlet's joys, delights, and minor victories.

Albert Camus, the French playwright and philosopher, pointed out that an actor's life is one of the world's most ideal existences, because the actor gets to taste the joys of all his character's lives; to Camus, to whom "what counts is not the best living but the most living," it is easy to see why this career should in fact be ideal. All actors must be open to this, for the joy of acting is not simply the joy of being an actor, but the joy of playing – and being – a character: you can experience the joys of living the character's life, and of relishing his or her best moments.

The actor's realm is that of the fleeting. [He] has three hours to be Iago or Alceste, Phèdre or Gloucester. In that short space of time he makes them come to life and die on fifty square yards of boards...What more revelatory epitome can be imagined than those marvelous lives, those exceptional and total destinies unfolding for a few hours within a stage set?

French playwright, novelist and philosopher,
Albert Camus[22]

What, though, defines a character's capacity for joy? What past associations may fill her memory and are capable of being sounded? What private audiences may beam at her from beyond? What sensory experiences fill her with delight? What smells make her happy? What sounds? What glances? What are her associations with twilight? With summer? With cold? How would she enjoy sitting on a tractor seat driving down a dusty road? Or on a porch swing in Louisiana? Or on Lady Macbeth's throne?

Actors should find, in each character they play, the thousands of moments to relish: the thousands of breaths that may be freely and fully taken in, the jokes laughed at and the wits exchanged, the fluid and responsive strokes and petting, the loving and interplaying. They should find – and experience – the *playfulness* of their characters: their joy in badinage and riposte, of gaminess and flirtation, of pillow-fighting and shy sidewise glances. They should find their character's enjoyment of gentleness, grace, affections, the quiet soundings, and delight in their presence. They should find, above all, the positive things about their characters and the positive things their character enjoys and revels in.

Let *yourself* experience and enjoy these things. Indulge them. Remember, it is only when you are allowing yourself to wallow in the character's despair that you can be accused of "indulging in your role" – a stagey and ineffective practice. By indulging in your character's joys, and by relishing her victories – insofar, of course, as the script and the other character's actions will allow – you are only engaging in the character's total life. And your enjoyment will engage the characters around you – and the audience watching you. Hamlet, though a "melancholy Dane" who centers a tragedy, enjoys moments of sheer exaltation, as when his college friends Rosencrantz and Guildenstern appear in the second act: "My excellent good friends!...Good lads, how do you both?" he exclaims. Had Hamlet not felt such joy at their arrival, his later dismissal of them would not appear to us, as it does, so disheartening, for one must have a heart in order to lose it. Likewise Laura's joy when Jim remembers her from high school and offers to dance with her, and Amanda's joy when Tom says Jim will be coming to dinner, and even Tom's delight in the movies that he sees, are essential to establish the depth of the profound disappointment these characters eventually suffer when their joys are dashed. You can't have one without the other.

If we look at this from an audience point of view for a moment, we realize that we are never so deeply in contact with strangers – and the characters in plays are indeed strangers to us – as when we see them ecstatic. Who among us has not felt a great surge of feeling while watching an athlete win a great race, or a bride accept her ring at the altar, or a President that we like be inaugurated, or an actor we like receive a Tony Award – even if we've never met these people in real life? Moments of true joy, moments that are relished to the fullest, radiate a grand transmission of sympathetic feelings. They make the most disinterested observer glow with a sense of identification and shared kinship. They can hush a crowd; they can inspire a populace; they can win an election.

Most beginning actors, however, have a tendency to emphasize the pathos of their characters, perhaps feeling that self-pity is the best way of stimulating sympathy – either from the other characters or from the audience. This is usually as ineffective onstage as it is in life. Far more powerful emotional bonds are evoked by the feeling of shared joys – no matter how trivial they may be – and with brimming happiness. Perhaps those joys are but moments in a long and dense tragedy. Perhaps, for Hamlet and for Laura, they seem insignificant episodes against the weighty circumstances and tragic events these characters ultimately contend with. But they remain the sparks that tie the characters to each other and to the audience – the sparks, ultimately, that fire the will to live and life itself.

Exercises: Relishing a character's life

Take any character and list all his or her victories in a single scene. Include such victories as:

- Being left alone.
- Being talked to.
- Greeting someone pleasant.
- Being challenged.
- Being admired.
- Being befriended.
- Being stroked.
- Being loved.

How does the character respond? Respond, in character.

What are the past associations of the character that would make him or her respond with relish to situations in the play? What memories of childhood are joyfully stimulated in the scene? Find them and play them.

What are the potential evils that the character has escaped? In what way is the character grateful for not being blind, not being crippled, not being old, not being unloved? What does he or she love about her surroundings? Find these and play them.

- Let your character admire the way he or she talks.
- Let your character admire the way he or she looks.
- Let your character admire the way he or she moves.
- Let your character admire her surroundings, and her place in them.

Pick another (but similar) character and go through the three previous exercises. See how many different behaviors are attributable to the different character.

Makeup: Self-transformation

We have covered in this section many mental processes involved in an actor's characterization of a role, focusing on the character's thinking, her vision, the outside world she perceives, the tactical masks she may wear, and the particular relish with which she responds to her world and its specific events. We have also discussed some external attributes, such as props and pieces of stage business, and how these, too, may become character-specific.

This is not all there is to characterization, however. In productions which do not entirely veer from realism,* Falstaff must still be seen to be fat, Lear to be old, Pantalone to be stilted, and Quasimodo to be hunch-backed. For these roles,unless actors do not themselves share their character's physical properties, they must physically transform themselves. This means, among other things, makeup, which has been with the theatre since its inception. "Makeup" is used here not only in the sense of greasepaint, but may also include "made-up" character voices, character movements, character physiques, and character props.

However, we should not think of makeup as either purely physical or purely a one-way, actor-to-others statement. Makeup is also psychological, and it leads to feedback which draws forth "characteristic" behavior. Makeup can be part of the whole interaction of a character, and it can induce characterization. Another way of saying this is that makeup can be a self-fulfilling prophecy. Both men and women who apply cosmetic makeup in their daily lives almost universally report that they not only think they look more attractive, they *feel* more attractive. And this feeling changes their opinions of themselves – and thus re-characterizes themselves – accordingly. Cicely Tyson, who astounded audiences and critics in the teleplay *Autobiography of Jane Pittman* by aging from twelve years old to a hundred and ten with total credibility, reported "after the first makeup session, when I looked at it in the mirror, I really *felt* that old," and went on to describe her resultant "internal feeling of old age." [23]

The point is that the actor should not simply apply makeup, she should *experience* it. She should see how others react to it, both consciously and unconsciously. She should perform improvisations in makeup (and costume, where possible) so that she learns from it.

We should never forget that making up means making *up*. Characters, like the rest of us, invariably want to look their best, not their worst. Quasimodo may be humbled by his hunched back, but there are certainly aspects of his appearance of which, at least secretly, he is proud. Makeup must accentuate this positive. Obese by the world's standard, Falstaff can still glory in his girth; it is, at least in part, an intentional obesity, and there was clearly much well-remembered joy in its creation. Beginning actors tend to think of makeup as a disfigurement of their already-perfect appearances; this is only another aspect of the "character assassination" approach to characterization mentioned at the beginning of this chapter.

Highly stretched characterizations, like Tyson's 110-year-old Pittman, require the planting of very well-studied obstacles and limitations. Viewers of that presentation could see Tyson's character struggling to overcome the handicaps of her physical and psychological systems: her brittle vocal cords, arthritic fingers, woebegone knee, hip, and neck joints, disobedient muscles, cloudy memories,

---

* Theatre productions do veer from realism, of course, and increasingly in the current theatre. This will be discussed in the following chapter.

waning attention, blocked hearing and seeing. It was Tyson's struggle *to overcome* these ailments that made them "characterizing" elements of old age – "real" to the audience, and "really" affecting. Dustin Hoffman's masterful Ratzo Rizzo in the film *Midnight Cowboy* is another example of a "stretched" characterization, also played by the actor-character's intense struggle to overcome the limitations of (planted) lameness, pain, ugliness, incontinence, physical helplessness, and fear.

Highly stretched characterizations require a great deal of research on behavior as well as on greasepaint, because the extremities of characterization are as much in the mind as on the body. For an affecting and honest portrayal of any characterization highly different from yourself, you must work very deliberately not just at finding how that person, or kind of person looks, but how she *thinks* she looks, and what that does to her.

Characterization by way of makeup has been left to the end of this chapter for a number of reasons, not the least of which is that, to a number of beginning actors, makeup is often mistaken for the whole thing. There is a tendency to think of characterization, and particularly highly stretched characterization, as the surest mark of greatness in an actor. Sometimes it is, of course, and the examples of Tyson and Hoffman given above are two of the thousands in the theatre's history. But the tendency to exaggerate the importance of "stretching" in this direction also has an escapist motive; beginning actors are frequently much more anxious to play a character's vulnerability than anything that could be mistaken for their own. This is not stretching, it is shrinking. The character in this case becomes a mere mask to hide behind rather than a living, breathing, sometimes ecstatic and sometimes suffering human being. Such superficial character acting is safe, chaste, and relentlessly "good enough," but it does not bring characters or audiences to life.

The best character acting is like the best slalom race, where the obstacles are planted to inspire a breathtaking performance, and where the performer goes all out in an effort to encircle them and win. That kind of acting is enchanting as well as accurate, involving as well as correct, powerful as well as perfect.

Summary of Chapter 3

Character acting is not solely, not even primarily, a matter of makeup, character "voices," and character "walks." It is the assumption of a character's thinking from the point of view of a character's own self-centeredness. Characterization is a subjective process: The actor characterizes the world as her character does, and then interacts reciprocally with that world as she has characterized it. She sees the world in terms of its offered victories (her ideal future, her finish line) and the obstacles in her path – physical, psychological, and physiological. In her homework for the role, the actor "plants" specific obstacles which will lead her through dramatically interesting contours and paths en route to her situational goals. She plants for herself a private audience that will influence her behavior unconsciously. She masks herself to the other actor-characters as a tactic to surmount her obstacles and achieve her victories. She enjoys those victories with a special and individual relish. Ultimately, however, the "character" that she is seen to play will be determined by the audience, who will determine her character by what they see of her future goals, the obstacles that she believes she faces, and the masks she dons to surmount her obstacles and win her goals.

4

PLAYING STYLE

"I used to watch Sir Laurence (Olivier) when he played Mr. Puff in *The Critic*. To the identical syllable, in each performance, he would take off his hat, take out the hatpin and stab the hat with the hatpin. He didn't vary a hair's breadth from performance to performance, yet it was always funny and always astonishing. It occurred to me that it is possible to be a well-trained instrument, to perform as a craftsman without ever becoming ordinary, and that if there is such a thing as perfection in acting it's worthwhile living for and striving for that perfection."

American actress Julie Harris[1]

As a word in our language, "style" defies attempts at definition. Everyone agrees that style refers in some way to the manner in which things are done, but from that point the word usually disintegrates into semantic chaos. It is used to denote technical modes of expression, as in "a flamboyant style." It is used to denote the shared characteristics of a historical period, as in "Restoration style." It may indicate a contextual theatrical format, as in "Expressionistic style." It may become highly mystical and epigrammatic, as in the classic French definition "Style is the man himself." Sometimes it describes an individual, as the "Bruce Springsteen style." Sometimes it describes a group, clan, or race, as "Divorce Italian Style." Sometimes, even, it can stand by itself without qualifier, as when we say a person "has style." In that case we are essentially saying that the person has "style style," and the word becomes its own modifier. It is no wonder that books on the theatre have foundered on the confusion of meanings of the word "style."

146

For the purposes of making the concept useful, "style" in this book describes the *shared behavioral characteristics of the play's characters*. It is, in other words, the play's *collective characterization*.

Or characterizations, plural, because there may be several groups of characters in a single play. Shakespeare's *A Midsummer Night's Dream* is written in what might be called an Elizabethan style, but the play contains three different groups of characters – the aristocrats, the fairies, and the "mechanicals" or workmen – and each of these groups has its own style: of dress, speech, education, ideology, and behavior. And the play-within-the-play that the mechanicals present in the last act displays another style altogether.

Style is like characterization in many ways. It is at the same level of the actor's structure of consciousness. It develops in childhood and, by the time of the play's action, it has been planted like the slalom designer's flags in such a way as to curve its characters' ensuing dramatic pursuits into interesting contours. It is as opposite from characterization, however, as a mirror twin: Characterization is a measure of how an individual character *differs* from other characters, while style is a measure of how much he or she *resembles* them. If one character speaks in witty epigrams, that is a mark of her character; if all the characters do, it is a mark of the play's – and usually the playwright's – style. If one character speaks in verse, or with a Brooklyn accent, or throws cream pies in other people's faces, this marks a unique character; if a group of characters behaves in those fashions, however, this becomes the collective lifestyle of the entire group.

Style is also a precondition of the whole play – of the various social and class values of the people (real or imaginary) the play concerns. And the overall interactions of the play's characters are governed, at least to some extent, by the preconditions of the play's overall style, including its geographical and historical settings.

The basic problem for the actor in a "stylized" play is one of the alignment discussed in this book's first pages. How does the actor, and the actor's character, enter into style exhibiting social and class values wildly different from her own – without losing her lifelike spontaneity? How, for example, does she play out of herself, with her own emotions and engaging in genuine relacom with the other actor-characters, and at the same time speak in rhyming couplets? Or in Wildean bon mots? Or with an Irish accent? Or in the lyrics of Oscar Hammerstein sung to the music of Richard Rodgers? How can actors from today's world step into the patterns of the past, or of some playwright's fantasy or director's imagination, without seeming "phony" to the audience, and, worst of all, without feeling artificial to themselves? How can actors avoid affectation when playing in styles that in today's world seem affected, or at least "elevated"? How can style, finally, be integrated with the actor's innate personality, and the actor-character's dramatic situation?

The answers to these questions are easier than we might think. If we look through some of life's own experiences, we can see that style is integral not only with life-situations, but often with our own survival. Style is no adornment; at bottom, it is a social necessity. We have been performing it all our lives.

Let us look, for example, at ourselves as first-time American tourists in France. We enter a small-town barroom and, being our American selves, we order, "Gimme a Bud." But the bartender just stares at us, shrugs his shoulders with an incomprehensible mutter, and goes off to wait on somebody else. We realize, to our chagrin, that he doesn't speak English. So we simplify. Wagging a finger in the air, we simply say "Beer!" The bartender brightens, goes to the bar, and returns with a glass of Byrrh. Not the same thing, is it? So we get a French phrase book and read the words from the pronunciation key: "oon bee-ayr, see voo play." Now, finally, we get our "bière." We have not changed our identity, however. We are still Americans. But we have changed our manner of *speaking*. We have therefore changed our style – for the spoken language in a culture is a part of its style; part of the *shared behavioral characteristics* of its people. And we have changed our style to get a very real reward. Employing style is *useful* to us; it is practical. Whether or not it is elegant is not of any concern. At the moment we use it, it is simply necessary if we want to order – and receive – a bottle of beer. Or to talk our way out of getting a French traffic ticket.

Now imagine that we cross the Channel to London. Here we are less concerned – after all, they speak English in England, don't they? We wander into a dockside pub, and again say, "Gimme a Bud." Much to our shock, we get the same stare, the same shrug, the same mutter! "Draw one," we say hopefully, "Got a beer?" Still no response. So we dig into a British phrase book and find the correct expression. Quoting it, we say, "I'd like a half and half, please." But no, still a quizzical expression and silence as the publican turns to someone else. Finally the Brit at our elbow looks up to the barman and says, pointing at you, "Geh' me mite an awf 'n' awf, guv'nuh!" And you get your beer. "Awf 'n' awf," you nervously say when later on you want a refill. Again you have changed your style; again you have used style to get something you wanted.*

But the London example makes us feel even stranger than the French one did. In France, they speak a foreign language, and pronounce their words differently, but in London they speak our language, don't they? So on this occasion we feel foolish, perhaps even affected, asking the bartender for an "awf 'n' awf" when we know damn well the phrase is "half and half." We feel like we're putting on an accent, "putting on airs" in a reverse sort of way. And that's how most actors feel the first time they tackle a part in blank verse or rhyming couplets. "This isn't me speaking!" "How can I be me and talk like this?"

You don't have to go to foreign countries to experience this feeling. When you go from grammar school to junior high, or junior high to high school, or when you first go to college, or to a school in a different state than the one you grew up in, or a frat house or sorority, you find you must quickly adjust to the prevailing

---

* OK, this would never really happen. Bartenders in England now know what "a beer" means. In fact, almost all of them in France do too. But let's assume it could happen and move on.

style of your new environment. People dress differently, talk differently and act differently, and while there may be "rule books" that specify the do's and don'ts of your new locale, there are no "style books" that tell you how to make the subtle adjustments of how you dress and how you speak in order to be fully accepted into your new culture. So you have to learn by observation and imitation. And that's how we have done it – from early childhood to maturity, and, in some ways, throughout our entire lives – even senior citizens face a behavioral crisis when adjusting to the collective behavior of their fellow residents in a new rest home.

Still, while it is totally irrational, we maintain – probably forever – the unconscious feeling that our own pronunciations are the "correct" ones and that only other people have "accents." Most Americans can remember the shock they felt when somebody abroad – particularly a Brit – mentioned their "American accent." All that time we had believed it was the Brits who had the accents! We also assumed that they would have had the intelligence to understand that!

What I'm talking about, of course, is the ethnocentrism that is shared by all cultures. Ethnocentrism is simply the plural of egocentrism. Americans, Brits, Turks, Japanese, and Peruvians all grow up thinking themselves the standard-bearers, and that all other cultures have somehow deviated from their "standard" way of speaking, dressing and behaving. Other cultures, most pre-adolescents throughout the world believe, are "weird." Long after we rationally realize this is not the case, we still carry these notions somewhere in our unconscious. Indeed, this is one of the causes of bullying, prejudice, and even wars. But it is also one of the reasons why theatre – and indeed acting – is an essential social activity. Plays, films and television – and performing in plays, films and television – have played a major role in improving human understanding among disparate cultures since the time of the ancient Greeks. Seeing how "other" people live, and that the most important aspects of their lives are not as different from our own than we once thought, can change social divisions into bonds. Learning to "play a style," and perform as though you had grown up in a different culture than you did, is more than a lesson in acting. It is a lesson in life.

The fact is, of course, that what we call "beer" is a physical thing, a liquid property, and it is no more "beer" than it is "awf 'n' awf" or "half and half," or for that matter "sigaloops" or "chowchowder." As long as it slakes thirst and provides nourishment, people will call for it by whatever name "works." That is the first lesson of style. We use whatever language, inflection, dialect, mode, manner, and format of behavior that helps us win our goals. Style, at bottom, is *what works*, or what we hope will work, when we address any society or culture or group. To get a glass of beer from a bartender we must enter his world; to get a kiss from a loved one, we must approach it from hers. And that a multilinguist can confidently order a beer in more countries than can a monolinguist only indicates that people who travel should learn more languages. When an actor can confidently speak in the languages of Shakespeare, Shaw, and David Mamet, it makes those actors who can't do it – but still would like to play a wide repertoire of roles – realize that they had better learn how.

149

Style, finally, is an action. It is neither a definition of self, nor a limitation of the self, but a resource for effective action within a group, class, or culture. It is a tool toward situational victory in the theatre and survival in life.

Style is not merely about geography, of course. Let us do a little time travel: Imagine yourself, like the Connecticut Yankee in Mark Twain's classic novel, transported to King Arthur's court in the sixth century. You would arrive with your present-day clothing and wallets stuffed with present-day currency, a smartphone, and credit cards. You would be friendless, though, and without usable financial resources. Your phone, currency, and credit cards would be useless. Your clothing and your behavior, should they be noticed by authorities, would probably mark you as a fiend from hell. There could be no thought of trying to explain that you were a time-traveler from another century; it would only be proof you were a demon, or perhaps a lunatic. Those who would survive such a transplant would undoubtedly be the ones who most quickly and effectively adopted the manifestations of the place in time. Shedding their polyester clothing and cellphones, abandoning their modern dialects and vocabularies, they would quickly seek to imitate the clothing, language, usage, employments, and even attitudes of those around them. They would not worry about appearing "affected" or "phony" when adopting these sixth-century behaviors; they would simply be fighting to survive, and they would only survive if they could make those around them accept them as fellow beings and not foreign or alien monsters.

They would not, however, stop being themselves. They would know that were they later to return to the twenty-first century, they would be able to return to a twenty-first century lifestyle. They would simply have picked up another language, like a multi-lingual tourist. The assumption of sixth-century social behaviors would not be a permanent personality change, only a way of getting food in their mouths and a roof over their heads.

There are many different styles – some quite formal – within different cultures, even in our twenty-first century world. The judicial courtroom is a good example. In an American courtroom, for instance, lawyers are constrained to rise on the bailiff's cue, to address the judge as "your honor," and to speak to the assemblage with prefaces like "May it please the court." Attorneys do not speak that way because they are "courtly" people but because they want to win their cases, since that is the language style which will most favorably impress the judge. In addition to its specialized language, courtrooms everywhere have specialized settings, costuming, and decorum. In America, the judges sit on elevated platforms and wear long black robes. In the United Kingdom, they add patently artificial white wigs. These formalities combine to form a consistent and identifiable style, and those who violate that style may find themselves forcibly removed.

But the courtroom is only one example of this stylization in everyday reality. Political clubs, religions, dormitory groups, coffee klatches, baseball teams, and the informal "worlds" of Wall Street, Hollywood, and theatre companies all have their styles, their "uniforms," and their collective characterizations, which their members must adopt to a greater or lesser extent in order to gain acceptance and eventually power within the group – and to avoid its potential punishments and ostracism.

Style, therefore, is not something that has been invented by the theatre or by the demands of art. While it is part of the dramatizing of the play, and of the playwright and director, it is also an aspect of human interaction. It is a special arena in which characters interact. It provides firm preconditions through which they must seek victories and struggle for survival. While the audience may see, or wish to see, certain styles as "affectations," the characters in the play do not. To them, their style is essential; it is fundamental.

Playing theatrical styles

The theatre contains a vast assemblage of styles. History, geography, culture, and the grand imagination of our dramatic authors have created a myriad of styles – some named, some unnamed, and some misnamed – which are the "special arenas" in which the interactions of most plays take place. How does the actor enter such a special arena, and how does she play style without sacrificing her own, out-of-herself credibility?

Playing theatrical styles is essentially a matter of the actor's understanding style in terms of the preconditions it places on behavior, then planting those preconditions between herself and her situational goal. The preconditions will then draw the appropriate style out of her. Like characterization, *style is performed reciprocally* rather than directly.

As in the life-examples above, the American tourist speaks Cockney not because she "feels" Cockney-ish, but because the pubican responds only to Cockney. The Connecticut Yankee wears woolen leggings not because he is intrinsically a leggings-wearer, but because Arthurian courtiers would accept them and would think that denim jeans were a sign of the devil. The attorney speaks deferentially to the judge not because he feels inferior, or because he is a timid person, but because the judge rewards deferential language. In every case, style is primarily adopted to please, prod, persuade, or terrify the *other person* in the interaction, not the person adopting it. Adopting a style, in a word, is tactical.

Naturally, this tactical stylistic adoption is not wholly conscious. Most of it, in fact, has developed over the character's lifetime and is habitual – even in many cases beyond the point of its effectiveness. Yet it remains intentional at the unconscious, if not the conscious level; style is intended by the character, and comes out of the same concentration on winning, intentions, and tactics that derive from the actor-character's situational pursuits. This, ultimately, is the key to how John-Hamlet will play "out of himself," and at the same time speak "in blank verse."

Because a character's style has developed in ways suitable to win the character's victories, it is also necessary to realize that style, when mastered by the character, is *enjoyable*; most characters can (and should) be seen to relish their own style. If we feel awkward at first ordering a glass of beer in a foreign language, we ultimately rejoice in ourselves when we have finally mastered that language. The deferential attorney will grumble for years at the "artificial" jargon he must speak, but as his experience teaches him the cybernetic tricks of his trade, he will ultimately revel in his withering "May it please the court" lead-ins. As a master craftsman will grow to love his tools as an extension of himself, and since style is the "tool" by which a character seeks her situational victories, so characters must grow to love their styles as they love themselves. Hamlet not only uses blank verse, he *loves* blank verse, and he loves using it and using it well.

In sum, the actor's essential mechanism for playing a theatrical style can be mastered in these four steps:

- She first analyzes the style in terms of its purposes and preconditions; what kinds of behavior are rewarded, and what kinds of behavior are punished; in short, she uncovers and creates the "world of the play" that is the particular framework (the special arena) in which the play's interactions take place, and by which they are regulated.
- She "plants" that world, with its special rules and mores, as a precondition for all her actions.
- She "enters" that world, as the Connecticut Yankee would have entered King Arthur's court, and tries to interact successfully within it, according to her intentions, goals, and situations from the play.
- She grows to relish that world, and her ability to interact within it, insofar as she can.

By this four-stage process, the actor is seen to be transformed – she no longer acts onstage as she does off, but her pursuit of real goals, genuinely and intently pursued, remains intact. As we see it, her identity seems to have altered; to herself, however, she is fundamentally unchanged as a person, just *behaving* differently. Her vitality is not only intact; it is enhanced.

That indeed may be the hardest problem for a young actor: *exploiting* her vitality, its essence, its exuberance, its power. Just as the American tourist may be timid when first ordering from a French bartender, so the beginning actor may be nervous in approaching a play by Molière. Like the foreign tourist, she is afraid of looking foolish; like the tourist she holds back, rigidifies, shrinks from her task. Trying to look inconspicuous, she only succeeds in what she fears the most: looking foolish. Only by understanding the situational *necessity* of style can the actor liberate herself into its most powerful expression.

Let us look at an example. James, playing Millimant in Congreve's *The Way of the World*, is instructed by the director to raise his leg, turn his calf inward, and place it on a bench. Granted, there are many pictures of Restoration gallants showing this posture, but it still seems a rather bizarre thing to James, a twenty-first century Iowan, to do – much less to delight in. Therefore James finds himself self-conscious and awkward. This, of course, is the hurdle of approaching an unfamiliar style.

But let's analyze it. In the Restoration, we find, the calf was considered by young women to be the sexiest part of a man's anatomy. This is the "precondition." Now all James has to do is woo Jane-Mirabelle *in an arena governed by such preconditions.* He raises his leg in the appropriate fashion, not because he is intrinsically a leg-raising person, or because "that's what they did then," but because, in his own mind, Jane-Mirabelle is going to be sexually excited by the sight of his proffered calf. So James not only does the gesture, he *enjoys* doing it; he relishes it. And that relish will almost certainly transmit to Jane-Mirabelle as well; if it does, the Restoration has come back to life, and the calf is sexy once again – it might even work in Iowa!

"In essence, there is no difference between classical and realistic acting. It's only that they do not take place on the same level."

French director Michel St. Denis[2]

Reciprocal stylization

In general, therefore, style is not something the actor plays because of her own predilections. She plays it because of the predilections of other people. Style, to the actor, is not in herself but in the other characters with whom she interacts. *They* are the ones who are stylized; she is simply reciprocating their behavior.

Thus, Juliet speaks love poetry to Romeo not because she loves poetry but because *he* does; this is the precondition that the actor paying Juliet plants in her consciousness. Like character, style is played *reciprocally* to planted assumptions. As the actor-character sees other people as characters (but not herself as one), so she sees other people as stylized (but not herself as such). She therefore does not stylize herself; she responds to the styles of others. She speaks the way she thinks they want her to, the way she thinks will gain her the most rewards. At the level of content, of course, she can disagree with other characters in the play, as can an attorney in the courtroom, but insofar as she stays in the play, she must stay in the special arena of the play's style. She must win her victories within the framework of the play's "world," and of the preconditions imposed on it, quite unconsciously by the society, and quite consciously (in most cases) by the playwright and director. She must win on *their* terms, not on her own, for without their acceptance there can be no victory. Pursuing your goals within a new social group, then, will create your new style without your even knowing it.

The world of the play

The world of the play is not a simple matter, and rarely can it (or should it) be reduced to a single word.

Several factors combine in a play's world and its style. These include the historical period or periods in which the play is set, the play's literary format (e.g., blank verse, Alexandrine couplets, prose), its presentational form (e.g., realistic, surrealistic, farcical, agitprop, postmodern), the author's primary goals (aesthetic, poetic, political, commercial), and the particular cultures or classes to which the play's characters belong, or to which they aspire. Sometimes these worlds are multiple. Jean Paul Sartre's *The Flies*, for example, portrays a historical world of archaic Greece through the language of 1940s existentialist dialecticalism. T. S. Eliot's *Murder in the Cathedral* portrays the historical world of medieval England in the spirit of contemporary Christian theology and the language of modern verse. Shakespeare's *Titus Andronicus* portrays Imperial Rome in tones of Elizabethan melodrama. Tony Kushner's *Angels in America* is, as its subtitle indicates, a "gay fantasia on national themes." The combinations of these stylistic components are perhaps infinite; what draws them together in the actor's mind is that they are all determinants of her character's tactics for achieving situational victory. They are defined operationally, and not necessarily verbally or intellectually.

Example: Man and Superman

Let us examine, by way of illustration, the world of George Bernard Shaw's *Man and Superman*. Written in 1903 and set in England in that era, its characters necessarily differ from most of us by nation, dialect, historical period, and/or social class. It is also a play whose world is somewhat imaginary, and not quite like any world that has ever existed outside of Mr. Shaw's own fertile brain. Here is a sample passage from that play in which the young Jack Tanner faces Roebuck Ramsden, the elder guardian of a young lady Tanner has interests in.

RAMSDEN (very deliberately): Mr. Tanner: you are the most impudent person I have ever met.

TANNER (seriously): I know it, Ramsden. Yet even I cannot wholly conquer shame. We live in an atmosphere of shame. We are ashamed of everything that is real about us; ashamed of ourselves, of our relatives, of our incomes, of our accents, of our opinions, of our experience, just as we are ashamed of our naked skins. Good Lord, my dear Ramsden, we are ashamed to walk, ashamed to ride in an omnibus, ashamed to hire a hansom instead of a coachman and footman. The more things a man is ashamed of, the more respectable he is. Why you're ashamed to buy my book, ashamed to read it: the only thing you're not ashamed of is to judge me for it without having read it; and even that only means that you're ashamed to have heterodox opinions. Look at the effect I produce because my fairy godmother withheld from me this gift of shame. I have every possible virtue that a man can have except—

RAMSDEN: I am glad you think so well of yourself.

TANNER: All you mean by that is that you think I ought to be ashamed of talking about my virtues. You don't mean that I haven't got them: you know perfectly well that I am as sober and honest a citizen as yourself, as truthful personally, and much more truthful politically and morally.

RAMSDEN (touched on his most sensitive point): I deny that. I will not allow you or any man to treat me as if I were a mere member of the British public. I detest its prejudices! I scorn its narrowness! I demand the right to think for myself. You pose as an advanced man. Let me tell you that I was an advanced man before you were born.

TANNER: I knew it was a long time ago.

RAMSDEN: I am as advanced as ever I was. I defy you to prove that I have ever hauled down the flag. I am more advanced than ever I was. I grow more advanced every day.

TANNER: More advanced in years, Polonius.

RAMSDEN: Polonius! So you are Hamlet, I suppose.

TANNER: No: I am only the most impudent person you've ever met. That's your notion of a thoroughly bad character. When you want to give me a piece of your mind, you ask yourself, as a just and upright man, what is the worst you can fairly say of me. Thief, liar, forger, adulterer, perjurer, glutton, drunkard? Not one of these names fits me. You have to fall back on my deficiency in shame. Well, I admit it. I even congratulate myself; for if I were ashamed of my real self, I should cut as stupid a figure as any of the rest of you. Cultivate a little impudence, Ramsden, and you will become quite a remarkable man.

RAMSDEN: I have no—

TANNER: You have no desire for that sort of notoriety. Bless you, I knew that answer would come as well as I know that a box of matches will come out of an automatic machine when I put a penny in the slot: you would be ashamed to say anything else.

(The crushing retort for which Ramsden has been visibly collecting his forces is lost forever...)

We can certainly see, in this passage, all the earmarks of what can be called "Shavian style." There is the very deliberate phrasing: no stammers, no sloppy reasoning, no grammatical sins. No one could mistake this for everyday speech, even everyday Edwardian speech; speech is rarely if ever transcribed with semicolons. Rather, this is Shavian-styled debate rhetoric. There is the building of assertion upon assertion, the use of rhetorical climaxes and extended outpourings of crescendoing epithets: "Thief, liar, forger, adulterer, perjurer, glutton, drunkard." There are multiple listings, such as Tanner's "ashamed's," and parallel phrasings, such as Ramsden's "I detest its prejudices, I scorn its narrowness, I demand the right to think for myself." There is literary allusion (to *Hamlet*), wit ("I knew it was a long time ago"), sophisticated irony ("Cultivate a little impudence"), simile ("as a box of matches will come out of an automatic machine when I put a penny in the slot"), and the "crushing retort" which is prepared but never delivered. The "Shavian style," however, does not apply to any one character as much as to *both* of them, even though they are individually quite different men. It is respected by both of them; it *works* on both of them – and that is why they use it. The world of *Man and Superman*, we see right away, is one where brilliant verbal rhetoric is going to be rewarded, and inarticulate bullying will prove hopeless. If Stanley Kowalski could walk out of *A Streetcar Named Desire* and into *Man and Superman*, he would be utterly ineffective in any pursuit.* The process of evolution and natural selection has gathered onto Shaw's setting only those characters who can survive in the glittering intellectual climate of Shavian discourse.

So the actor assuming the role of Tanner must play toward dual goals. At the content level, he must win his control of Ann's guardianship. At the relationship level, he must make clear to all concerned (and particularly to Ramsden) that he is cleverer, smarter, better read, more quick-witted, more pursuasive in debate, and in short, more "Shavian" (Shaw-like) than Ramsden. Ramsden, however, pursues the identical goals. So the battle between them goes on at both content and relationship levels, for as they argue over who shall control Ann's future (the content debate) they are simultaneously trying to achieve the *superiority of style* which would entitle them to dominate the relationship, and therefore win a final victory at the content level. They are trying, in other words, to gain control of Ann (content) by "out-Shawing" each other (style): their situational victory, therefore, is entirely dependent on their stylistic excellence, and their levels of behavior are fully in alignment with each other's.

That alignment is what makes "stylized" acting possible without any sacrifice of power or credibility, but rather with their enhancement. Style is not "something added"; it is instrumental to the situation. Actors engaged in Shavian situations must learn Shavian debate tactics. They must master them, perform them, improvise them, and absolutely delight in them. Above all, they must make the Shavian tactics *situationally* useful; they should make them tools in their character's behalf. As Shaw says in the preface to this play, style is nothing but "effectiveness of assertion." It is that which has impact and focus, that which *works*.

---

* On the other hand, if Marlon Brando had walked out of *Streetcar* into *Superman* he would probably have been terrific. The famous male star of *Streetcar*'s 1947 premiere had been a sensation the previous year playing Marchbanks in Shaw's *Candida*.

"Effectiveness of assertion is the Alpha and Omega of style. He who has nothing to assert has no style and can have none: he who has something to assert will go so far in power of style as its momentousness and his conviction will carry him. Disprove his assertion after it is made, yet its style remains."

Irish/British playwright George Bernard Shaw

Style as a weapon

Style is a situational tool even in totally non-naturalistic styles. It is hard to imagine a less naturalistic style than opera singing, for example, but the great soprano Maria Callas explains that "the voice is a weapon, the voice should serve the person [character] you are on stage." What could be sillier, from a naturalistic point of view, than a Japanese lady named Butterfly singing a Puccini aria (in Italian, yet) as her American sailor-lover Pinkerton goes off to sea? Playwright David Henry Hwang ridicules this idea in his *M. Butterfly,* and yet Callas sang her way into our hearts because her Butterfly could sing her way into Pinkerton's.

Given Callas' rationale that "the voice is a weapon," we may presume her mechanism as a planted precondition: that Lieutenant Pinkerton is an opera fan – indeed, a Puccini fan! This plant lets her sing her heart out to him. It lets her try to be successful with her singing as well as with her song; with her form as well as with her content. Callas-Butterfly not only sings the aria, she sings singing; she is "saying" not merely the words of the song, but conveying the relacom message: "I am a great singer. If you leave me you will never hear an aria like this again!" So Callas' magnificent voice becomes Butterfly's weapon; we, the audience, are merely the observers and vicarious co-participants in this intense musical-dramatic experience.

"The performer is obliged to make the concern of the character he is portraying so unconditionally and consistently his own that to him and to the audience all basic musical functions – rhythm, meter, harmony, tempo, dynamics – do not appear to be prescribed by the score or the conductor but seem to be determined by his, the character's, intentions and sensations."

German opera director Walter Felsenstein[3]

Relishing the world of the play

Style is not only a weapon, of course, nor only a tactic. These are only the foundations of style, the reasons why styles develop. In the final analysis, the style of a play becomes a magnificent world to *experience*. And this leads the actor toward one of her deepest and most profound glories – the joy of inhabiting a new and magnificent world. Like the old cliché about travel, acting "in style" is broadening.

As our American tourist finally makes himself at home in the Cockney pub, he finds out not only that he can order himself a glass of beer with relative ease, but also that he can share in the values, language, humor, feelings, culture, and spirit of a world previously foreign and inaccessible to him. For most people – and all actors – this can be an exquisite experience. The style of a culture, whether the "real" culture of a local bar, or the imaginary cultures of Shaw's or Puccini's worlds, is a shared set of understandings among people and their societies – understandings that have profound, if unspoken, connections. Style, ultimately, is a fellowship, a union of cultures, a transcendental social relationship. It is a cultural and spiritual conflation of values, history, modes, and philosophy. It is an escape from the confines of our own environment, and from the narrowness of our own understandings. As Michel St. Denis, celebrated French director and institutor of New York's Julliard Drama School, suggests, "Style…is the expression of real understanding, of deep communication with the world and its secrets, of the constant effort of men to surpass themselves."[4]

Therefore it is the task of the actor to consider an assignment in style as a voyage into a strange, wonderful, and vast new world, one in which she can discover new things about her capabilities, and devise new tactics to work through new preconditions. She must meet with relish the challenge of dealing with new people, new ideas, new values, and new modes of expression. The worlds of *Man and Superman* or *Madame Butterfly* are not necessarily better ones than our own, but they are wildly different; they are whole in themselves, and to their inhabitants the life within those worlds is thrilling indeed. The joy of living in those worlds, the thrill and relish with which style is played and experienced, will radiate through any cast and any audience.

Shakespeare's speaking styles

So far we have been speaking of overall styles – Shavian and operatic, for example – which form the arena of manners for their particular plays and pieces. This is not to say that every play – or even any play – can be reduced to a single style. Shakespeare is a playwright who, perhaps more than any other, provided an extraordinarily broad palette of styles in every play, a variety of dramatic languages in which content and relationship, form and function, are inextricably entwined. The overall stylistic format of Shakespeare is a combination of earthy prose, blank verse, medieval doggerel, rhyming iambic dimiter, anapestic tetrameter, Elizabethan song, witty stichomythic repartee, Senecan melodrama, Marlovian bombast, and Lylyan balance. These are not "real world" linguistic formats in any way, but rather dramatic constructs created by an author of unprecedented linguistic skills. Shakespeare uses the speaking styles of his characters to enormous situational effect; his characters are defined as much by how they speak as by what they say.

Hamlet provides us a very good example of this, and shows us a great many speaking styles that relate directly to situation, or to plot points. In the world of *Hamlet*, which is a theatrical world, not a real-life one, blank verse is the accepted mode of speaking among educated and royally connected Danes. Prince Hamlet speaks blank verse because it has been spoken to him all his life; one gets the feeling he has been uttering iambic pentameters almost since he learned to speak. But blank verse is not the only way he speaks. When trying to persuade Polonius that he is insane Hamlet speaks prose; and corrupted prose at that ("For if the sun breed maggots in a dead dog, being a god kissing carrion, – Have you a daughter?"). Hamlet's stylistic change is far more shocking to Polonius than the content of his remarks: it makes Polonius think Hamlet has been afflicted with madness, "though there is method in't." Which there certainly is.

Hamlet's "mad" prose is, just like his blank verse, chosen from his "stylistic verbal repertoire" for pragmatic ends, not because they happen to be "Shakespearean." Hamlet switches from verse to prose throughout the play, and always as it suits his purpose: as he does when he welcomes those not directly connected to the royal court – the players, Horatio, and the two gravediggers – and at other times to confuse and taunt his quasi-royal and verse-speaking adversaries (Polonius, Osric, Rosencrantz, Guildenstern, and even Ophelia). In a remarkable scene (IV, ii) with Claudius, Hamlet speaks prose to the King while the King speaks verse to Hamlet – dispatching him to England for what he expects to be Hamlet's death. Not only are Hamlet's lines blithely insubordinate (calling

Claudius his "Mother" for example), so is his utter abandonment of the blank verse that is, by this time in the play, clearly established as the official court language: Claudius and Gertrude, as well as Laertes, Fortinbras, and the ghost of King Hamlet, for example, speak nothing else. Hamlet's use of prose here is more insulting to Claudius than what he actually has to say.

Hamlet's linguistic versatility – his ability to range between sparkling verse at court and inelegant (though brilliant) prose in the graveyard – testifies to his wondrous stylistic variety and his ability to don various masks as occasions require. While aware of all the "forms, moods, shapes" that are "actions that a man might play," Hamlet realizes that none of them can "denote" him, but rather that they can help him move toward his situational goals. And so he adopts whatever stylization of his speech will move him forward.

"Shakespearean style" is not, however, simply a matter of prose versus blank verse. We must speak, first, of Shakespearean styles in the plural, and identify the varieties of behavior that characterize a play's world. *Hamlet* demonstrates numerous speaking styles, for example, which are tactical in their very syntactical construction. For example:

> HORATIO: Stay illusion!
> If thou hast any sound, or use of voice,
> Speak to me.
> If there be any good thing to be done
> That may to thee do ease and grace to me,
> Speak to me.
> If thou art privy to thy country's fate,
> Which, happily, foreknowing may avoid,
> Oh, speak!
>
> (II.ii. 126–35.)

Comment: Rhetorical pleading. The ghost of a late King would hardly listen to adolescent whining or verbal threats. Horatio's repeated phrases form a singsong incantation, increasing in its insistence as it goes along, to pierce the silence of the apparition. When the plea fails, Horatio cries to Marcellus to stop it, and Marcellus strikes at it with his spear. Neither the rhetorical interrogation nor the show of violence works, but they are both used as attempts to win situational advantages.

> HORATIO: But look, the morn, in russet mantle clad,
> Walks o'er the dew of yon high eastward hill.
> Break we our watch up, and by my advice
> Let us impart what we have seen tonight
> Unto young Hamlet, for upon my life,
> This spirit, dumb to us, will speak to him.
> Do you consent we shall acquaint him with it,
> As needful in our loves, fitting our duty?

Comment: Poetic elaboration The first two lines, justly famous, have frequently been cited as examples of Shakespeare, in his outdoor theatre without realistic stage decor, "painting the scenery with words." But there is a situational point here, too. Horatio is asking Marcellus (and Bernardo) to break up their watch and to go with him to the palace and talk to Hamlet. His introductory phrase about the morn serves as a turn-taking device to focus attention on himself, on the new business at hand, and on his own eloquence which will be needed to carry this matter to the prince. Horatio does not "throw off" this line as though it were not eloquent; rather he uses it to enhance his own position with his cohorts, and to establish his right to a position of authority. Apparently, Marcellus and Bernardo respect poetic eloquence, and that is why Horatio uses it.

> CLAUDIUS: Though yet of Hamlet our dear brother's death
> The memory be green, and that it us befitted
> To bear our hearts in grief and our whole kingdom
> To be contracted in one brow of woe,
> Yet so far hath discretion fought with nature
> That we with wisest sorrow think on him,
> Together with remembrance of ourselves.
> Therefore our sometime sister, now our Queen
> The imperial jointress to this warlike state,
> Have we, as 'twere with a defeated joy—
> With an auspicious and a dropping eye,
> With mirth in funeral and with dirge in marriage,
> In equal scale weighing delight and dole
> Taken to wife.

Comment: Regal address The tortuous syntax of this opening of Claudius' first speech – two sentences with multiple dependent and independent clauses spread over fourteen lines – indicates a man who can say what he wishes without fear of being interrupted, and who is assured that his listeners will take it upon themselves to unravel his meaning. If "the time is out of joint," as Hamlet believes, here we have Claudius explaining how, with his new "jointress," he is reuniting the kingdom; and he is saying this in a complex linguistic construction as well as a literal message. His blanched phrases, his alliterations ("sometime sister," "delight and dole"), his oxymorons and antinomies, all seek to create the appearance of a completed syntactical and genealogical complex which proves to the hearers that the throne of Denmark is rock solid. The tactic apparently works – on everybody but Hamlet.

> OPHELIA: He took me by the wrist and held me hard;
> Then goes he to the length of all his arm,
> And, with his other hand thus o'er his brow,
> He falls to such perusal of my face

As he would draw it. Long stay'd he so.
At last, a little shaking of mine arm,
And thrice his head thus waving up and down,
He rais'd a sigh so piteous and profound
As it did seem to shatter all his bulk
And end his being. That done, he lets me go,
And with his head over his shoulder turn'd
He seem'd to find his way without his eyes,
For out o' doors he went without their help
And to the last bended their light on me.

Comment: Broken heart Ophelia has just come into a palace room where she finds her father, Polonius. This is immediately after she has experienced an unexpectedly horrific encounter with Hamlet, whom she had hoped to marry but now says looked "as if he had been loosed out of hell." Her speech, however, utterly breaks down as she delivers it. Its first four lines are written in perfect, ten-syllable, iambic pentameters, but the fifth line comes to a dead halt right in the middle ("As he would draw it.") After taking a breath, Ophelia manages to finish the fifth line, and then delivers another four lines of perfect pentameters – but again comes to a complete halt halfway through the tenth one ("And end his being.") After taking another mid-line pause she finishes the line, and then concludes the speech with four more pentameters, but the last line ends in what we can only call six syllables of pure prose ("…bended their light on me.") The brutally broken verse pattern clearly echoes Ophelia's broken heart, and her inability to maintain the regular blank verse structure that she, as the Lord Chamberlain's daughter, had been speaking for most of her life – and in all her earlier scenes.

CLAUDIUS: Give me the cups,
And let the kettle to the trumpet speak,
The trumpet to the cannoneer without
The cannons to the Heavens, the Heaven to earth,
Now the King drinks to Hamlet.
Come, begin.

(V, ii, 285–90.)

Comment: Incendiary oratory The King, having poisoned the drinks as well as Laertes' sword, now tries to intoxicate the duelists (as well as the spectators) so that his murder of Hamlet will happen in a welter of drunken confusion. Claudius' crescendoing phrases (trumpets are louder than kettledrums, cannons are louder than trumpets, and the great sound of heaven – a thunderclap – is louder than cannons) are incitements – not only for the duel to begin, but for everyone who sees the duel to get so excited that they will not notice, after Hamlet is killed, what had actually happened. Of course, Claudius' tactic does not succeed, but it is clear what his goal is.

FORTINBRAS: Let four captains
Bear Hamlet, like a soldier, to the stage.
For he was likely, had he been put on,
To have proved most royally. And for his passage
The soldier's music and the rights of war
Speak loudly for him.
Take up the bodies. Such a sight as this
Becomes the field, but here shows much amiss.
Go, bid the soldiers shoot.

Comment: A show of grief Regardless of whether or not Fortinbras feels true grief at Hamlet's death (it would be surprising if he did: he never knew Hamlet, and Hamlet's father had killed Fortinbras' father), he recognizes that it is politic to show some. Fortinbras, a Norwegian, is about to take over the Danish crown, and he could lose any advantage he might have if, at this moment, he seemed overly gleeful or overly "rehearsed" for what he is about to do. Thus his verse, in this speech which ends the play, is strikingly broken in its prosaic and overlong (twelve-syllable) fourth line and its abruptly curtailed sixth and ninth lines. The rhyming couplet ("this" and "miss") is Fortinbras' manner of concluding the event, assuring himself of having the final word about it. Rhyming couplets are common in Shakespeare at the end of scenes. They should be played as such – as attempts to conclude conversations in one's own favor – of having the last word and shutting out the other characters.

There are many more possibilities of relating the syntax of speeches in *Hamlet*, or in any play, to the situational involvements of the characters who speak them, and to demonstrate the tactical use of these syntaxes, which form the basis for the verbal style of each characterization, and in sum, of each play. This discussion only creates the beginning of an analysis of Hamlet's stylization, and does not even touch upon the visual stylizations of dress, manners, postures, and expressions which might find their way into the stylization of a production. But the analysis of these six speeches should suggest the deep integration of speaking styles with plot situations – particularly in the work of a master playwright.

"[The English language is] so rich and cruel and beautiful, like a fireworks display, and yet it can be so subtle and so crude. Marry that to the stage and something mysterious happens. Don't ask me what. It's magical."

British actor Alan Rickman[5]

Physical styles

To this point, we have concentrated on speaking styles, specifically in Shaw and Shakespeare. There are, of course, physical styles as well, having to do with costume, carriage, movement, bearing, posturing, gesture, and comportment. In fact, these are the stylistic attributes we learn in infancy, before speaking; it is to physical stylization that mothers refer when they instruct their children to "mind their manners."

Physical styles, like speaking styles, are behaviors that are directed toward situational victories. We have already seen that the Restoration rake's elevation and turning in of his calf was an attempt, on his part, to display what his lady would consider the most suggestively erotic portion of his anatomy; it is a gesture identical in function to Stanley Kowalski's stripping off his shirt in A *Streetcar Named Desire*, an act differing in outward form but not in purpose or intent. The actor playing the rake "plants" in his mind the precondition of late seventeenth-century desmoiselles being excited by the calf, instead of the chest, and plays his situation accordingly.

Gesture, in most cultures, is frequently as specifically communicative as spoken language. It is therefore intentional rather than simply expressive. The Italian who purses his fingers and shakes them is not merely releasing his feelings, nor is he trying to "look Italian"; he is, instead, communicating a very specific message in the physical language he has been brought up with. Even non-specific gestures – shrugs, grunts, waves of the hand – are usually socially derived and represent attempts, if unconscious ones, to *do* something rather than to *be* something. In studying and adopting the gestures of a culture (historical stylizing) or of an imaginary theatrical format (theatrical stylizing), the actor must search for the intention and purpose of the style; whom it is directed to, and what it is intended for. Only then can she transform her gestures into the stylized ones with the requisite authority and power.

Costume is, of course, one of the great hurdles for many inexperienced actors; and this is easy to understand. Most of us initially feel uncomfortable putting on rented tuxedos or formal gowns; it is only natural, then, that we will be even more uncomfortable wearing doublet and hose, or hoop skirts and petticoats for the first time. Almost nothing marks the amateur production of Shakespeare as much as young actors fiddling with their costumes, and obviously wishing they were able to wear their rehearsal jeans and T-shirts. It is the actor's old enemy, egocentrism, that creates this hurdle; the actor's innate belief that her everyday clothes are "real," and that ball gowns, tuxedos, doublets, periwigs, togas, and zebra skins are "stylized" – unreal, affected, and peculiar. Jeans and T-shirts, however, would be just as stylized and unreal to an Elizabethan or an ancient Greek. Costumes must be worn as *clothes*, and enjoyed as such. That does not mean they should be worn as we wear our own clothes, but rather that they should be worn for the purposes for which they were built, either in past historical eras or future imagined ones.

For the style of dress we adopt, like everything else in style, is intended and intentional. Characters who can be presumed to have chosen their own clothes – which includes almost all dramatic characters other than paupers or prisoners – *like* what they wear. They have ordinarily *chosen* what they wear. Some dress for specific effect, some for comfort, some for fashion, some to fit in, others to stand out: but the fact is that no dress is wholly purposeless and no costume is wholly without a tactical consideration.

To wear a costume of a style different from our own, however, requires that we understand the reason why the character would wear it. The actor, instead of seeing her costume as an awkward embarrassment, must see how it gives her a source of strength, how it can be an emblem of her power. She must *love* her costume – unless the play specifically indicates that she has been forced to wear it. Indeed, costumes can become the character's weapons. Tennessee Williams gives Stanley Kowalski a pair of bright red silk pajamas so he can dazzle Blanche; Shakespeare gives Hamlet a "suit of inky black" so he can shame the court; Molière gives Monsieur Jourdain a grotesque turban so he can awe and impress his family. Actors should therefore learn the potential uses of their character's costumes and seek to win their goals by wearing and using them.

Carriage, movement, and deportment are similarly physical styles that present problems when the actor is required to move out of her own time and place, or her own (usually limited) vision of the world of the play. One of the great curiosities of the modern theatre was the insistence of certain mid-twentieth century American "method" actors on performing a Shakespearean script with the shrugs, grimaces, stammers, and halting, sluggish movements common to their own time. This could perhaps have succeeded if the plays involved had been reset into a more contemporary period, but they were not; the actors had simply been instructed – or had decided themselves – to use "real" movements instead of "stylized" ones. But of course this is ridiculous – egocentricity again – for no style of movement is intrinsically more "real" than any other, except as viewed from the relative and narrow perspective of one's own habits and the habits of one's surrounding society. A shuffling, muttering, foot-dragging Henry V could hardly inspire the English army through the gates of Harfleur; and a sloppy, mean-spirited Hamlet could hardly enlist Horatio's aid, Ophelia's love, or Laertes' eventual respect. Elegance, in King Henry and in Hamlet, is simply a prerequisite for effective action within a royal arena – if that is where the play is set (as it was in Shakespeare's time). Conversely, regal-like elegance would be ineffective around Stanley Kowalski's poker table, where another style of movement and bearing is required, and where even Mitch's clumsy efforts at eloquence are futile.

Learning to play styles

Learning to play a particular style demands, at the outset, a thorough understanding of the world of the play, including its period and locale; the political and social environment portrayed; the special preconditions which the author has imposed upon his characters; and the dramaturgical devices that affect the play's format and presentation. This ordinarily involves a good deal of research, some of which might be suggested by a director or dramaturg – research that may involve the study of pertinent and related works of art, music, philosophy, science, religion, and literature that help reveal the texture of life in the author's world. And, of course, the actor must understand the mental mechanisms for translating her knowledge of a play's – and the production's – style into the "plants" that will make it play.

But to understand all this, unfortunately, is only a first step in playing style. Even if we fully "understand" from Mme. Callas that the voice is a weapon in behalf of the character, we cannot simply go from there to be able to sing like Maria Callas. Nor does our understanding of Jack Tanner's rhetoric, Hamlet's versifying, or King Henry's regal bearing lead us directly to the capacity to perform in these styles. Understanding provides us with the base, the mental alignment, and the liberation from egocentrism which makes learning possible; but of course, these are only foundations.

Essentially, the actor learns style in a way similar to the process by which the character would have learned it. Style, after all, is *acquired* behavior; it is not innate or genetic. Environment, not genes, determines whether a child will speak French or Cockney or Brooklynese. Tanner, insofar as we consider him a real person (or even as an author's idea of a real person), was not born rhetorical, he learned to be rhetorical, just as King Henry learned to be regal and the Restoration rake studied how to be rakish. The learning processes for all of them involved at least three things: instruction, imitation, and real-life trial and error. And while these processes must be telescoped down in time for the actor, all three will still apply.

Learning of style by *instruction* is, of course, the most obvious way, if also the hardest to find. Jack Tanner went to school; the actor playing Tanner, most desirably, would simply go to an accelerated program in the same school. Unfortunately, however, schools like Tanner's don't exist any more, so the actor is forced to find what kind of comparable instruction she can. Classical acting styles, along with dialects, verse speaking and scansion, period dance, and like skills, are taught in major acting conservatories, where student actors work under the tutelage of professional classical actors. There is certainly no effective substitute, in the development of a classical actor, for personal instruction by an experienced master. Written analyses of particular styles, such as those above with regard to *Man and Superman* and *Hamlet*, are also instructive in isolating the purposes and uses of a certain style, which when coupled with the actor's imagination and self-application, can produce marvelous results. A combination of academic study and conservatory training is a proven producer of fine performers who can be flexible and capable in a variety of physical and vocal styles.

Imitation cannot be ignored in the development of style either, however, because imitation is the process by which we learn most of our day-to-day behavior. Therefore, it is also how characters in plays may be assumed to have learned their behaviors. Tanner not only went to school, he spent a great deal of his childhood observing people like Ramsden, and fashioning his behavior after them. We all, in life, find and imitate role models. The child, after all, learns to speak by imitating others. She also learns and retains her dialect by imitating others, and the actor who wants to play that dialect will invariably learn it, at least in part, by the same process. Likewise, the young debutante learns deportment from fashion models, the Prince learns regality from the King, and the young athlete mimics the moves of his childhood hero. Imitation is the means by which we pick up countless attitudes and behaviors that are not important enough to talk about formally, but which comprise the bulk of our daily actions. Imitation, therefore, is indispensible in learning styles..

Imitation, though, of what? Obviously the actor cannot directly imitate another actor's performance without a mammoth sacrifice of her own creativity, spontaneity, and even credibility. The actor who tries to play Hamlet by simply copying Kenneth Branagh's movements and inflections as seen on YouTube will almost certainly fail, because he would simply be imitating a performance of life rather than life itself, and would so sacrifice his own personality – his individual contribution to the role – that the result would be a caricature, not a character. Where possible, the actor learns style from living exemplars. Stanislavsky, when he directed a play set in a brothel, took his cast to live in one for a couple of weeks.

"I sometimes think that if professional actors reflected a little more on how we all learn acceptable social manners, it would be a valuable guide to many of the techniques of their craft."

British director Tyrone Guthrie[6]

Imitating recordings of native speakers is a once-removed technique for learning a dialect – although, if listening to recordings of stage productions, they should be of plays other than the ones you plan to be performing in! You can learn bearing, deportment, and other physical styles by studying paintings and photographs. These can include both candid photos, which show their subjects when not posing, and portraits, which show them as they are hoping to be seen – and trying to be seen. The latter are helpful because this might be exactly as *your* character, were she a real person (which is how you will play her) might "want to be seen." But there are better ways.

Exercise: *Play opposite Olivier*

The problem with imitating other actors through recordings, pictures, film, or even live contact is that it is a second-removed technique, and, if this is all you have, will probably stultify, not enhance, your performance. You simply cannot watch a filmed Olivier performance and then "play Olivier." But there is a terrific alternative: Watch a filmed Olivier performance and play *opposite* Olivier! Find a recording of a two-person scene with Olivier (or any other actor working in the style in which you are planning to perform) as one of the two characters. Re-record it, taking out the lines of the other character. Then, after learning those deleted lines yourself, "play" the scene with Olivier (or any other actor you have recorded). Try to impress him! Appeal to him; debate with him; dominate him! You will not be trying to imitate Olivier's individual voice, you will be trying to compete with it. You will still be you, but you will be entering his world – the world that the Oliviers (or the Brandos, or the Streeps) inhabit. You will become a member of this world just as Jack Tanner became a member of Ramsden's world.

The imitation in this exercise is indirect and reciprocal. It is the same imitation we do in ordinary life, both in growing up and in adapting to new situations and new people. The actor must grow into her character, of course, in a much shorter time. Her task must be to synchronize herself with the Olivier style (or whatever style is attempted) – to master it for her tactical approaches, to relish it, and finally to be able to break out of that synchronization when she is ready to grasp the particular victory that her own character needs and desires.

Trial-and-error, of course, is the cybernetics of behavioral development. It is how our behavior is shaped from birth – day by day until it becomes second nature. Trial-and-error informs and redirects both instruction and imitation. The actor uses trial-and-error as a technique for getting into a stylized world in concert with other actor-characters; she must, in addition to using her style as a weapon, continually evaluate and improve her weapon's effectiveness. Style is not rigid and not fixed; it is a fluid, ever-adjusting attempt to find the best vehicle, the best tactic, toward victory.

Note, however, that in the examples above, the characters' stylistic approaches are rarely successful. Tanner does not really close out Ramsden's arguments, Stanley Kowalski does not in fact dazzle Blanche. Hamlet's inky black suit does not really shame the Court. Monsieur Jourdain's turban does not really awe his family – indeed, it makes him look like an idiot. Nor does the Restoration rake always excite his damsel, and Maria Callas' Butterfly has never been able to keep her Pinkerton from leaving. Style is a weapon, but it is not all-powerful; it is attempted rather than simply displayed, and it can never be proffered glibly.

Trial-and-error, therefore, is important in the actor's development of style because it is important *to the character* as well. If actors find that performing in a style new to them is a struggle, and if their early efforts end in failure, they may be comforted to realize that their characters are struggling as well. Their characters are as afraid of failure as they are. The fear of failure underlies every effort for success. It is not that Claudius would rather be speaking prose in his opening speech to the Court. As a pretender to the throne, he would have been speaking blank verse for years. But Claudius is *struggling* for his regality. It does not come easily to him. That his political situation demands him to speak regally, and his dramaturgical situation demands him to speak in verse, does not mean that he is facile at these highly-styled presentations. He must concentrate and he must *work*, just as the actor playing him must work to create royal authority and superhuman confidence and to make his "effectiveness of assertion," in Shaw's phrase, seem to pour effortlessly out of his mouth. It is all too easy for us to ignore the struggle for expression experienced by characters who speak and act differently than we do; we usually assume, say, that they are "Shakespearean people," or "royal people," and that this sort of language simply rolls off their lips. Perhaps it comes more easily to them than it does to us, but it is still *work*. Characters as well as actors strain against the limitations of style. They struggle to perfect it and to make the best use of it. The actor's struggle toward victory, therefore, takes place not only at the plot and situation level, but also at the level of style. Style is a critical part of relacom, and the actor who struggles to achieve victory in his situation must also struggle to achieve victory in her style.

Exercises: *Playing style*

These exercises do not teach styles; as should be clear from the foregoing discussion, styles are acquired only by an effective combination of personal instruction, apprenticeship, imitation, and trial-and-error. The exercises will liberate stylizing mechanisms, however, and demand an understanding of the tactical use of style.

Group domination

In an improvisation, or in an imaginary self-exercise, try to dominate a group by being its very best member in the eyes of the group. Avoiding parody, try to become:

- The belle of the ball.
- The king of the mountain.
- The star of the show.
- The chief of the ratpack.
- The chairman of the investigation.
- The bishop of the archdiocese.
- The Speaker of the House.
- The sweetheart of Sigma Chi.
- The team spokeswoman.
- Miss America.
- Mr. America.

- Big Man On Campus, 1920s style.
- Ditto, 1960s style.
- Ditto, the style of ten years ago.
- The best poker player in Stanley Kowalski's (*Streetcar*) gang.
- Your father's best friend.
- Your mother's best friend.

Analyzing group styles

Take any of the groups mentioned above and analyze them by answering the following questions:

- What draws the attention of these people? What holds it? What makes them look up?
- What makes these people respect me?
- What kind of words do these people respond to? What is their slang? What is their span of verbal attention? Do they fear eloquence? Do they admire it? Do they respond to it? Does it annoy them?
- How do they respond to casualness? in dress? in speech?
- How do they respond to the expression of feelings? of passion?
- What puts these people down? How does it make them feel?
- What shuts these people up? What happens to them when they shut up?
- Who are their allies?
- How frightened are they of physical force?
- How repressed are they? How open to seduction? What are their professed morals? What are their real morals? What do they desire from me?
- What turns them on?
- What turns them off?
- What frightens them most? How do they react when frightened?
- Do they have a sense of humor?
- Do they like to have fun? To be seen having fun?
- What do they like in people?
- What makes them trust people?
- Do they treat their friends well?
- Who are these people?

Analyzing historical styles

Ask the same questions, above, about the following historical groups. Research the answers, and where research fails, speculate:

- Hamlet's Wittenburg schoolfellows.
- Courtiers to Charles II (English Restoration).
- Courtiers to James I (Jacobean England).

- Courtiers to Oedipus (archaic Greece).
- Courtiers to King Lear (archaic England).
- Judges of the Spanish Inquisition.
- Jews in the Ghetto of Renaissance Venice.
- Moscow aristocrats before the 1917 Revolution.
- Courtiers to Caligula (Imperial Rome, Decadent era).
- German weavers during the Industrial Revolution.
- French followers of Robespierre, during the Revolution.
- Puritans in Salem, Massachusetts, during the witch trials.
- Slaves in Alabama.

Creating imaginary styles

Ask the same questions about a wholly imaginary group, and by your imaginative answers, define a wholly imaginary style evolving from the group. For example:

- The fairies in A Midsummer Night's Dream.
- The ondines in Ondine.
- The trolls in Peer Gynt.
- The frogs in The Frogs.
- The Furies in The Eumenides.
- The gods of The Good Person of Sczechuan.
- The Seven Dwarfs in Snow White.
- The Characters in Six Characters in Search of an Author.
- The three madwomen in The Madwoman of Chaillot.
- Martians.
- Witches.
- Talking trees.

In an improvisation, **integrate with the group** as you have analyzed and defined it.

- Opera – Go back to the contentless scene or the Woyzeck scene from Chapter 2, or any simple two-person scene that you and a partner have memorized. Improvise, without parodying, an operatic version of the scene. Improvise it as a Mozartian, Puccinian, and Wagnerian opera by turns. Listen to recordings of various operas with your partner, and try to make your opera improvisation fit into the operatic structure that you hear. Do your opera improvisation with the recording playing in the back ground. Use your singing to win situational victories.
- Blank verse – Memorize any of the speeches in this chapter. Perform them according to the tactics described in the accompanying commentaries. Make the style of the speech useful to the character and the fulfillment of the character's intentions. Master the style, revel in it, take delight in its

171

usefulness. Concentrate not on yourself, but on the character or characters you are speaking to – and also to your private audience. Do not judge yourself, and do not judge whether you are doing the exercise well. Just do it.

- Play opposite a modern actor as you played opposite Olivier.
- Learn a dialect. Learning dialects is identical to learning styles: dialect is a style – indeed, it is the first style we spoke of in this chapter, and it is invariably part of every style. Not only is it a useful exercise in style, it is a practical tool for getting an acting job. And once you learn a dialect, you will have it for the rest of your career. You can learn by phonetic study and imitation of live or recorded examples, of course, and there are many dialect books and websites with vocal recordings. But you can also learn and use dialects by going into public areas frequented by appropriate linguistic groups. When you learn the dialect, try to "pass" with it.
- Face down a portrait – Get a book of the paintings of various periods, preferably with a large number of portraits. Find a full-page portrait with the eyes looking straight out, and put the portrait at about eye level with yourself. Stare down the portrait. Try to dominate the person you see there. Try to seduce the person that you see. Try to figure out what frightens him, what excites him, what appeals to him. Get to know him, and in so doing, adjust yourself to get to know him better. Develop an intense relationship; repeat the exercise a day later. Stare down the portraits of the famous people that you can find in art museums. You will find yourself adopting the style of the person you try to dominate. Find full length portraits when possible. In staring down the person in the portrait, imagine yourself wearing comparable clothing.
- Wear a costume – Borrow some garments from an obliging wardrobe department or find some at a thrift shop. Walk around – stride boldly, creep on tiptoes, enter a room in high heels and (simulated!) fur wraps. Do a mirror exercise with yourself in front of a full-length mirror. Speak to your image in the mirror. Let yourself "grow into" your own costume. If the costume has pockets, put your own possessions in the pockets. Write a letter to someone while wearing the costume. Watch TV; make yourself breakfast. Return to the mirror and do another mirror exercise with yourself. Spend a day by yourself in the costume.

Style: the actor's directorial function

We have concentrated in this discussion on the mechanisms for a single actor discovering, analyzing, and "entering" a specific style, or set of styles which will integrate her into the general style of the play, or segment of the play. But there does have to be a determination, at some point, of what the "general style of the play" is to be. And that is usually determined by a director – although a director working in close collaboration with a team that includes producers, designers, dramaturgs and, once they are cast, the actors themselves.

When this book was first written, there were two major "general styles" for producing plays that were written or set in previous eras (e.g. Edwardian, ancient Greek) or in different and nonrealistic theatrical formats (farce, verse, operetta). These were "conventional" productions and "unconventional" ones – the latter also called by dozens of other names, both generic and specific: experimental, avant-garde, surrealistic, expressionist, poetic, agitprop, absurdist (Beckettian), epic (Brechtian) and many others. As I write the current edition, there are even more labels in the unconventional category (the catch-all "postmodern" and "conceptual" chief among them), while the "conventional" category has all but disappeared, except in a few community theatres and summer stock companies. Even France's historic Comédie Française and England's celebrated National Theatre and Royal Shakespeare Company perform their Molière and Shakespearean classics with motorcycles roaring across the stage, video projections behind them, thunderous sounds emitting from the speakers around the house, and costumed with everything from Nazi uniforms to nudity to the latest offerings of Diesel and Urban Outfitters. But in almost every case, there is a desire on the part of both the theatre and the audience to have a *coordinated* style of production – so that the characters, even if they don't know each other as individuals, can sense each other's collective style. And this requires some collective shaping of the production, normally led by the director.

But even conventional classical productions raise enormous stylistic questions. To say that a play will be produced in the "conventional" style of ancient Greek tragedy for example, is to say almost nothing at all. Does that mean the heroic-poetic style of Aeschylus or the cynical-realistic style of Euripides? Does it mean focusing on Apollonian (rational and aesthetic) or Dionysian (mystic and sensual) elements of ancient Greek culture? Does it mean choral chanting or choral speaking; a chorus of one hundred (as in Silviu Purcarete's production of The Danaiads) or a chorus of one (as in Olivier Py's production of Prometheus Bound)? Do the actors wear masks, half-masks, or no masks? Colored or white himations…or yet more ancient garments? Is there scenery or no scenery? A raised stage or no stage? Is it performed indoors or outdoors? As a mass spectacle or an intimate arena staging? Set in the fifth century BC (when the plays were written) or the tenth century BC (when the stories of the plays were thought to have been created)? Will the chorus speak in unison or be broken into semi-choruses and soloists? All of those possibilities could be – and have been – justified as a "conventional" classic Greek tragedy style.

And an "unconventional" style – which is what almost all directors aim for in the twenty-first century – means there will be a thousand such questions asked and a million possible answers that could be given. Obviously, a guiding hand must ultimately make the decisions upon which everyone's performance will be able to rest comfortably. And that hand is usually that of a director – and usually before the actors have even been cast, much less have started rehearsals.

Nonetheless, the actors have a role in shaping and finalizing this general style, not by working on their own, but by working in concert. Playing opposite Olivier would make you aim at pleasing (or defeating, or encouraging) Olivier, but it would also make Olivier work at having an effect on you! Style, we remember, is reciprocal. And the real interactions between real people, which become the performed interactions between performing characters, are always at minimum a two-way street, even when the persons on opposite sides may be of radically different proportions. Style, again, is a *collective* characterization. Actors who truly interact with one another on the stage or the film set discover, through their characters, the tactics and goals that are common to each other, that *work* on each other and that, collectively, create the core of the style of the production. They thus, working in concert, have a *directorial* function as well as an acting one.

Summary of Chapter 4

Style is the collective characterization of the play. It is those behavioral characteristics covered in the previous two chapters that are common to the characters in a play, or to a group of those characters. Sometimes it is historically derived, and sometimes it is a wholly imaginary creation of the playwright or the director and the design team. The actor playing in a given style makes a transformation from her everyday behavior, but there is nothing unreal about the behavior she then performs. It is only different. The actor plays style by understanding its situational purpose, and how it may prove effective in winning her character's goals. She then plays that style reciprocally; it is drawn from her by the goals her character seeks, and the preconditions (which she plants) that regulate interactions within the group in which she seeks them. Playing style, the actor begins to relish it. She begins to enjoy and appreciate the world she has entered. Her style becomes her weapon and her love; she can play powerfully and without embarrassment or tentativeness toward situational victory within the framework of style.

Style is a struggle, not an accomplishment – for the character as well as for the actor. Neither the actor nor the character will ever totally master any style; no one does. We, in our own lives, are always trying to top ourselves. We are always reaching for style; we never completely arrive, we do not stop trying until our final breaths.

Specific styles, such as speaking dialects and performing in period costumes, are learned by research, by instruction, by imitation, and by real-life trial and error. We are always adjusting and perfecting the styles which become part of our behavioral equipment, part of our acting versatility.

Style is built into a play by the director, the design team, and eventually the actors who set up the "common denominators" of ideal futures, tactics, dialects, private audiences, and characterizing of others; these serve as the universal preconditions that determine, to a greater or lesser extent, each character's thinking. Whether this is done formally or informally, it is the responsibility of each actor to adapt, by reciprocal mechanisms, her actions and behaviors to the demands of a world thus "stylized" in its appearance and in its intrinsic and extrinsic "rules."

5

PLAYING THE PERFORMANCE

"Performing is far more than a couple of actors speaking words to each other. The people who have no lines in the play are performers nonetheless. They are…contributing by virtue of the very slightest nuance of the movement that they make… We are a performing species."

American philosopher/psychotherapist/playwright
Fred Newman[1]

It is a temptation to think, in some American acting classes at least, that when the actor successfully plays the dialogue, the situation, the character, and the style, she has done everything she needs to do. This is not correct. The actor must also perform. She must play the performance. She must create an effect on an audience.

What, exactly, does this mean? What does it entail? Among other things, it means that the actor must be heard in every seat in the theatre house and with every nuance that can be picked up in the film studio's microphone. And this is a bare minimum, a passive responsibility. She must also make the audience know what her character is all about. More than that, she must make the audience *care* what her character is about, and must make them guess what her character *could be* about. She must create, in addition to the external behavior of her character, the character's potential. And she must create this with impact. These are active responsibilities, and they take work to accomplish.

When we look at it freshly, we realize that acting is not simply a job that must be done competently; it is an art form that must be executed brilliantly, ravishingly. It must not only satisfy an audience's expectations, it must exceed their expectations; it must indeed raise their expectations. It must excite its viewers; it must electrify, entertain, and transport them. It must be hilarious enough to make them laugh, or engaging enough to make them think, or empathic enough to make them weep, or intense enough to make them gasp – or, indeed, it should have many or all of these attributes. Acting that fails to achieve any of them fails to fill the theatre – or the film multiplex – that houses it. There is, after all, no requirement that people attend the theatre, no requirement that the theatre even exists. Theatre blossoms only because it is overwhelming, and when its acting is astonishing. Where a theatre and its acting are merely "good," merely "correct," merely "in the proper style," both die a slow death.

But all this, of course, presents the actor with a potential problem. She must perform her role at the same time that she acts it. She must "sell" her character at the same time she "becomes" it. And this touches the very "paradox of acting"* we have thus far avoided: How does the actor "perform" without sacrificing her credibility? How does she electrify, ravish, and excite her audience without mugging, indicating, hiding, flag-waving, and all the hammy, performative gimmickry we will see as anathema to her situational involvement? How can she be "theatrical" without disgracing herself, her characterization, or her style? The answers to these questions can be approached only by examining a final level of acting behavior: the performance level, the level of theatricality.

Stanislavsky

First, why is this issue a paradox? Why should an actor's skills in performing before an audience conflict with her credibility? Much of the problem stems from an over-reliance, mainly in America, on a handful of comments – some later retracted – by Konstantin Stanislavsky.

Since the early years of the twentieth century, there has been a strain of acting and acting instruction, particularly in the United States, that considers the audience the enemy of acting, inhibiting the actor's honesty and truthfulness onstage. Stanislavsky was famously frightened by the audience, believing for a while that his stage fright could be alleviated by intense inner concentration that would provide him "public solitude." In his major acting text, Stanislavsky explains, "There, in the circle of light, as in your own home, there is no one to fear and nothing to be ashamed of…In such a narrow circle of light, with one's attention focused, it is easy to observe things in precise detail and live one's most intimate feelings and thoughts, and perform the most complex actions."[2] There, he said, "in a performance, with a thousand eyes on you, you can always retreat into your solitude, like a snail in its shell."[3] Eventually, however, Stanislavsky

---

* Diderot's famous text of that name (*Le Paradoxe sur le Comédien*), mentioned earlier in this book, was written in 1773 and published in 1830, and argued that actors should feel real emotion only in rehearsal, never in performance.

realized he was cheating those who came to see his work. Emerging from a St. Petersburg theatre late one winter, where his Moscow company was on tour and had been holding a late-night rehearsal, he saw a huge crowd of people lined up at the box office for tickets for the company's performance that would open on the following day. "My God," he later recalled to his colleague, Vasily Toporkov, "I realized what a responsibility we are taking...to satisfy the spiritual needs of these people who are freezing here all through the night... I realized that beyond the super-objective of the play there must be a *super*-super-objective. I cannot yet define it, but that night I felt that those people who stood on the square must get still much more than what we had prepared for them."[4] Stanislavsky finally realized that the audience deserved more than to see his onstage actors retreating into solitude like snails in their shells.

Of course, Stanislavsky's stage fright was in no way associated with a lack of adequate technical ability. Indeed, he was an absolute master of stage technique, beginning his career as a flamboyant actor in romantic epics, farces, and operettas – with great acclaim in the latter for his Nanki-Poo in Gilbert and Sullivan's *The Mikado*. His potential as an opera singer was so extraordinary that Tchaikovsky offered to write an opera for him. The entire second half of his masterwork, *An Actor's Work*, is almost totally devoted to purely technical aspects of acting, including advanced stage-speaking techniques and instructions that employ operatic terms like *forte* and *fortissimo*. His stage idol was the thunderous Italian actor, Tomasso Salvini, whose answer to the question "What are the most important three things about acting?" was "Voice, voice, and more voice," and whose famous motto was "I can make an audience weep by reading them a menu." Stanislavsky knew, and in his youth practiced, all the technical skills of performance that we use today – but he never, at least in his published writings, found a way to merge them with his deep devotion to truth, authenticity, and honest emotion.

Stanislavsky's commitment to honest emotion, however, has remained fundamental to acting. And rightly so; he was not wrong about this, nor was his American disciple, Lee Strasberg. And we are now able to demonstrate a neuroscientific basis to this. A series of experiments by Giaccomo Rizzolatti and his colleagues at the University of Parma in the late 1990s discovered that specific neurons in the brains of macaque monkeys that fired when the monkey was picking up a piece of food also fire in other monkeys who merely *see* the monkey pick up the food. Subsequent experiments indicated that human beings do likewise. "Anytime you watch someone doing something, the neurons that your brain would use to do the same thing become active – as if you yourself were doing it," explains the distinguished neurologist V.S. Ramachandran.[3] This helps explain how emotion is transmitted among humans: when we see others in pain, what are now known as *mirror neurons* make us experience pain of our own.

We are, it turns out, brain-wired for empathy. The mirror neuron discovery has become a neurological basis for Horace's dictum two millennia ago, that the actor can only move the audience when he himself is moved. Mirror neurons give a solid foundation to the core teachings of both Stanislavsky and Strasberg, and to those distinguished actors and acting teachers who followed in their footsteps. For theatricality in a realistic Chekhov play, a Shakespearean soliloquy, or a Gilbert and Sullivan operetta (all of which Stanislavsky mastered as an actor) provides FedEx deliveries of the actor's emotions directly to the audience's eager eyes and ears – via the mirror neurons in their brains.

Theatricality: the final level of acting behavior

"Etonne-moi!" ("Astonish me!")
Classic slogan of Russian impresario
Sergei Diaghilev

"Theatricality" is not a bad word at all. It is essentially the short form of "the theatrical process," or "the theatrical arrangement." It is the specific way in which actors and audience are linked.

Theatricality is not a mere vehicle. Nor is it simply an outward gloss that a director or actor grafts onto situation in order to make it palatable to an observing audience. Nor is it the sugar coating of the play's medicinal theme. Rather, it is intrinsic to the play, and it is played with the play, not on top of it.

Theatricality therefore cannot be dismissed from the actor's mind. The crucial question is how does it fit into the structure of the actor's consciousness? How does she "play the performance" as well as the part?

Example: The Olympic skier

Before addressing these questions directly, let's return to our analogy of the downhill and the slalom racers. The downhill skier, who pursues her intention (the finish line) in any way she can, with a total commitment to victory (getting there first), is analogous to an actor simply playing a situation, and pursuing her goals in the quest for a victory. This is the first level – the "life level" of acting behavior. The slalom skier, who has the same goals and commitment to victory, must do so around obstacles, and via a curving path shaped by the flags of the slalom designer and governed by the rules of the slalom. She is therefore analogous, as we have seen, to an actor whose path to victory has been complicated by the

178

considerations of characterization and style placed in her way by the playwright, the director, the costume and set designers, and usually the actor herself during her period of homework. This is the second level – the dramatized level – of acting behavior.

Now let us take this analogy to its third and final level: a slalom run in the midst of *a crowd of rooting spectators*. This becomes the theatrical level. Imagine her in an Olympic race. She sees the finish line far down the hill, the flags scattered down the course, and she both sees and hears thousands of cheering, yelling, rooting partisans lining her route. As she approaches them, their cheers increase; as she passes them, they cheer even louder. Her pulse, elevated to its seeming extremity by the race itself, surges even higher. She cuts closer to the poles, takes riskier chances, and almost becomes reckless as she displays a previously unseen daring that the crowd brings out of her. The cheers of the crowd fill her brain, they boost her speed; she begins to feel a burst of superhuman spirit that tempts her to challenge the very limits of human endurance. She seeks to win this medal now, not just for herself but for her fans, her crowd, her country, and, if she believes in one, for her God!

Persons unacquainted with "performance," whether in sports or on stage, may doubt the effectiveness of the crowd's cheers upon an athlete, particularly upon one so professionally skilled and disciplined, but that effectiveness is quite real. It is even measurable. Hard-nosed and skeptical bookmakers, who set their odds on facts, not theories, figure the "hometown advantage" in precise numbers when they make their point spread calculations, knowing that the athlete – or team of athletes – with the most loyal rooters will get a solid and calculable boost from them. "Boosters," in fact, is the name of some of the "rooting clubs" that follow their chosen athlete-heroes from competition to competition.

The psychological reasons for the boost the fans provide include, at the least, four features:

First, they raise the athlete's expectations, and allow her to share in the crowd's highly idealized expectations for her. These become tugging, cybernetic forces urging her on, compelling her to victory. Much of this is purely physiological. The cheers stimulate the secretion of adrenalin: the heartbeat increases, the spleen contracts and releases its red blood cells, the liver releases its sugar, the visceral organs release blood to the muscles, and the bronchi dilate to deepen respiration. All these add up to greater physical energy, greater muscular power, and greater stamina and control.

Second, the crowd encourages recklessness. By declaring itself at one with the athlete, the crowd also declares itself a supporter for the athlete should she overextend herself. The cheers and screams encourage the athlete's fearlessness, and induce, in her, a greater willingness to take chances in the pursuit of superhuman physical attainments.

Third, hundreds in the crowd are boldly waving her national flag, stimulating every ounce of her patriotic pride as she anticipates standing on the victory podium while her national anthem is played.

And finally, the crowd threatens punishment for a failure of effort. Having, by their cheers, raised her to a position of eminence, the crowd implicitly suggests to the athlete that they now count on her – that she is carrying their honor and their hopes, and she therefore *must not let them down*. The effect of this implicit punishment for failure, coupled with the reward for her recklessness in the pursuit of victory, is a tremendous spur to the athlete; it can compel her beyond the merely "good" to the truly "great."

Yet the skier is never "playing to" the crowd. She is not trying to directly engage her fans, her boosters, or even her God, though the presence of all of them fill her mind. Indeed, she never gives them so much as a glance – and were she to do so, the rooting would cease, and she would be seen not as a hero but as merely a showboater or grandstander. Her total conscious concentration is on the finish line, and on gaining speed and executing the best and fastest possible route around the flags. The feedback loop between the skier and her fans is overwhelming, but in no way will she openly acknowledge it. Unconsciously, however, and inevitably, she knows they are helping her win her victory. And she will learn, perhaps unconsciously, how to cultivate this wildly supportive "home town" audience.

It is the same with all athletes: while they *produce* for their teammates they *perform* for their fans, and their fans egg them on to perform even better. When the boxer successfully lands a blow, his fans roar in approval and he is doubly-energized to "hit him again, harder, harder!" When the hometown baseball player races ahead of the ball toward home plate, the crowd roars and the player focuses every muscle in his body to slide in safe. Eventually, what the athlete finally realizes is this: the more she stimulates the crowd, the more they will stimulate her, and the more they stimulate her, the more she can stimulate them. It is a self-feeding, self-fulfilling, cybernetic cycle of increasing energy. It becomes a symmetrical feedback loop; the athlete and her fans will win together or they will lose together; each uses the other to bring out the best performance of each.

Crowd and athlete, then, seek the same thing: victory at the finish line. "Winning is not everything; it is the only thing," as Lombardi's saying echoes again and again. But winning – as opposed to cheering – is also a one-way street. The crowd looks at the boxer, but if the boxer looks at the crowd, he will be knocked out in two seconds. If the skier looks for her mother on the sidelines, she will crash into the flag, or end up way wide of the mark. The crowd can only get its victory from the skier; the skier cannot get hers from the crowd. So the skier is not looking for an award from her fans; she is looking for an award *for* them. If she fails to achieve her victory, they are useless to her; all the "nice tries" and pats on the back are the dimmest, saddest of consolations. She does not stimulate the crowd, then, for any reason but to assist her winning, to add fuel to her feedback fire that will draw from her that last burst of spirit, that last full measure of devotion that will help her win her goal.

But what if there is no crowd of spectators? What if this is not the Olympics but a mere practice run, with no one but her coach looking on? What if observers are there, but rooting for someone else? Anyone who has ever performed in an athletic contest knows the answer to these questions: the athlete *imagines* rooters, and will be "boosted" by her imaginary rooters almost as much, sometimes, as by real ones.

Imaginary rooters accompany us all, and they may take many forms. They can be the grand but wholly imagined crowds we dream up as attending our efforts and cheering us along. They can be the imaginary radio or television announcer who breathlessly reports our every action to a nationwide audience: "And here he comes around the bend, *nailing* that turn and heading for home plate!" Children at play are quite uninhibited at becoming their own announcers: "Johnny takes the sign, nods his head; now he's going into his windup..." says Johnny to himself as he takes the sign, nods his head, and winds up on the pitcher's mound. And of course they will include our private audiences (see Chapter 3), meaning our parents, teachers, siblings, deities, past and present sweethearts, rivals and role models. The athlete stimulates herself by imagining herself observed, encouraged, and egged on. And so can an actor.

The actor theatrical

The actor in the theatre is in many ways analogous to her athletic counterpart. Like the athlete, the actor can stimulate a crowd of observers; also like the athlete, she can be stimulated by them. No one can expect an actor to be oblivious to this; it is the fundamental dynamic of the theatre, as it is of spectator sports.

The actor can, therefore, "use" the audience in much the same way that the athlete can, but there is one absolutely crucial understanding that must precede this "use." It is simply this: the audience will only support and stimulate the *character*; they will not, until the curtain call, directly support the *actor*.* During the performance, an audience does not root for you to be a good actor, but for your character (if you are a good actor) to win her victory. Insofar as an actor "plays to the audience," she does so strictly *on behalf of her character* and her character's struggle. She uses the audience to *help her character win*.

As with the athlete, the actor-character seeks her victory through the situation of the play, not (except in soliloquies, or direct addresses to the audience, discussed later in this chapter) by directly performing to her surrounding audience. But, also like the athlete, she performs *for* her surrounding audience. There is quite a difference.

Let us begin with a real-life example. If, say, Jill and John are having lunch at a café and get into a debate about their differing hopes for an upcoming election, it is common for each of them to raise their voices, if unconsciously, to silence

---

* OK, there are exceptions. When a star actor first appears onstage, it is customary in some venues (a very bad custom, in my opinion) for the audience to applaud him or her. The same can happen when singers in a musical freeze at the end of their song until the applause dies down – hardly something their characters would do.

each other's argument and thereby prioritize their own. Their debate becomes an argument, and arguments tend to escalate in volume, as induction tactics turn to threatening ones. But there is another reason they raise their voices: so that others seated nearby can hear their arguments. And why do they do this? So they can gather a crowd of "rooters" for their positions. John, for example, is hoping that surrounding diners – people he does not know and never looks at – will not only hear but accept the argument he raises, and perhaps generate a "support group" behind him that will even nod approvingly at his brilliant line of reasoning. But Jill hopes the same thing; *she* raises her voice in return, though still looking right at John, hoping (again, usually unconsciously) to get a support group of her own. For the fact is, complete strangers tend to look at other persons' public arguments and fights whenever they occur. On an elementary or junior high school playground anywhere in the world, no fistfight ever begins without a crowd of onlookers quickly gathering around the fighters, often within a matter of seconds. Conflict is fascinating, and that's why great drama – which is about great conflicts – is fascinating. We raise our voices because we believe what we say is *right*, and so as to attract a following for our point of view.

So while John and Jill are *interacting* with each other, they are also *performing* for the café diners. And they are doing both of these activities *simultaneously*; neither mode of communication is disentangled from the other. That Jill is performing does not mean that she doesn't "believe" in her argument. Quite the contrary, it means that she *really* believes it; she doesn't just want John to vote for the candidate she likes, and she doesn't want anyone else in the café to do so either. And John likewise wants everyone in the restaurant to take his side. Like Jill, this only makes him *more* earnest about his position, and more powerful in expressing it.

And this is how an actor plays her role on stage. She *interacts with* those directly involved in her situation, and *performs for* those people, real and imaginary, who she senses may possibly be within hearing – again, their real and imaginary hearing. And this would be true if there were no one in the dining area of the restaurant, because there could still be people back in the kitchen, or people could be watching them through the window and maybe even a word or two could be heard from outside the building.

For the fact is, most of our waking lives are lived in public. This was particularly true in the earlier eras of drama, certainly up until the twentieth century. Before the era where we found ourselves riding around in enclosed, air-conditioned and audio-equipped automobiles, living in freestanding multi-bedroom homes with soundproofed walls and double-paned windows, and considering personal privacy our all but inalienable right, the vast majority of human beings lived outdoors or in tiny hovels or in jammed-together tenement buildings, and they traveled almost entirely in public and on foot. Privacy as we know it today was all but unknown: people mostly lived, ate, worked, and even bathed and relieved themselves in public places or outdoor facilities. Homes, for most who could afford them, were miniscule, and you could hear just about everything happening in them – and in the close-by neighboring ones as well. Shakespeare's birthplace, for example, which still exists in Stratford, was then (and remains now) a small two-story wooden house with just two tiny bedrooms; it was home not only to Shakespeare and his parents and five siblings but also to his father's tanning shop on the ground floor – where their sheep also slept during cold winter nights. Even the royal palaces of those eras, such as Versailles, were drafty structures that were filled with hundreds of full-time servants that were necessary to make the occupants – in the ages before electricity, machines, plumbing, or toilets – reasonably comfortable. Totally private conversations in such eras, therefore, were almost unknown.

It is no surprise, then, that the great bulk of the dialogue in plays written prior to 1900 is presumed to be spoken in public venues. Plays had large casts, often including a large number of non-speaking servants and "attendants," and while these supernumeraries were not given lines to say, they certainly could – and should – be assumed to be listening to what is being said by others. Consider the example of the extraordinary scene in Shakespeare's *Richard III* when Lady Anne, following the corpse of the late King Henry VI as it is being taken to the funeral ground, has the pallbearers "set down" the coffin so she can mourn the King, who has been murdered by the Duke of Gloucester. Hardly has the coffin been laid down, however, when the Duke himself arrives and, astonishingly, begins to seduce Lady Anne, whose husband he had also murdered. Anne reviles him, curses him, spits on him, but eventually caves in and accepts his ring. What most readers (and not a few literature professors and even directors) ignore is that the pallbearers, having set down their load, *remain onstage for this entire scene*, thus witnessing Anne's condemnation of the Duke and the Duke's perverse seduction of the woman whose husband and father-in-law he has brutally killed. The pallbearers never reappear in the play, but if we are to take the scene seriously we must realize they would surely tell all their friends about the amazing interaction among royals that they have witnessed. Any actor playing Gloucester or Anne in this scene would have to understand that their characters are not merely interacting with each other but also "performing" for these silent pallbearers – as well as any passersby that may be watching from a distance, since the scene is set outdoors on a public London street. For both the Duke and the Lady are public personae – politicians in fact – and they will do whatever they can to bring the public onto their side in the scenes that must inevitably follow their amazing discourse.

Even realistic family dramas of the nineteenth and early twentieth century – in the era of Chekhov, say – usually had large casts with lots of social gatherings where even the most intimate exchanges could, and usually would, be overheard by other characters. All four acts of Chekhov's *Three Sisters,* for example, contain gatherings – parties, really – in and around the family home, and when paired characters think they are alone together for a minute or two, they are almost immediately greeted by other characters who inconveniently arrive to break up the intimate and "private" conversation.

What I am hoping to show, therefore, is the precise opposite of our conventional dramaturgy which holds that the theatrical event is a dramatized situation. On the contrary, a dramatic event is, more often than not, a theatricalized situation. The *actors* are not playing to an audience; their *characters* are. They are playing to a wide, wide world. They are playing to *our* world; the audiences' world.

"All the world's a stage, and all the men and women merely players."

Jacques in As You Like It, *William Shakespeare*

Erving Goffman made a superb series of realizations in this regard in his seminal sociological study, *The Presentation of Self in Everyday Life*. This 1959 book creates what Goffman described as a "dramaturgical analysis" [5] of human interaction, the central thesis being that during our waking hours we are all performing, all the time. Based on Goffman's realization that "human interaction [is] in some ways very much like a grand play," sociologist Peter Kivisto, in 1998, praised Goffman as "arguably the most original American theorist of the second half of the twentieth century." It is a warranted accolade.

Goffman's basic position, elaborated over some 250 pages, is that human beings transform their "activities into performances." [6] A theatrical context is then not added to the dramatic situation, it is *part* of the dramatic situation. In acting, the point is to bring the audience into the world of the play, not bring the play into the world of the audience. This is why "conscious performing" is not contrary to "real" acting, it is *part of* real acting. We do it in life, and our "living" characters do it on a stage.

The circles of audiences

People act to and for many different audiences. These include, among others, persons we're talking to, persons overhearing us, unseen persons who could *possibly* be overhearing us, and persons or spirits who – even if known to be far away or dead – we fantasize as hearing us. The separate audiences for whom a character interacts and/or performs can thus be laid out in a series of "audiences" that can be ranked on various circles that surround the (properly egocentric) character in sort of a "Ptolemaic system" of interacting and performing characters – as seen in the below "map" of the character's (and thus the actor's) communicants.

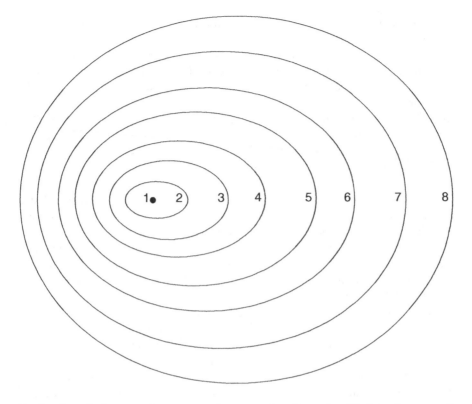

In this "map" of an actor's universe of perceived and imagined "other characters," the numbers represent:

1   You (the dot), as your character.
2   The character onstage to whom you are speaking – and with whom you are directly interacting. You and this character occupy the core (the "sun") of this neo-Ptolemaic universe; all the other levels are peripheral "planets" that exist at further and further distances from the core.
3   Actors onstage, representing characters in the play who are directly involved in the interaction, but not speaking at this time.
4   Actors onstage, representing characters in the play that you know can hear you but are not *directly* involved in the interaction at this time, as servants, for example.
5   Characters in the play you know to be *offstage* (e.g. in the next room), and expect can hear you. When Gertrude speaks to Hamlet in the Queen's Closet scene, for example, she is at level 1, Hamlet is at level 2, and Polonius, whom she knows is behind the arras, is at level 5.
6   Characters in the play you know who could possibly be within hearing distance (e.g. upstairs, across the hall) and who could possibly be overhearing

you or spying on you without your knowledge, but who you have no idea where they may be at this moment.

7   Characters in the play, or unidentified persons not in the play, who might by sheer chance be walking on the outskirts of the setting (say a public square or street), and who, though offstage and completely unnoticed, could be within hearing distance.

8   Persons or figures in your own private audience (see Chapter 3) of persons, living or dead, and/or of guardian spirits (e.g. God, angels, St. Joan's "voices") that you believe are not physically within human sight or hearing, but whose imagined opinion you care about.

The way in which the actor's character interacts with these "audiences" can determine not only the apparent naturalism of her immediate (core) interactions, but the style and theatricality of her performative ones.

It also creates a "public" aspect to all acting. One of Stanislavsky's most famous dicta was that acting "is being private in public."* Your author suggests instead that acting is mainly "being *public* in public." And sometimes, as we will see, "being public in *private*."

Within this topography, there will be a continual feedback between the characters and their respective "audiences," which can create dynamic interactions in which goals and tactics are always in flux, always being adjusted and refined, and in which the character's goals, situations, and expectations are continually evolving. This creates the live intensity, style, and theatricality of (public) performance. When, in *The Glass Menagerie*, Laura is dancing and talking with Jim O'Connor in the parlor, she is also aware that her mother is in the kitchen washing the dishes, her brother is on the back porch smoking a cigarette, and her teacher at the Rubicon Business School is still mad at her for quitting the course. By trying to please *all* of these characters at the same time, Laura – and the actor playing her – will be experiencing a very full and active life. She will thereby convey her entire universe of both fears and expectations to everyone watching her, which – happily for the show's director – will include those seated in the theatre audience.

Playing to audiences

In the first court scene in *Hamlet,* the Prince has little to say until his mother asks him why his father's recent death "seems so particular" to him. Hamlet replies with his first speech of more than one line:

---

* Lee Strasberg's most famous exercise was "the private moment," in which a member of his Actors Studio would go onstage, alone, and perform an ordinary private action – such as shaving or putting on makeup – in front of a live audience.

HAMLET: Seems, madam, Nay, it is. I know not 'seems.'
'Tis not alone my inky cloak, good mother,
Nor customary suits of solemn black,
Nor windy suspiration of forc'd breath,
No, nor the fruitful river in the eye,
Nor the dejected 'havior of the visage,
Together with all forms, moods, shapes of grief,
'That can denote me truly. These indeed seem,
For they are actions that a man might play;
But I have that within which passeth show—
These but the trappings and the suits of woe.

Hamlet is, of course, talking to his mother, but he is talking to her in public; there are nine named characters in the courtroom, plus as many attendants as the theatre company can place there. Hamlet is well aware that everyone in the room is listening to him. His real target at this moment is not his mother but her new husband, King Claudius, who has just made what Hamlet considers the hypocritical speech (cited in the previous chapter) in which Claudius pretended to be mourning Hamlet's father's death. Hamlet is letting Claudius know that he sees through this pretended grief and woe; that these are "actions that a man might *play*," but that he, Hamlet, has "that within which passeth *show*," i.e. *real* emotions rather than simulated grief and woe.

But Hamlet, even if he looks at his mother the entire time, is also speaking to the *entire court*, and letting them know that he sees through Claudius' pretended grief. He is performing for *them* as much or more than speaking to his mother, and in doing so he is publicly undermining the King's authority in front of his Lord Chamberlain, his ambassadors and even his lowly attendants – while Claudius, forced to pretend to love his new stepson, can only stand there silently and do nothing about it. And the actor playing Hamlet is therefore performing Hamlet's "performance" (which is to accuse his uncle of only *playing* those "actions that a man might play").

Hamlet's audience is larger yet. He is speaking indirectly to other people. His girlfriend Ophelia, if not present (although most productions have her on the stage at this point, she is not in the published cast list), will surely find out what he said from her brother Laertes. The ambassadors and attendants, though they make no comments at the time, will surely be telling their friends about Hamlet's "seems" speech as soon as they leave the Court. And Hamlet is all but certainly talking to his father, who, though dead, clearly lives on in Hamlet's private audience – and will soon be in Hamlet's *literal* audience as well when, as a ghost, he makes his way to the castle battlements.

And, of course, Hamlet is talking to God. Just four lines after the King and his courtiers depart, Hamlet, finally alone on stage, cries, as we have already seen, "O God! God! / How weary, stale, flat, and unprofitable / Seem to me all the uses of this world!" Hamlet's saying "God" twice in succession makes this not merely an appeal to God, but an *insistent* appeal. He is trying to *make* God listen to him.

For the actor playing Hamlet, these various "audiences" of his "seems" speech will embolden him mightily. Though directly addressing his mother, he knows that many other people are listening to him. And so performs for them as well. And thus, as he speaks, his tactics will become firmer, braver, more dynamic. As he detects that he is successful in humiliating his uncle, who remains silent, his confidence in performing, his sense of an incipient victory to come, will egg him on further. Insofar as he realizes that some people on stage (Polonius, certainly) will be strengthening their support of Claudius, his cutting edge will sharpen, his wit will dig in more deeply, and his speech will glisten with increasing ironic brilliance. Thus the court setting, with its audience of potential supporters and potential rivals and enemies onstage, and its private audience alive in Hamlet's mind, will bring the best possible "performance" out of Hamlet. It will also bring the best "Hamlet" out of the actor playing Hamlet.

Now let us simply expand that court to include the theatre audience! Let the actor playing Hamlet seek *their* support as well. Such support will redouble the actor's force and energy. Hamlet will not merely reach Claudius and his court, he will reach the theatregoers attending the performance, who will become, in his mind, the Danish populace that, as Claudius will later say, are the "general gender" that bear him "great love." Hamlet is performing for this audience. His speech will reach Claudius *through* them. It will tell Claudius: "Look, these people are against you, these people find you shameful." Hamlet's virtuoso performance, his sheer theatricality, has a situational function which is only amplified by his theatrical one. And this will set up a valuable rapport between him and the theatre audience, to whom Hamlet will speak directly, and at some length, several times before the play is over.

What about Claudius? He, of course, is trying the same thing. His tactics in the scene are a demonstration of political force and pragmatic rationality. He, too, is trying to convince the Court that he is the appropriate man for the throne, and fully deserving of their support. He is trying to convince the larger audience as well – but his hands are somewhat tied because he's also trying to convince them that he loves his new stepson. Both characters, in their battle with each other, are playing for all-out victory, and are bringing in both the onstage and offstage audiences as weapons in that struggle. They are performing. And this is the performance mechanism that is at the very heart of a vigorous, credible, and aesthetically consistent theatricality.

This mechanism does not depend on the presence of an actual onstage audience, such as the Court. The "plant" of an audience of rooters can be made even in a one-character play. It is a mechanism, and it becomes the basic precondition for theatricality, for performance. The actor does not, in the case of most realistic plays, play directly to the audience any more than the Olympic skier looks at the crowd around her. But she knows that they are watching, and she takes advantage of that fact on behalf of her character, and on behalf of her character's quest for victory. Insofar as the audience seems to be rooting for her character, she exploits this and attempts to increase it. Insofar as they are neutral, she tries to stimulate them to action. She identifies them with members of her character's own private audience, and tries to stimulate and please them. Insofar as they are hostile, she tries to change them into being supportive and loyal. She need do none of this consciously; the feedback loop exists, and it cannot not operate. She must only allow the loop to perform in its only effective way: on behalf of her character's intentions.

And the fact is, in twenty-first century theatre, realistic dramas contain far more characters speaking to the theatre audience in direct address; looking them right in the eye, and proving the point that even in realism, characters can perform directly to audiences without being considered "unreal" or "phony."

The character as hero

"Occasionally, an actor can completely dominate any house, and so, like a master matador, he can work the audience the way he pleases."

British director Peter Brook[7]

Goffman's notion that we are all performers – that all the world's a stage – is a simple extension of the psychological phenomenon of human egocentrism, our feeling that we are all the heroes of our own plays. The slalom skier considers herself the hero of her fans, and if fans do not in fact appear on the slopes, she imagines them there. She is, in any event, a hero to her private audience; and she is quite able and willing to imagine her private audience as part of her public one. The actor, in the same way, imagines her character not only as the hero of the play, but as "heroic" and worthy of the audience's support, encouragement and cheers. Even Osric, a relatively minor character, should himself feel that "*Hamlet* is a play about Osric"; but even more than that he also should feel that any fair-minded audience will identify with Osric more than anyone onstage. He is, in his own mind, not only the hero of the play but the hero of the play's audience. This is Osric's and only Osric's subjective opinion, of course, utterly unconfirmed by objective analysis, but it remains a dominant theme in Osric's egocentric mind. All characters, like all people, assume the inevitability of final validation.*

This is an aspect of universal human egocentrism. Fundamentally, all persons innately think of themselves as "right;" "right," in our minds, is essentially defined as "what we do." While we may be consciously aware of our faults, our flaws, our regrettable habits, foibles, and affectations, and that other people have accused us of these imperfections in our behaviors, yet we still feel that if there were an all-seeing, all-knowing, all-just observer of our thoughts and actions we would find ultimate vindication. Insofar as we find ourselves ridiculed, unappreciated, or despised, we feel ourselves, deep down, to a like degree misperceived. Egocentrism is a holdover from earliest infancy. Piaget, the child psychologist, has shown that the infant "feels that others share his pain or his pleasure, that his mumblings will inevitably be understood, that his perspective is shared by all persons, that even animals and plants partake of his consciousness."[8] The infant, in other words, feels she is at the center of the world, with all eyes upon her and her alone. Maturity gives rude shocks to these infantile delusions, but it does not eradicate them. Rational development diminishes, but does not destroy, our egocentricity; it remains a precondition for all our thinking.

Characters in plays share that precondition. No matter how vile, despicable, or malicious they might be in our eyes, they themselves feel confident that we will, given the whole story, take their side. Iago, in Shakespeare's *Othello*, is a fine example of this; one of Shakespeare's most loathsome characters, Iago often addresses himself to the audience through soliloquies. It is clear in those soliloquies not only that he delights in himself, but that he fully expects us to delight in his delight. In the many confidences he shares with us, he charms us with his wit, his frankness, and his unabashed contempt for the witlessness of the other characters. He appeals to our sense of justice, to our appreciation of his intellectual superiority, and to our prejudices. He acts as though we admire his ironic style. With every speech he gives us a message that says, "I know you can't admit it out loud, or to the person you're sitting next to, but you know I'm right, don't you? You share my sense of irony, you admire my cleverness and resourcefulness – in fact you like me, don't you?" And, if the performance is sufficiently powerful, we *do* like him; grudgingly perhaps, but genuinely. No matter how feeble, how reviled, or how downtrodden, we all share the essential feeling of innate self-righteousness. Even suicide, to its practitioner, is seen as a heroic act, expressing not the suicide's unworthiness in the face of society, but society's unworthiness in the face of him. If we could read the letters and the diaries of the world's great villains, castoffs, and unappreciated souls (Adolf Hitler, Arthur Bremer, John Wilkes Booth, Sirhan Sirhan), we would find a

---

* There is a hoary theatre joke about a young actor cast as Osric in his college production of *Hamlet*. He calls his mother to tell her he's been cast in *Hamlet* and she asks him what the play is about. "Well, there's this guy Osric..."

feeling of ingrained, heroic self-approval that is quite equal to that of the announced heroes of our time.

Egocentricity is the phenomenon that cements the character's relationship with the audience. It allows the character to make the basic assumption that the audience is on her side, eager to overhear, and ready to approve the logic of her position and the superiority of her manner. No matter what her part, the actor may presume that the audience is prepared to "root" for her character. She can encourage this rooting. The audience is, to begin with, fair. It is objective. It is everything the character could want in a final "judge." The character need not be defensive with the audience. Insofar as they may be predisposed, they will be predisposed for her, not against her. They will want her to win. They will identify with her victory; her victory will be theirs. She will be their hero. For this reason her attitude toward them is one of confidence and positive expectation. She has their initial support, she needs only to preserve and develop it.

This is the basic mental precondition for an immensely powerful and theatrical performance. And, since the precondition is based on the solid foundation of the character's situational victory, it elicits a theatricality that is entirely real to the play, honest to the character, and credible to the audience. It is a theatricality totally aligned with situation, style, and character; it is utterly different from mugging, showing-off, and amateurish contextual self-indulgence.

Exercises: *Playing to the audience*

In theatre, the audience exists. Trying to pretend that it doesn't is simply a double-bind; you cannot "not know" what you do know – and you do know that it is there. So accept it. And use it.

The following two exercises, if you can arrange them (they require several colleagues), will allow you to use the audience in a way fully aligned with your actor's concentration on your character's situational intentions. In them, you need not conspicuously play to the audience, but you should try to have them take your side, work for you, and root for your success in achieving your goals. Make them encourage other characters to support you.

- Battle for supremacy – Two actors learn and prepare the wooing scene between Kate and Petruchio in Shakespeare's *Taming of the Shrew*. As written, there would be no one else on stage during the scene, but understand that almost everyone in Padua knows that Petruchio has come to town specifically to woo Kate, and that the home of Baptista (Kate's father), where the scene takes place, will be filled with people who have a major stake in how his wooing succeeds. They – Baptista, Petruchio's servant Grumio, Kate's sister Bianca, Bianca's wooers, and all the house servants – will therefore be listening in from just outside the doors, since this promises to be the most exciting event in Padua in years! Perform the scene, therefore, with an "audience" that includes Baptista's family, Bianca's wooers, and servants, all surrounding the action. Let the male audience members become partisan "rooters" for Petruchio, and the females partisans for Kate, and let them join in the action by vocally expressing their support, cheering on their favorite character, and trying to help their chosen character "win" the scene. Invite the women in the audience to laugh at Kate's jokes and the men to cheer on Petruchio's. And let Kate and Petruchio, while they bicker and tease without taking their eyes off each other, simultaneously "perform" their actions and speeches to strengthen the support of their fans, proving to their rival that they have the strongest "team" on their side.

- Political speech – Memorize a mesmerizing political speech, historical or from the theatre world, such as Marat's address to the Assembly in Peter Weiss' *Marat/Sade*, or John F. Kennedy's Inaugural Address, or Henry V's speech before Agincourt, or Martin Luther King's "I have a dream" oration. Deliver it to an audience of cheering supporters. Then deliver it to an imaginary audience, but with cheering supporters behind you – you being their spokesperson. Then deliver it to an imaginary audience without any real cheering – but hearing cheering in your mind. See if you can carry over the real cheers into your imagined ones.

The audience as chorus

The Greek tragedians endowed the theatre with a device of great theatrical utility – the *chorus*, which serves a dual function as both party and witness to the play's major lines of action.

While the chorus may ally with one character – or group of characters – during the course of a play, it does not deny its ear to any claimant, and serves as a sounding board and judge for all the play's characters and all the play's claims. Therefore, all the characters in Greek tragedies look to the chorus as a source of potential support for the struggles in which they find themselves engaged.

We can see this very clearly in the great arguments between Oedipus and Tiresias, Oedipus and Creon, Creon and Tiresias, Creon and Haemon, Oedipus and Polynices, all in the familiar Theban plays of Sophocles. These arguments take on added urgency and piquancy when we realize that they are not private debates in close quarters, but public ones, staged outdoors and in full daylight, and that they are waged, ultimately, for the final opinion of the chorus.

Haemon, particularly, exploits this in his defense of his fiancée, Antigone, to his father, Creon, in Sophocles' *Antigone*:[9]

CREON: Would you call it right to admire an act of disobedience?
HAEMON: Not if the act were also dishonorable.
CREON: And was not this woman's action dishonorable?
HAEMON: The people of Thebes think not.

CREON: Since when do I take my orders from the people of Thebes?
I am King, and responsible to myself.
HAEMON: A one-man state? What sort of a state is that? You will be an
excellent King – on a desert island.

Haemon has succeeded in goading Creon into making a disastrous remark in
front of the wrong audience, for when Creon denounces the right of the "people
of Thebes" to tell him how to rule, he has forgotten that he is speaking in the
midst of a chorus that represents the very people of Thebes he is railing against.
This is, in fact, the turning point for Creon, whom the chorus of Theban
citizens had supported until this moment, but who will now turn against
him. The chorus, though not speaking at the time, becomes an "audience" that
totally changes the direction of the entire play.

In a larger sense, however, the chorus is also a representative of the Athenian
audience that *attends* the play. For while in its dramatic function as a "collective
character" the chorus of *Antigone* is composed of Theban elders in the archaic era
of Oedipus (say the tenth century BC), in its theatrical function as an audience it
represents "contemporary" (i.e. fifth century) Athenian citizens during the time
of Sophocles. The judgments the chorus makes in the play will be the same
judgments the audience makes while watching the play. The chorus, then, is *both
part of the play and part of the audience*.

This relationship echoes the physical arrangement of the Greek theatre, with
the chorus in a circular "orchestra," located between the audience in the
"theatron" and the actors on an elevated stage behind them. The physical
relationship between actor, chorus and audience, therefore, means that when
Haemon speaks to the chorus he is also directly addressing the audience behind
them. So the ancient Greek actor's relationship with the audience, whether by
direct address or by indirect behavior, is simply an extension of his character's
interactions with the chorus.

The Greek device of the chorus is immensely useful to the actors in Greek
plays. It establishes a theatricality that is perfectly aligned to the play's
situation. The character's interaction with the chorus and the actor's interaction
with the audience are identical; they are shared. Whatever is addressed to the
chorus is simultaneously addressed to the audience; the arguments that move
and impress the chorus will move and impress the audience, and the more
persuasive the character, the more theatrical the actor. With this sort of
alignment, performances of great power and eloquence can come through with
an unfiltered impact. It is unfortunate, perhaps, that we have lost this device
through the break-up of the classical conventions; modern choruses, like
Anouilh's in his modern *Antigone*, are interesting for what they tell us, but they
don't listen very well.

"There is always a chorus. There is always a play-within-the-play… A dramatic hero is always surrounded by a social group, actual or implied, who press upon him with extraordinary attention, extraordinary threat, just as the audience in the theatre does. Even in one-character plays… the character must direct his remarks to a real or imagined audience whom he makes take on a choral role."

American theatre theorist Michael Goldman[10]

The concept of the Greek chorus can be useful to the actor in the non-Greek play as well, however. It can become a metaphor for her performance context. Suppose the actor were to invent an imaginary chorus? This would be identical to the skier on a practice run creating imaginary "rooters." We have explored the theoretical principle that the actor, in becoming "theatrical," in leaping to the final level of acting behavior, and in her own mind becomes the hero of the play. If she is a hero, she needs a heroic chorus. The creation, in the actor's imagination, of a silent chorus *in the audience* is a potent mental device for liberating a theatricality that is totally aligned with situation – just as it is for Creon and Oedipus. The presence of an imaginary chorus "brings the audience on stage" in exactly the right place: as each character's confidante, supporter, and appeal judge.

Exercises: *Audience as chorus*

Memorize and perform any of the classic debates of Greek tragedy, in the midst of a "chorus" that surrounds the action. For example:

* Prometheus and Oceanus in Aeschylus' *Prometheus Bound*.
* Haemon and Creon in Sophocles' *Antigone*.
* Oedipus and Tiresias in Sophocles' *Oedipus Tyrannus*.
* Electra and Clytemnestra in Sophocles' *Electra*.
* Electra and Clytemnestra in Euripides' *Electra*.
* Theseus and Hippolytus in Euripides' *Hippolytus*.

Let the **chorus be characterized** (for example, as Theban elders, or palace women) but not rehearsed or directed; let them make up their minds as they wish at the time. Repeat, but this time have four people from the "chorus" become an "audience," and have them take seats a few steps behind the remaining chorus members. Perform the scene.

Now **reverse** this, and have the "chorus" stand behind, and the "audience" around the performer. If the exercise is done in a theatre, have the "chorus" in the back row of the house, the actors and "audience" on stage. The point of this exercise is to show that, for the actor-characters, it makes no difference whether the faces around them are labeled "chorus" or "audience." The same should apply despite changes in magnitude occasioned by real performance, in which there might be a chorus of fifteen and an audience of one thousand; from the actor's perspective the two groups, structurally, are indistinguishable.

- Repeat the first exercise with a wholly imaginary chorus and no audience.
- Repeat the first exercise with a wholly imaginary chorus and a real audience.

Memorize and perform one of the following scenes in the same manner as the previous two exercises: with each character imagining his character's own "tragic chorus" surrounding him, and both with and without a real audience observing the scene:

- Tom and Amanda in *The Glass Menagerie*.
- Willy and Charlie in *Death of a Salesman*.
- Blanche and Stanley in *A Streetcar Named Desire*.
- George and Martha, opening scene, in *Who's Afraid of Virginia Woolf*.
- Ramsden and Tanner in *Man and Superman*.
- Woyzeck and The Jew in *Woyzeck*.
- Any scene of strong conflicting values and interests.
- The contentless scene in Chapter 2.

Repeat the previous exercise, imagining the chorus in the back of the house.

The Shakespearean soliloquy

Shakespeare never used a listening chorus (in some plays, notably Henry V, he employed a speaking chorus), but he did use a convention common to his time which served a similar function. This was the direct address, or the soliloquy.

What exactly is a soliloquy, however? The Merriam-Webster dictionary provides only two definitions: (1) "the act of talking to oneself," and (2) "a dramatic monologue that represents a series of unspoken reflections." But human beings don't talk to themselves in long poetic stanzas or extended paragraphs. And nothing could be less dramatic, much less theatrical, than a character's "series of unspoken reflections." So spoken words uttered by actors who are merely "talking to themselves" or "thinking aloud" are, in most cases, unreal, non-dramatic, and non-theatrical. Yet soliloquies have been featured in hundreds of plays since the time of the ancient Greeks, and are more common in twenty-first-century theatre than at any time since the Renaissance. Why have they retained – and indeed increased – their popularity?

Forms of soliloquies

Soliloquies come in two major forms. The first is the *apostrophe*: a speech directed to a non-present but at least potentially sentient being; a god, a spirit, or someone in your private audience that you can at least imagine could possibly hear you, see you, or in some way sense you physically. The apostrophe is common in poetry, as Lord Byron's "Roll on, thou deep and dark blue Ocean – roll!" A prayer is the most common apostrophe. When Hamlet says, "O God, God" in his soliloquy after his "I know not seems" speech before the court, he hopes his words that follow may reach the God in whom he believes, and whom he hopes might be listening to him.

The second form of soliloquy is the *direct address,* in which an actor speaks directly to the audience. These include, most obviously, prologues (which begin Act I and Act II of *Romeo and Juliet*), epilogues (as spoken by Rosalind in *As You Like It*), choruses (as those preceding the five acts in *Henry V,* and one spoken by Time between Acts III and IV in *The Winter's* Tale), plus *asides* (short interjections directed to the audience, particularly common in Restoration comedies).

Both of these forms are worth exploring. I will reference each with works by Shakespeare, not only because his are the most renowned soliloquies in drama, but also because Shakespeare's texts are easily available and because Shakespeare, a life-long actor as well as a playwright, knew better than anyone how to write speeches for actors.

The Apostrophe: Juliet and the Fiery-footed Steeds

There are literally hundreds of apostrophic soliloquies in Shakespeare, of course. Some are comic. Bottom, playing the role of "Pyramus" in a play-within-the-play of *A Midsummer Night's Dream,* apostrophizes a wall ("O wall! O sweet, O lovely wall!" he wails). But most are serious. As we have seen earlier, Lady Macbeth, alone on stage, calls for night ("Come, thick night…") to descend and hide the crime she is planning, and her husband likewise calls for the stars to disappear ("Stars, hide your fires…") to keep anyone from discovering this bloody act. Juliet, alone on her balcony, also calls for night to come, but in an utterly different context:

> JULIET: Gallop apace, you fiery-footed steeds,
> Towards Phoebus' lodging: such a wagoner
> As Phaeton would whip you to the west,
> And bring in cloudy night immediately.

Juliet is asking the horses that, in Greek mythology, draw the chariot of the sun across the sky, to speed up night's arrival – as they did when young Phaethon took the reins and sped them forward to the "lodging" where the sun would disappear.

Young actresses often play this speech by throwing their arms rapturously around themselves, even closing their eyes to show the audience how deeply in love they are. But if we instead see Juliet *trying to see* horses in the sky and urging them to go faster, and *trying to see* Phoebus' lodging in front of the horses and the cloudy night behind them, we will more deeply engage in this 13-year-old girl's wondrous passion and imagination. Her fearlessness in seeking to break the barriers of reality to command the heavens themselves will thrill us. This is far more compelling than simply re-enacting a clichéd gesture of hugging oneself or treating the steeds and lodgings as mere poetic metaphors. For when the horses have run their course and the sun has set, the Spirit of Night – in this case a "sober-suited matron" of Juliet's imagining – will come, bringing with it, as she now apostrophizes, Romeo and the apocalyptic brilliance of his love:

> [JULIET:] Spread thy close curtain, love-performing night…
> Come, civil night…with thy black mantle…
> Come, night; come, Romeo; come, thou day in night!

In her soliloquy, then, Juliet is not trying to *show* something but to *do* something. She is trying to speed up the sunset, and Romeo's arrival, so she can relish the "day in night" with her lover/husband.

And *we will see this with her*. We will look where she is looking. Our mirror neurons will mirror hers. We will root for her to succeed in her goals – even knowing that no one can make the sun go more quickly forward, and (as the prologue has told us) that her victory, if achieved, will be short-lived. We, in short, will be *transported* to Juliet's world, which is the ultimate goal of acting.

The Direct Address: Oh, What a Rogue…

Not all soliloquies are apostrophes, however. Some seem to have no target other than the character who speaks it, as the Merriam-Webster definition suggests. Hamlet has several. "Oh, what a rogue and peasant slave am I!" he utters, alone onstage. To whom, if not himself, is Hamlet speaking? At whom is he looking? With whom is he (and thus the actor playing him) *interacting* – when not only is there is no one else on stage, but no spirit, or divinity even implied?

The answer is simple: Hamlet (and therefore the actor playing him) is speaking directly to, and interacting with, the theatre audience.

This is the *direct address*, but it is not merely an address. The actor is not merely speaking to the audience but is also asking them questions – "Who would bear the whips and scorns of time…?" "Who would these fardels bear…?" – and begging the audience to give his character a response, even if it is just with their eyes.

The direct address is in fact a two-way street. The *character* speaking it is also quizzing the audience, charming them, often entertaining them with jokes, often dazzling them with his or her aperçus, but always seeking to invoke their respect, their warmth, and their approval, and hoping to sense their bodily clues, their changes in breathing, the excitement in their eyes, the attention of their consciousness, the favor of their expression. She wants their help!

"The audience knows the difference between being talked to and being talked at."

American playwright Sarah Ruhl[11]

Shakespeare wrote a great many direct addresses. Obvious ones include his prologues and choruses, and Elizabethan versions of "program notes" or even "apologias" from the playwright, such as the first chorus of *Henry V* in which an actor comes forward to apologize for the rudimentary scenery with which the company is staging the great fifteenth-century battles between England and France.

Other direct addresses come from characters who come forward to tell us their plans for the future. The Duke of Gloucester begins *Richard III* with a monologue which tells us of his unhappiness that is about to be lifted ("Now is the winter of our discontent..."), and Benedick's comic speech in *Much Ado About Nothing* after he is tricked into thinking Beatrice loves him ("This can be no trick...") is clearly directed to those in the audience attending the play. The actors playing these parts look us right in the eyes, and we look right into theirs.

However, it is virtually indisputable that *all* soliloquies in Shakespeare's plays, other than apostrophes delivered to non-present and/or imaginary characters, spirits, or gods, were spoken *directly to the audience*. How – without having any sixteenth-century photographs – can we know this? Because in the roughly circular Globe Theatre of Shakespeare's company, there was simply no place an actor could look *without* directly facing the upwards of 3000 spectators that surrounded him on all sides! The Globe audience extended at least 300 degrees around the actor, left to right (one scholar says it was a full 360 degrees[12]), and from down at his toes (these would be the "groundlings" standing in the "pit" below him), to far above his head – those seated in the top row of the three-tiered Globe. Moreover, all this was in broad afternoon daylight, which illuminated the actors and the spectators equally. So *of course* Shakespeare knew that his soliloquizing actors, when not staring at the sky or the floor, or looking for the Spirit of Night, or God, or Phaeton's steeds, would *by necessity* be gazing straight at members of the sunlit theatre audience as they spoke.

And why would they do otherwise? Watching a character muse aloud to himself while looking vaguely off into the middle distance is about as exciting as watching a stranger muse aloud to himself on a street corner. Most of us simply turn our heads and scurry past when this happens. But watching Hamlet looking directly at us when he cries out, "Oh, what a rogue and peasant slave am I!" will grab us powerfully. After all, we've been involved with Hamlet and his desires and difficulties since the second scene of the play. Hamlet has talked to us before and we know he will talk to us again; by now, we fully agree with him that "something is rotten in the state of Denmark" and we are rooting for him to "set it right."

The benefit to the actor playing these soliloquies as interactions with the theatergoers is immense, for both actor and audience. Try it yourself: Stand in front of a group of people and say aloud, but looking over their heads as if speaking to yourself, "What a jackass I am!" Then say the same sentence to the same people while looking directly at them. Try to make them *respond* to you instead of merely sharing a personal rumination on your shortcomings. The intensity, complexity, and emotional tone of your line (and particularly the way you say the word "jackass") when you *see these people seeing you* will double, even quadruple. If you don't believe it, ask them; they'll tell you.

Then do the same with Hamlet's "O what a rogue" line. It will almost certainly feel more impassioned, more engaging, and more intelligent – and will be spoken with far better diction and precision – than will your "thinking aloud" version. It will be received thus by your listeners as well. What audience would not prefer this second manner of acting the speech?

Indeed, actors now perform non-apostrophic soliloquies mostly this way in professional Shakespearean productions. Their soliloquies then become *interactions with the audience*. When Hamlet offers his "To be or not to be" question on today's stage, he is rarely debating with himself, he is far more often seeking our support. Throughout the play, he poses us similar questions: "How stand I, then…?" "Must I remember…?" "Who calls me villain…?" "What is a man, if his chief good and market of his time be but to sleep and feed?" Literary analysts often call these "rhetorical questions" because they do not stimulate a spoken reply – but in the theatre, the audience's bewildered silence *is itself a reply*. Our reluctance to respond tells Hamlet, "Wow, this is a tough one!" And it *is* a tough one. In a melodrama, when the villain comes down to the audience, twirls his moustache, and, pointing to the damsel in distress, asks us, "Shall I let her go?" we holler, "Yes!" When Peter Pan asks us to applaud if we believe in fairies, we applaud mightily and tears come to our eyes. But when we are silent after Hamlet asks us "What is a man…?" we cannot speak because we are just as conflicted about the question as he is. And when Hamlet, looking us squarely in the eye, tells us that "conscience doth make cowards of us all," it is clear that he is not only talking to us, he is talking *about* us – all of us. Who amongst "us all" will not be drawn deeper into the play, and into Hamlet's (and therefore the actor's) mind, when these soliloquies are played in such a manner? We want to answer him, but we can't.

And sometimes, the audience does answer! Samuel West, who played Hamlet for the Royal Shakespeare Company in 2001, recalls an evening when he asked the audience "Am I a coward?" and a man in the balcony hollered back "Yes!" West describes this as "perfect… I could play the next line, 'Who calls me villain?' while scanning that part of the house looking for him." By meeting the audience's eyes, West explains, his Hamlet was essentially telling them, "I'm talking to you. I can't go on with the play until I talk to you."[13]

So when Hamlet's soliloquies are not apostrophes to God ("O God! God!…"), or to his absent mother ("O most pernicious woman!"), or uncle ("Bloody, bawdy, villain!"), or father ("Ay, thou poor ghost…"), they are proposals to the audience. He is looking at us for a response, perhaps a smile, a laugh, a tear, a puzzled frown, a nod of sympathy, or even a holler from the back row. He is creating a dialogue with us, studying us for our reactions, asking for our help. We are his private audience, and his public audience as well.

When Shakespearean characters address us so directly, they invite us to share – not just hear – their thoughts. Often they invite our participation in planning their future actions. In *Twelfth Night,* Viola is confronted by Malvolio who gives her a ring, explaining that his Lady Olivia has commanded him to "return" it to her; once he departs, Viola turns to us and says, "I left no ring with her: what means this Lady?" Viola is asking *us* what Olivia had in mind – for after all, we saw the previous scene after Viola had left the stage, when Olivia gave the ring to Malvolio and told him what to say. And in the next 25 lines she asks us our opinions about all this: "How will this fadge?…What will become of this?" The Duke of Gloucester (Richard III), Aaron in *Titus Andronicus,* and Iago in *Othello* all develop their malevolent plots right in front of us, looking at us as if to determine how they should proceed. Aaron, alone on stage, explains to us how he will seduce Tamora: "I will be bright, and shine in pearl and gold to wait upon this new-made empress." Then, seeing that we have raised no objections to this plan, he becomes bold enough to improve on what he just said: "To wait, said I? To *wanton* with this queen!" He is using *our* silence to intensify *his* revenge. Iago all but asks us to collaborate with him as he improvises his plan to betray his rival Cassio right before our eyes: "Cassio's a proper man: let me see now: To get his place and to plume up my will, in double knavery – How? How? Let's see…I have it!" Iago's "Let me see now" and "How? How?" make clear that Iago has begun his speech without knowing how he will end it. He is making decisions based on our moment-to-moment reactions to his evolving plan. And we, by witnessing all this and not "calling the police," as it were, have become Iago's partners in evil. For, against our better natures, we have delighted in this monster's cunning! This is the strange magic of theatre.

The (Focused) Self Address

Do characters *never* talk to themselves? Well, yes, sometimes they do – but it is almost always (if not always) some special *part* of themselves, physical, or spiritual, that they address. Juliet cries to her heart: "O, break, my heart! Poor bankrupt, break at once!" Hamlet cries to his mind: "My thoughts be bloody, or be nothing worth!" Othello speaks to his soul: "It is the cause, it is the cause, my soul." Macbeth speaks to his hand, which is closing in on the dagger he thinks he sees before it: "Come, let me clutch thee." And King Lear cries out to the anguish in his loins that "swells up toward my heart." "Hysterica passio!" he roars to it, "Down, thy climbing sorrow!" Indeed, Menenius (in Shakespeare's *Coriolanus*) even describes a metaphorical "conversation" that takes place among the body's major organs: specifically the "crowned head, the cormorant belly, the vigilant eye, the counselor heart, the arm our soldier, our steed the leg, the tongue our trumpeter." Even when talking to "ourselves," Shakespeare implies, we generally narrow our focus onto individual body parts.

We can characterize such soliloquized fragments as "focused self-addresses," because they are focused on just a single part of the speaker's own physical or mental self. In his famous soliloquy on the heath, which he considers a prayer ("I'll pray, and then I'll sleep," he has said just before beginning it), Lear alternates apostrophes with a carefully focused self-address:

> LEAR: Poor naked wretches, wheresoe'er you are,
> That bide the pelting of this pitiless storm,
> How shall your houseless heads and unfed sides,
> Your loop'd and window'd raggedness, defend you
> From seasons such as these? O, I have ta'en
> Too little care of this! Take physic, pomp;
> Expose thyself to feel what wretches feel,
> That thou mayst shake the superflux to them
> And show the heavens more just.

The soliloquy begins as an apostrophe to the "poor naked wretches" who, though not present at the moment, populate the heath. "O, I have ta'en too little care of this!" is most likely an apostrophe to the gods in whom Lear believes (having referred to "the great gods, that keep this dreadful pudder o'er our heads" earlier during the storm). But the remainder of Lear's speech is clearly directed to his own pomposity, or to "Pride" – one of the Seven Deadly Sins with which he seems preoccupied, having used the term previously to insult Kent, Cordelia, Goneril, and Oswald when he believes they have done him wrong.

Breaking this speech into separate formats is important not just because it classifies Lear's varied targets, but because it makes clear that every sentence he speaks is *part of a dialogue*, not a monologue. Lear is both looking in and reaching out. He is alternating his remarks to wretches, gods, sins, and to anyone that might be in hearing distance (the silent Kent is there with him and the Fool has just ducked into the shelter), and he wants all heaven to know what he is doing. And from each of these targets he hopes for a response. When, shortly after the speech, he yanks off his clothes ("Off, off, you lendings! Come, unbutton here"), he turns his words into physical actions. His "soliloquy" is an attempt to communicate with his entire universe.

The Soliloquy – from the Greeks to Tony Kushner

Let's move away from Shakespeare now. Although his soliloquies are the world's most famous, almost *every* playwright in theatre history has written such speeches. Soliloquies were common in ancient Greek tragedy where, as in Shakespeare's Globe, they could not *not* be spoken to the audience, since the audience was seated directly behind the chorus to which the characters were presumed to be speaking. So, as we have noted, when Oedipus speaks to the chorus of (fictional) tenth-century BC Theban citizens, he simultaneously speaks to the (real) fifth-century BC citizens of Athens watching the play. Soliloquies were even more common in ancient Greek comedy – indeed, *every* comedy of Aristophanes featured a long soliloquy (called a parabasis) that was delivered directly to the audience, possibly by Aristophanes himself. Medieval English dramas – which Shakespeare's audiences grew up on – routinely featured characters that spoke directly to the audience; a fifteenth-century actor playing Herod, for example, leapt off the stage and ran about the spectators, yelling at them; and Noah and his Wife, in the various medieval plays about them, argued ferociously about the respective duties of husbands and wives as argued throughout rural England of that era. From ancient times to the Industrial Age – through the *commedia dell'arte* of the early Renaissance to the subsequent plays of Molière, Goethe, the English Restoration and nineteenth-century European and American farce and melodrama – characters have spoken soliloquies and asides directly to the audience. Even when realism reared its head around the 1870s, dramatists worldwide continued the practice. Henrik Ibsen, sometimes known as the playwright who "killed off the soliloquy," had his title character in *Hedda Gabler,* alone on stage, burn a rival's manuscript in the fireplace while apostrophizing the rival's girlfriend: "Now I'm burning your child, Thea! You, with your curly hair! Your child and Eilert Lovborg's!" But, of course, Thea is nowhere to be seen – only the audience sees or hears this line. And the great master of modern realism, Anton Chekhov, included soliloquies in almost all his plays, from one-acts like *Swan Song* and *On The Harmfulness of Tobacco*, to his major masterpieces *Ivanov, The Seagull*, and *The Cherry Orchard*.

Even famous mid-century American realists have used them. Tennessee Williams ends *Glass Menagerie* with Tom's apostrophe to his absent sister ("Blow out your candles, Laura"). In *After the Fall*, Arthur Miller places an imagined "psychiatrist" in the midst of the audience so that his principal character (and hence the actor playing him) can make his confessions a dialogue with his invisible "therapist in the house," along with the spectators conveniently surrounding him. Postmodern drama has vastly increased the presence of soliloquies in today's theatre. The European surrealists, absurdists, meta-theatricalists, and followers of Bertolt Brecht's "epic theatre" have made the apostrophe and direct address virtual staples of their work in the twentieth and twenty-first centuries. In today's drama they are everywhere, in Tony Kushner's *Angels in America*, Julia Cho's *The Language Archive*, Sarah Ruhl's *The Clean House*, Tracy Letts' *Superior Donuts*, Brian Friel's *Faith Healer*, and of course in one-person plays, including Neil LaBute's *Wrecks*, Jay Presson Allen's *Tru*, Willy Russell's *Shirley Valentine* and Doug Wright's *I Am My Own Wife*. The soliloquy today is as common on stage as it was in the Greek *theatron* and Shakespeare's Globe.

The question remains, however, how is the soliloquy to be performed in modern realism? Apostrophes are not much of a problem: no one today thinks twice about watching Hedda speak, as it were, to the absent Thea as she tosses her pages into her fireplace. But the same can be true of the direct address. While most American productions of Chekhov stage his soliloquies in the Merriam-Webster fashion, as dreamy (and I'm afraid often dreary) ruminations on the character's woes, I have found that actors performing Kostya's pre-suicidal soliloquy in *The Seagull* as a direct address to the audience can completely enrapture both the actors who speak them and the spectators who hear them. It turns out that audiences no longer need to be continually shielded from realizing they are in a theatre watching a play. In the age that follows Brecht, Beckett, and their kin, just as in the eras of Aristophanes and Shakespeare, we live comfortably in more than one place at a time. Today we watch mini-advertisements of upcoming shows that sneak into the lower corners of TV dramas. In films, we hear the final spoken dialogue in one scene overlapping the initial visual images of the next one, and have learned to flash back and flash forward without blinking an eye or re-adjusting our time frames. TV editors even cut to brief soliloquies in sitcoms spoken right to the camera (as in "The Office" and "Modern Family"). We no longer need to wait for the curtain call in order to co-exist, in the same time and space, with the actors on the stage or screen. The soliloquy has come out of the closet and out of the confessional booth. It is an action, an *interaction*, and it is very much alive on stage.

Exercise: Shakespearean soliloquies

Memorize and perform a Shakespearean soliloquy to a real audience, considering the soliloquy as an interaction between yourself and an audience-chorus. Try, with your soliloquy, to convince the audience-chorus of your character's rightness, your character's great intelligence, your character's superior wit, and your character's overall winsomeness. Try to develop a bandwagon effect on the audience/chorus, and convince them that you are going to win, and that it is to their advantage to join with you now. Try any of the following soliloquies, drawn from comedies as well as tragedies:

- The Duke of Gloucester in *Richard III*. His opening soliloquy is a particularly difficult one, since it is usually played with the actor obviously intending to show us how loathsome Richard is. Play it, however, *as* Richard instead of *about* him, and show us how *marvelous* you are. If you must tell us that you are "rudely stamp'd," then do so either for our sympathy or for our amusement (which you share). When you tell us that "dogs bark at me as I halt by them," either make that a sarcastic joke (meaning "The world says all kinds of slanderous things about me – that dogs bark at me when I pass, that sort of stuff – but you and I know different, don't we?") or as a testament to your unflagging self-knowledge and superior honesty ("Look, I know who I am, which is a heck of a lot better than the other characters in this play"). Emphasize that you, as Richard, "delight" to "descant on mine own deformity;" explaining that you like one thing above all else, which is to make lovely music (a descant) out of your physical handicaps, and that the plots and murders you are now planning before our eyes are really a glorious fugue which the audience will be privileged to admire. Play Richard's soliloquy, then, as a *positive, goal-oriented interaction* with the audience, and try to get them on your side.
- Viola's "I left no ring with her," from *Twelfth Night*. Try to get the audience-chorus's assistance to "untangle this…knot" that leaves you in such great distress. Make the question "What will become of this?" a real question to the audience-chorus, try to make them give some sort of answer, with their eyes, their expression, their interest. Try out various hypotheses on them; try to get their help.
- Petruchio's "Thus have I politicly begun my reign," from *The Taming of the Shrew*. Here your goal is to convince the audience – which you expect to be male and male chauvinistic – that you are the cleverest marital expert of all time and that your plan is the best, most humane, most inspired ever invented. When, at the end of the soliloquy, you demand of the audience "He that knows better how to tame a shrew, now let him speak," make that a genuine challenge; make the audience want – and fail – to answer!
- Romeo's "He jests at scars that never felt a wound," from *Romeo and Juliet*. This speech is not ordinarily played to the audience; as an exercise, however, do play it to them, trying to get their moral support for your pursuit of your beloved Juliet. Convince them – now your private audience, your "personal chorus" – that your love is great enough to transcend the obstacles you will face wooing a Capulet. Make your tentative and sometimes contradictory self-commands a test. When you say "Her eye discourses, I will answer it" and then reverse yourself with "I am too bold, 'tis not to me she speaks," try to sense which course of action your audience-chorus will support. Bolt forward when saying "I will answer it," and then quickly retreat for cover on "I am too bold" so as to *ferret out* your audience-chorus's position on your very delicate and confused situation. Get their help – for most of them are older and wiser than you are!

There is an interesting quirk to this scene. Juliet appears above at Romeo's first line, though Romeo apparently does not see her. It is not at all unrealistic, however, to assume that Romeo might be having this interaction with the audience-chorus in order that Juliet, in her bedroom, would overhear it! This will reverse the ordinary theatrical relationship: the audience will become the chorus, and Juliet will be Romeo's intended "audience." Play the scene, then, as an *interaction* with the audience-chorus and as a *performance* for the (hidden) target of his remarks, Juliet.

- Hamlet's "To be or not to be," or "Now I am alone," or "Now might I do it pat," or "How all occasions do inform against me," or Ophelia's "O, what a noble mind is here o'erthrown," or Claudius' "O, my offence is rank, it smells to heaven." All of these, of course, are from the play of *Hamlet*. They are perhaps among the most famous soliloquies in dramatic literature, but they are not, for that reason, mere poems played upon a stage. There is a political nature to this play, which concerns not just fathers and sons, kings and princes, but general public opinion. Claudius explains to Laertes that he cannot act directly against Hamlet not only because of "the great love the general gender bear him," but because they, "dipping all his faults in their affection, would...convert his gyves [defects, literally "fetters"] to graces." Claudius also worries about "the people muddied," and Laertes comes in leading a "rabble" of them. Clearly, there is a general public to be persuaded in this play, and these soliloquies can and should be performed, at least in part, as the characters' efforts to win the support of the Danish populace, men and women, and to gain the love of the "general gender."
- Lady Macbeth's "The raven himself is hoarse," in *Macbeth*. The soliloquy is ostensibly addressed to the "spirits that tend on mortal thoughts." Place those spirits in the audience-chorus. When you ask them to "unsex me here," try and make them do exactly that. Do not play these statements as mere rhetoric, make them invocations for real action. Demand results!
- Iago's "Thus do I ever make my fool my purse," in *Othello*. Try, with the speech, to make the audience share your disdain for Cassio and Othello. Make them laugh with you. Make them enjoy you. Enjoy them!
- Edmund's first soliloquy ("Thou, Nature, art my goddess") in *King Lear*. Taunt the audience directly with your repeated questions: "Why brand they us / With base? with baseness? bastardy? base, base?" Make them realize how prejudiced your society is (and perhaps your audience members are). Look them right in the eye! Make them uncomfortable!
- Othello's "It is the cause, it is the cause, my soul." Try to make the audience validate your intended action, and the moral rightness of your cause. Make a pitch to God that you should go to heaven with this speech.
- Beatrice's "What fire is in mine ears?" from *Much Ado About Nothing*. This is really a quadruple-target soliloquy, first directed to the audience, then to her own sins, then to Benedick. and finally to Benedick's friends, and perhaps the audience as well. Note all four targets of her speech. The first is right after

Beatrice, in hiding, overhears what she believes is a casual conversation (but is in fact a rehearsed one) between her two friends indicating that Benedick, with whom she has been sparring for years, actually loves her. When the friends depart Beatrice asks the audience to verify what she has just heard:

> What fire is in mine ears? Can this be true?
> Stand I condemn'd for pride and scorn so much?

Hearing no objections from the audience, Beatrice then apostrophizes to her earlier sins of Wrath and Pride, disowning them both:

> Contempt, farewell! and maiden pride, adieu!
> No glory lives behind the back of such.

And then she delivers an apostrophe of love to the non-present Benedick:

> And, Benedick, love on; I will requite thee,
> Taming my wild heart to thy loving hand:
> If thou dost love, my kindness shall incite thee
> To bind our loves up in a holy band;

And finally she shares this apostrophe with the friends she has just overheard, and others in the play who, she realizes, have been supporting Benedick all along:

> For others say thou dost deserve, and I
> Believe it better than reportingly.

The imaginary audience-chorus

The Greek chorus is decidedly real, since it consists of costumed actors who actually speak lines and express specific opinions about matters. In the Shakespearean soliloquy, the chorus is imaginary. In the mind of the character who addresses them in a soliloquy, the "actor-character" is addressing an "audience-chorus."

The audience-chorus does not disappear, however, when the soliloquy ends. Iago, who addresses the audience directly on many occasions, does not suddenly become oblivious to their presence when Cassio enters. He continues to "play to" the audience-chorus in the ensuing scene; he continues to solicit their support. The analogy might be made with a trial attorney in a criminal case. The attorney will sometimes address the jury directly, as in his summation speech. In that case, he interacts with the jury, and speaks and performs directly to them. This is his direct address. But he is playing to them, performing for them, at every moment of the trial: when he is cross examining a witness, approaching the bench, or merely sitting at his table with his client. His only goal is to win his case, and the only way he can win it is through the jury. Performing in almost every play can be summed up as its characters each trying to "win over" the theatre audience, not with their acting skills but with the rightness of their cause and the appeal of their character's personality.

We can now take this a step further. There is no reason at all why this need apply solely to soliloquies. The fact that Iago turns to Cassio when Cassio enters at the end of his soliloquy does not mean that Iago stops playing for the audience's approval, and the fact that Cassio never soliloquizes to the audience does not mean that Cassio does not also play for their approval. Indeed, he has presumably seen, from behind, the last words of Iago as he talks to the audience, and he obviously is aware that there is "an audience" out there, even if he never directly addresses it. The soliloquy, when it exists, is only a segue as a character turns from one audience (Iago to the audience) to another (Iago to Cassio). This imaginary audience-chorus-other is a fabrication of every character, whether a soliloquizer or not. It is an imaginary fabrication, but at the same time it is as real as anything "mental" is real; it is as real as hope, fear, and headaches. It stems from psychological realities, particularly the universal egocentricity by which each character feels in the presence of a favoring audience-chorus. We all feel that the world – at least *our* world, which is the only one we really deeply care about, day-by-day and minute-by-minute – revolves around us. We all feel that the people in the world are eager observers of our behavior – or at least should be – and are, potentially, the "general gender" that we hope, in the final analysis, will rally to our support.

The actor's job, then, in "theatricalizing" her character, is to develop the character's audience-chorus, to characterize them, to plant them, and to play to them. Two marvelous mechanisms tie this all together in one final, perfect, alignment:

- the audience-chorus can be the character's "private audience," (see Chapter 3) and;
- the audience can be planted in the back rows of the real audience.

These mechanisms pull theatricality out of the actor together with characterization and style. They provide the preconditions which make theatricality a necessity of the character's situation rather than an exigency of the actor's context, and which make theatricality real and dramatic reality theatrical.

The private audience in the public one

The private audience, as I have presented it, are those people a character carries about in her head – both the individuals who draw from her the unique inclinations and incentives that determine her character, and those who induce from her the collective social behaviors that define the play's style.

Having created and internalized that private audience, the actor's next – and final – mental task is to "plant" that audience in the public one. She plants them as the audience-chorus to her character's behavior, not in the first rows of the public audience, as a Greek chorus, but in the back rows as well. From that point on, she never has to look at them directly, talk to them directly, or acknowledge their existence in any way. Her relationship to them is like the skier's relationship to her partisans lining the route. But she will know they are there. She will project to them. She will stimulate them. She will play for their highly specialized, highly special support, and toward their highly-characterized and highly styled demands.

Example: Man and Superman

In Shaw's Man and Superman, for example, the actor playing Jack Tanner should create Tanner's private audience. He should imagine them in full embodiment and then should "plant" them in the real audience watching the Man and Superman production. This audience is composed of the persons he most admires: his socialist teachers and fellow students at Oxford (where he could be imagined to have studied), his brilliant friends in the socialist Fabian Society (to which Shaw belonged), and his disciples in his soap-box speeches given at Hyde Park Corner (where Shaw gave speeches). In arguing with Ramsden, he will be talking to Ramsden, but he will probably also be performing for his friend Octavius (Tavy) who he presumes is somewhere in the house, and for the house's servants, who, unlike Ramsden, are probably socialists too, although they cannot admit this in their boss's presence. And he will also be speaking to, and on behalf of, his private audience who he imagines is somewhere out in the auditorium. And he may also be rehearsing his upcoming speech to a college debating society. He will use all of these imaginary or potential "audiences" to help him get the most out of himself. And by so doing he will be working simultaneously toward a specific characterization and a specific style calculated to win himself a great victory over Ramsden, which will be conveyed to the real audience with a tremendous and infectious theatricality. And if he really believes he is *right* in what he is saying, and tries to convince his private audience that he is right, he will be heard loud and clear both in the wings of the theatre and the back row of its house – and probably in the dressing rooms below.

The real audience then becomes a real weapon in Tanner's quest for the Ramsden defeat. Every laugh Tanner gets from the real audience is another blow to Ramsden. Every shudder he gets from them for his brilliant rhetorical twists digs the knife deeper into his foe. Every gasp at his stunning linguistic reversals makes Ramsden all the more abashed, because Ramsden knows that he is now outnumbered as well as out-smarted! Even his servants can see that he's losing this debate. Even the audience of strangers in front of him are coming to realize he's a loser. Tanner's very theatricality serves the character's purpose as well as it serves that of the actor playing him.

"All you have to be concerned about is whether or not you've got something to say; if you've got something to say, they'll hear you. That's how you approach a role: Find out what it is you've got to say."

American actor Sean Penn, on
"How to be heard in the back row"[14]

The actor using the imaginary audience-chorus as his stimulus for theatricality, therefore, does not play to the "real" style of the "real" audience, but to an imaginary audience sitting in the real seats. The transformation the actor makes, then, is not in herself but in the audience. She doesn't characterize herself; she characterizes *them*. She stylizes them. In Jack Tanner's case the actor is not trying to make the audience see him as a Shavian character, but to see *them* as a Shavian *audience*.

Theatricality, like character and style, is thus played not directly but reciprocally. Theatricality comes from assumptions and preconditions planted in and about the real audience – essentially, the precondition that the real audience is the character's own private audience, and that it can be addressed as a wise chorus to the character's wise remarks, and a brave and heroic chorus to the characters' brave and heroic behaviors. In making these plants, these preconditions, the actor becomes the ultimate creator of her own performance. She becomes an artist.

Example: Restoration comedy

The comedy of the Restoration period affords us a grand example of the potential for this transformation. We know the nature of the English audience in the Restoration era from a variety of contemporary accounts. It was composed of a highly-elite crowd of sycophants to the court: a group characterized by wit, bitchiness, amorousness, competitiveness, pseudo-regality, anti-intellectuality, and a widespread contempt for all classes beneath the aristocracy. Peasants were accounted positively vile. Physical beauty was in great demand, particularly when displayed with great artifice. The city was the epitome of the life force; the country was a vast, unendurable wasteland, and the only existing civilized society outside of London (and then but dimly) was in Paris.

Actors during the Restoration catered blithely to this audience, both onstage and off. The comedies were as much about the audience as for them, and the plays were filled with local and immediate allusions, references to members of the audience, places at which the audience would gather after the performance, and, more than anything perhaps, love affairs and sexual escapades between the actors and their patrons – including the King. Although the theatres were indoors, the audience area was almost as brightly illuminated as the stage.

In creating the special Restoration theatricality of the seventeenth century, then, it is necessary to create not merely the Restoration "style," but the Restoration audience. The actors must address the audience not as a collection of twentieth-century theatregoers, but as a court of sycophants to Charles II. What this does is quite astonishing: it makes the audience act! If the actor-characters address the audience as though the audience were a group of Restoration fops and mistresses, the audience will consider itself a group of Restoration fops and mistresses! Then the male actor can "fop" at them and the female actors (the first in English history since medieval times) can flounce at them with all the confidence, enthusiasm, and foppishness at their command. A truly theatrical experience of this sort, with a communion of actors and audience, has the effect of changing the audience's collective pre-conception of itself, of "transporting" the audience to another world. The audience members at a successful Restoration comedy staged in our own era, for example, should not feel so much as though they were twentieth-century "peekers-in" at a Restoration happening; they should feel that they themselves are in the Restoration, even if the play is staged in modern dress. That, of course, is why people come to the theatre in the first place: not to watch something, but to have an experience – which, essentially, is to act. This is the final – and most laudable – goal of theatricality: to liberate the audience, to transport them into a different world, to make them feel witty, to give them not a moving picture of reality but a real experience in living. And in "acting."

Example: Realism – The Zoo Story

Theatricality is not, of course, limited to the highly stylized productions of Shaw or the Restoration. It is equally essential in realism or naturalism, for in both of these styles the actors must make their principal points clear and engaging to the real audience.* In both styles the actors must project meaning, characterization, and intensity.

We may look at Edward Albee's *The Zoo Story* as a well-known, realistic play that can exemplify this. In the play a hyped-up social outcast (Jerry) meets a timid, middle-rank publishing executive (Peter) on a bench in Central Park. Jerry badgers Peter into talking with him, and after a long, rambling, seemingly discontinuous conversation, Jerry prods Peter into fighting with him, and

---

* Naturalism is usually described as extreme realism; there are differences, but none pertinent to this discussion. Occasionally persons consider "style" as something that is distinguished from naturalism or realism; both, however, are themselves styles and cannot really be considered otherwise.

eventually killing him. Most of the dialogue is conversational, and while the play has philosophical, social, and religious themes, it can certainly stand as a credible, if unusual, interaction between two mid-twentieth century individuals.

Jerry's private audience is obviously a strong factor in his behavior, since his long rambling speeches are clearly not addressed, in the main, to his present hearer. Jerry's private audience must include, primarily, his parents, who in his mind abandoned him at an early age. His private audience is exemplified by the two empty picture frames which, he explains, adorn the wall of his rooming-house garret. There are also his faithless and deserting lovers, rooming-house neighbors, a sister, and a dog. And there is God, who, Jerry says, "turned his back on the whole thing some time ago." Clearly much of Jerry's extended conversation, while aimed at Peter, is mainly intended for Jerry's private and imaginary audience. Peter too has a private audience, at whose composition we can only guess. There is his wife, who presumably resembles his mother, and is something of a feared and dominating figure. Then there is his executive supervisor, and the authors whose work he is required to read and, eventually, resent. Then there are his disappointing parents. Finally, there are common members of both of the men's private audiences: the unseen but clearly nearby Central Park policemen and passersby, to whom much of their mutual behavior is directed. When Peter says, at one point, "I feel ridiculous," and Jerry replies "You look ridiculous," it is in the eyes of the imaginary Central Park passerby that this "ridiculousness" takes shape.

The actors in Zoo Story can bring out the theatricality of their situation (which, like the situation of any good play, is theatrical) by planting those "private audience" members in the back row of the house, and by playing the Jerry-Peter interaction as though it were being overheard and overseen by those particular individuals. Jerry, we soon realize, is still trying to please his (dead) father; Peter is still trying to impress his long-given-up wife. If the actors imagine these non-present individuals sitting in the back row of the theatre, there need be no further question of the play "getting across the footlights." It will get across, and with its credibility not diminished but enhanced.

Example: Brecht and Verfremdungseffekt

The theatre of twentieth-century playwright and director Bertolt Brecht illustrates another type of theatricality, one somewhat more complex than either the Restoration or realistic type.

Brecht's revolutionary "epic theatre" formulation is best known for its use of what Brecht called the Verfremdungseffekt, which translates best as "distancing effect" – or, in earlier translations, "alienation effect." Brecht's idea was that the actor should remain a solid step apart from her role and should not try to "become" her character as much as represent her. According to Brecht, the actor "never forgets, nor does he allow anyone to forget that he is not the one whose action is being demonstrated, but the one who demonstrates it."[15] The theory was controversial in its time (Brecht first formulated it in 1932) and remains controversial today, particularly among followers of Strasberg and Stanislavsky. The fact remains, however, that its basic tenets can be seen in most European and British stage productions today, and a great many American productions – even commercial ones – as well. It is not, however, in any way inconsistent with the basic principles of this book; indeed, it is closely wedded to them.

The distancing in epic theatre acting is dual: there is a sense of separation between the actor and her role, and a similar separation between the audience and their feelings. A "distanced" audience, Brecht reasoned, should not be swept up by the play's story, and the emotions it may arouse, so much that it would cause them to neglect the more important social issues that comprise the play's theme. Social themes, not personalities or "stories," are the ultimate focus of Brecht's plays, at least in the playwright's intention. And a "distanced" actor can allow the audience that focus. The actor, Brecht insisted, "does not allow himself to become completely transformed on the stage into the character he is portraying." He must rather "stand alongside the role" and present it to us as one might present the details of a car accident.

The theatre of distancing usually employs various epic theatre mechanisms – songs, signs, direct address, and other plot interruptions – an open acknowledgment of the audience's presence much like in the Shakespearean soliloquy convention. But what distinguishes the theatre of distancing above all is that the theatre audience and the character's private audience fully become one and the same. The characters in Brecht's plays – Mother Courage, Grusha, MacHeath, Polly Peachum, and the dual character of Shen Te/Shui Ta – perform to each other and, with equal force, to the theatre audiences that come to see them and to learn from them. There is therefore a strong community between the actors and the audience, which also includes the playwright and the production's design team. This is the "ensemble" (in the sense of "together") that is the core of Brecht's famous theatre, the Berliner Ensemble. Such an ensemble of theatre practitioners and theatergoers narrows the characters' reliance on their everyday psychology and fixations, and enlarges their commitment to social and political principles, theses, and themes. It makes them demonstrators as much as fleshed-out human beings.

The audience in a Brecht play is not expressly characterized. Rather, it is seen as an audience of contemporaries, presumably predisposed to Brecht's socialist humanism (or why would they be coming to a Brechtian play?). The Brechtian actor sees the Brechtian audience as part of her own extended family, as interested as she is in the progressive development of a humanized, socialized civilization. The Brechtian actor-character will look at the audience, speak to them, and share her feelings, gestures, ideas, and dialogue with them. More importantly, she will listen to them. She will study and observe them, and openly receive feedback from them. She will make them as important, in the play's development, as she is herself. The distancing in Brechtian theatre is not at all between the actors and the audience, as a few misguided American directors seem to think. Quite the contrary, it is between the actors and their characters, for between Brecht's actors and Brecht's audience there flows great mutual trust, great love, and a great spirit that says "together we will build a better world." At least when things are going well, I suppose.

One of the ironies of early Brechtian productions in America was the seeming reversal of this idea, where, going by the mistranslation of *verfremdung* as "alienation," actors were encouraged to despise the audience as being tasteless dopes or perhaps rich plutocrats. In some early American "Brechtian" productions, when the actors would come forward in the curtain call and the audience would applaud, the actors would snarl at them and, in nasty mockery of their applause, pound their palms together as if squashing bugs, and treat the audience as if they were a bunch of dolts, fascists, racists, or worse. Nothing could be less "Brechtian," or less epic. Brecht's plays and his productions were never intended to be diatribes against the people who came to see them.

But it is also true that Brechtian theatre did not seek, as does much American drama and theatre, to make its actors deeply realistic or its characters likeable. Epic theatre pays little attention to an individual character's unique psychology or random idiosyncrasies; rather, it concentrates on social orientations and political themes. It also concentrates on *interactions* over solo displays of feelings, thoughts, and behavior: Brecht insisted that his actors should replace the word "lines" that they used in regard to their speeches, with the word "rejoinders," which indicated that "each remark or reply contains an element of opposition."

Thus there is, in Brecht's theatre, a recognizable distance between the unique human actor and the generalized social character. That character is *demonstrated* more than individually *inhabited* by the Brechtian performer. This is the "estrangement" of the *Verfremdungseffekt*; it is a filter between the actor and her role. What Brecht finally intended was to dissolve the difference between dramatic interaction and theatrical performance, and make his actors and audience communicate on a level field.

Does it work? Doesn't the Brechtian still "become" the character she demonstrates? Brecht insisted no, but that might simply be rhetoric: Brecht's own "performance" as he strived to distinguish his theory as unique and thereby become known as a theatrical revolutionary. Which he certainly did. But becoming a character certainly involves engaging in the character's interactions, and this the Brechtian actor clearly does. In fact, Brecht's own plays succeeded almost in direct relation to the degree to which the audience accepted the actor as the character she played, much to Brecht's chagrin. At the premiere of his *Mother Courage and Her Children* in Zurich, Brecht claimed to be dismayed when the audience wept when Mother Courage loses her beloved son in the final scene. For the revival, he replaced the actress in that part with his wife, Helene Weigel. The audience was in tears again. So Brecht did not finally dismiss emotion. "The representation of human behavior… is bound to release emotional effects," he eventually admitted. "Epic theatre…by no means renounces emotion."[16]

213

The effect of Brecht's epic theatre can be absolutely staggering, and its great influence on contemporary staging and acting theories is a fact of modern theatre history. The Brechtian theatre, when artfully produced, transports the audience into a state of social indignation and awareness. In treating his audiences with enormous respect, Brecht made them respect themselves – particularly for sharing his views. His theatre is called "didactic," but it does not lecture as much as Ibsen's theatre, nor harangue as much as Shaw's. Rather, it induces, by the process of direct interaction, the development of its audience's social consciousness. It is this audience that must be the actor's private audience in Brecht, and this audience that she must see in the auditorium seats before her. Then her performance takes on the "alienated theatricality" that Brecht intended; alienated not from the audience and not from the play's ideas, but from anything extraneous to their coming together.

Brecht and Stanislavsky

Brecht and Stanislavsky are considered the polarities of contemporary acting theory. Brecht considered that Stanislavsky wanted actors to act "by hypnosis." "They go into a trance and take the audience with them," he said. Stanislavsky, on the other hand, believed that the actor's primary task was to be "living the role" (*perezhivanie* in Russian), and that her "prime task is not only to portray the life of a role externally, but above all to create the inner life of the character."[17] But their differences have been grossly exaggerated. Both are known for the extent to which they "went to the edge" on their own theories, but they probably shared the 90 per cent of acting theory which is somewhere between their most extreme positions. And they knew it. Towards the end of his career, Stanislavsky retracted many of his more radical notions, and even condemned them. To Stella Adler, he famously said, "If my system doesn't work for you, don't use it." He critiqued one of his MAT actors by saying, "What's false here? You're playing feelings, your own suffering, that's what's false. I need to see the event and how you react to that event, how you fight people – how you react, not suffer...To [do what you are doing] is to be passive and sentimental." And when an actress asked him about "emotional recall," Stanislavsky's response was: "What idiot thought that up?" But Brecht too was quite willing to relinquish his theory when an actor came up with something better. "Acting [should not be] made into something purely technical and more or less inhuman by my insistence that the actor oughtn't to be completely transformed into the character portrayed," he once wrote. "This is not the case. Such an impression must be due to my way of writing.... To hell with my way of writing."[18]

For the separation between "actor" and "character" is, after all, a pure abstraction. There is but one body, one face, one voice. Impersonation, no matter in what spirit it is undertaken, carries an undifferentiated impact.

Role Distance

There is yet another connection between Stanislavsky's and Brecht's notions that shows them to be deeply interconnected in the human psyche. For this I would like to advance the idea of "role distance," as developed by Canadian sociologist Erving Goffman, mentioned earlier in this book for his dramaturgical approach to human interaction in his masterful *The Presentation of Self in Everyday Life* and its indelible connection to acting on the stage.

In a later essay, called "Role Distance," Goffman discovered a surprising change in the behavior of children at various stages in their lives when riding merry-go-rounds. While two-year-olds are too physically immature to enjoy being on a whirling carousel, he discovered, three- and four-year-olds undertake the task "rapturously." "The rider throws himself into the role in a serious way, playing it with verve and an engagement of all his faculties," Goffman explains. For them, "*doing is being*," and the three-year-old "fully embraces the performer's "role." This is, of course, Stanislavsky's notion of the actor "living the part." [19]

But by age five, everything has changed. "To be a merry-go-round horse rider is now apparently not enough, and this fact must be demonstrated out of dutiful regard for one's own character," Goffman discovered. By five, "irreverence begins," and the child "leans back, stands on the saddle, holds on to the horse's wooden ear, and says by his actions: 'Whatever I am, I'm not just someone who can barely manage to stay on a wooden horse!' The five-year-old is hence 'apologizing,' for playing the role." He therefore places "a wedge between the individual and his role, between doing and being." This wedge is role distance.

In the ensuing years, the role distance gets greater. The teenage rider considers the ride solely as "a lark, a situation for mockery." Adult riders carry role distance even further: when riding with their three-year-old offspring, the parents "wear a face that carefully demonstrates that they do not perceive the ride as an event in itself," making clear that they're only there because of their child. This is the ultimate role distance.

This change *exactly parallels* the difference between Stanislavsky's "living the part" and Brecht's distancing effect. The three-year-old lives the role of the zebra-rider, while the five-year-old presents it in a distanced fashion.

The gist of Goffman's essay, then, tells us that difference between Stanislavsky's *perezhivanie* and Brecht's *verfremdung* is not merely a theatrical dialectic but a direct parallel of a totally normal process in human maturation. We are all "living the role" at age three, and "distancing ourselves from our roles" at age five and beyond. Both behaviors are equally "real" – just reflective of different ages of our existence. When people say, "all actors are children," they are talking about the Stanislavskyian elements of acting. Brecht, however, wanted a theatre of, by, and for adults! And all of us, like Stanislavsky and Brecht, have both of these characters – the child and the adult – buried within us. And so do our audiences.

215

Summary of Chapter 5

The performing of a role – whether in realism, Sophocles, Shakespeare, Shaw, Chekhov, Wasserstein, film, opera, TV sitcom, or *cinema verité* – is a matter of creating and planting an audience and then using them as a tool on your character's behalf. It is a two-way street: the actor presents herself to the audience as the hero and partisan of their interests, and she asks that the audience become her supporters. This aligns characterization, style, and theatricality. If you play Madame Butterfly, you must imagine the audience as partisan to your predicament, and also disposed to an elegant soprano. Then you can align the soprano to the character, the style to the situation, without hesitancy, and without internal conflict, and can perform your role with everything you have within you – to both the front and back of the house.

6

ACTING POWER: A SYNTHESIS

"You cannot give theory when you want to teach somebody
acting. You have to do it. You have to work, work, work."
Swedish actor Max von Sydow[1]

This book begins with the notion of an actor's alignment of the various elements
required for a great and, in the book's term, powerful performance. When that
alignment is perfect, the results can be staggering. But it takes a lot of work – and
work on oneself.

We have turned, from time to time in this study, to sport for examples of this
alignment. Sporting events provide a valuable metaphor for the theatre; they
are "games" in which there is situation and context, and they are public events
that attract great followings. Sport and the theatre, in fact, have had an
intertwined history since the beginnings of recorded time. The Greeks had two
great festivals, a Dionysian one for theatre and an Olympian one for games. The
Romans presented plays and games simultaneously in their circuses; the
Elizabethans presented them alternately in theatres designed to hold bear-
baiting contests on days when no plays were performed. Today it is sporting
events and tele-dramas that, together, occupy the vast majority of television
time in the major Western nations. The great actors must compete successfully
with the energy, the excitement, the open-ended passion, even the "drama" of
a great sporting event.

"Acting is a sport. On stage you must be ready to move like a tennis player on his toes. Your concentration must be keen, your reflexes sharp; your body and mind are in top gear, the chase is on. Acting is energy. In the theatre people pay to see energy."

British actor Clive Swift[2]

The example of Dr. Roger Bannister is illuminating in this context. Bannister, in 1954, became the first man to run a mile in less than four minutes. This was not just an ordinary athletic record; for years people had said that the four-minute mile was a physical impossibility, that its demands exceeded human capability. Yet, after Bannister ran his sensational mile, his feat was almost immediately bettered. Within a few months, four-minute miles were common; people ran four-minute miles and came in third. At the time of writing, in 2013, the record is 3:43.13. The breaking of the four-minute mile was not, obviously, merely a physical feat. It seems to have required not only the speed and stamina of the athlete, but the daringness, the sense of creative discovery, that we expect from the artist. Bannister described the final moments of his run thusly:

My mind took over. It raced well ahead of my body and drew my body compellingly forward…There was no pain, only a great unity of movement and aim. The only reality was the next two hundred yards of track under my feet…I drove on, impelled by a combination of fear and pride…The noise in my ears was that of the faithful Oxford crowds. Their hope and encouragement gave me greater strength…There was fifty yards more. My body had long exhausted all its energy, but it went on running just the same…The faint line of the finishing tape stood ahead as a haven of peace, after the struggle. The arms of the world were waiting to receive me…I leapt at the tape like a man taking his last spring to save himself from the chasm that threatens to engulf him.[3]

Bannister's description is quite obviously the one we have been pursuing in this book with the analogy of the skier and the actor. His mental state at the time was purely cybernetic. He is looking only ahead; his mind is already there, drawing his body "compellingly forward." Nothing exists except the future, the next two hundred yards, the finish line. The crowd is "faithful." It is his private audience and also his public one; it is the "Oxford crowds" in attendance and it is also the "arms of the world" in his fantasy. It is real and it is imaginary, provoking in him both pride that he is their champion and fear that he may let them down. His spirit transcends his body, his energy seems to come from an external source, from the cheers of the crowd and the arms of the world. In the final leap to the tape everything comes together; there is no second thought, no holding back, no hesitancy, rather, an alignment, "a great unity of movement and aim." He is aligned for superhuman power.

It can be the same with acting. Great acting, like great athletic performance, comes from a transcendent effort, in which everything – audience, character, style, dialogue, costume, staging, self – comes together in complete accord. Alignment can create the accord. The actor must make the transcendent effort.

Effort is sometimes underrated as an actor's tool. There is an inclination, perhaps a defense, to consider an actor's talent hereditary or God-given; a "gift" that one has or one hasn't and there is nothing to be done about it. Nothing could be more deceptive. Heredity, training, psychological background, and cultural experience might all be vitally important in the growth of the actor, as they may be in the development of a track star, and I would hope that reading this book will be helpful as well, but none of these activities outweighs sheer effort; all they can do is make the effort easier and more spontaneous. Malcolm Gladwell, in his bestselling 2008 book, *Outliers,* put forth his all but indisputable "10,000 hour rule," generated by research indicating that the vast majority of the most successful athletes, musicians, inventors, and business executives in the world – people like Bill Gates and the Beatles – had reached the very top of their fields not so much by native talent or intelligence but by putting in a full *ten thousand hours* of hard work while learning and perfecting their respective crafts. Sheer effort, powerfully and effectively aligned with the character's situation, is the directive of acting energy. It is the dynamic of stage presence.

Presence

Great acting is often said to involve "presence." It is easy to say this, but hard to say exactly what it means. Audiences, who are more willing than actors or aestheticians to discuss the concept, consider that a performer has presence if and when she is "convincing," "commanding," "captivating," or "charming." In each of these cases, however, the audience is describing not the actor but themselves: they are saying, in effect, "I was convinced," "I was commanded," "I was captivated," "I was charmed." They are saying that the actor made them have an experience. This, of course, is the entire goal of theatricality in the first place.

The American drama critic John Lahr gave one of the most acute analyses of a captivated audience – himself – when he described his reaction to the singer Tina Turner:

"Hi, Tina!" we say, forgetting where we are...She is toying with us; but that's why we came – to be played with...She lifts grown men out of their seats; they wave at the stage; they talk to it...She comes up against the audience with a street-fighter's lust for battle. And she wins. (We want her to conquer us.) And wins completely...People are coaxed out of isolation and into a community...She has enough life for a whole auditorium. People move toward this luminous presence like moths to a light. Her energy is superhuman. The audience is feeling something. This, obviously, is presence.[4]

Presence derives from the word "present," and can be considered to mean something like "now-ness," or "present-ness." An actor trying to win a victory in a situation is experiencing his action at that moment, in the absolute present. Jean Louis Barrault says that, "The actor lives uniquely in the present; he is continually jumping from one present to the next...Characters...are continually in action and reaction. They reason, they plead, they argue, they fight with or against others, even with or against themselves. They dispute, answer back, dissimulate, deceive others or themselves with greater or less bad faith; but they never stop."[5] Being in the present – having "now-ness" or "present-ness" – being engaged in the experience of the situation and the feedback of the situation at the moment you are performing the situation – this is the precondition for presence. It is what allows the audience to be transported, to be moved, to experience and feel.

Being in the present, of course, means concentrating on the future, on the road immediately ahead. Paul Claudel, the French playwright, reminds us that, "Often we are moved not so much by what the actor says as by what we feel he is about to say." Expectations are no less real than actions. Expectations, after all, are what make the world go around, what make people act. Expectation is the soul of the human potential.

Potential

Jean Paul Sartre famously said that "we are our acts and nothing else." This may have (and I think does have) philosophical validity, but only as seen by an outside, objective observer. It has no validity from our own subjective perspective however: We "know" we are more than our acts, and that knowledge is no less "real" because it is subjective.

Helene Deutsch, the great Viennese psychiatrist, looked back over her immensely long and rich lifetime and wrote: "Everyone lives two lives simultaneously. One of them is devoted to adapting to the outside world and improving one's external circumstances. The other consists of fantasies, longings, distortions of reality, undertakings unfinished, achievements not won." The objective, existential analyst looks only at the first life. The person *in* life, however, and the character representing her, and the actor playing *her*, and the audience empathizing with all three of them, see and "know" the second. That knowledge of our human *potential*, the knowledge of things that have *not* been done, is the subjective reality of life. It is usually the most interesting aspect of any individual; it is *certainly* the most theatrical. In order to create a character with presence, it is necessary to create that character's *potential*, to create potential itself.

Where does the actor find that potential? Ultimately, she finds it in herself. Finally, the source of an actor's power is herself; this is the key that links her to her character and to the here-and-now of the present, and to the extraordinary potential of the future.

Acting, at bottom, is the most personal of arts. Not closed-in personal, in Stanislavsky's snail-in-his-shell mode, but open-minded, looking out, exploring potentials in the present and imagined victories in the future.

Peter Brook, the English director, suggests this quite clearly in his famous essay on "The Immediate Theatre," which, he argues, is a theatre directed to "present-ness." As Brook says, "The actor is giving of himself all the time. It is his possible growth, his possible understanding that he is exploiting, using this material to weave these personalities which drop away when the play is done." The actor must exploit her own personal possibilities, her own potential. This is the wellspring of a profound creativity.

And what is the actor's personal potential? Obviously it includes the actor's instincts for fulfillment, which are always engaged as she participates in feedback with the other actors. It includes her continual trying to win in her situational involvements, her relationship communications, and her dramatic and tactical endeavors. The hopes, wishes, lusts, longings, expectations, and commitments of the actor – which are shared with the character – all become a vital part of the actor's and character's potential, of the actor's and character's life and vitality. But that is not all.

Throughout this book we have concentrated on the actor's positive efforts; her win-directed behavior. That is because these are the character's concentrations. Now we must turn to a grayer and less conscious preoccupation: the character's fears, and his or her facing the threats of death and destruction. For these, too, lie within the realm of human potential. While they may be peripheral rather than central to our daily vision, they are nonetheless galvanizing in their effectiveness. Runner Bannister's conscious focus may have been on the finish line ahead of him, but his report is also of a "chasm" that threatened to engulf him from behind. The human potential is as much for disaster as it is for glory.

Great actors always manage to give the audience a sense of that potential, impending disaster. Of Marlon Brando, certainly one of America's finest actors, critic Ronald Hayman has written:

> Brando's acting is exciting because it seems so dangerous. There may be a framework of conscious preparation, but he keeps it well hidden and he looks likely to burst at any minute through the walls of any situation that contains him. Like Olivier, he has a volcanic quality and he makes us feel that if he erupts, there is no knowing where the flood of lava will stop.[6]

The comparison with Olivier is particularly apt, for the "volcanic quality," the "dangerousness," is the main link between the twentieth century's most celebrated "method" actor and its greatest "technical" performer. Nothing so distinguishes great acting – in any style, in any historical period – than the feeling that the actor has the potential to "go off" at any moment, and to unleash an explosion – a flood of lava, that will be totally out of the frame, totally uncontrolled and uncontrollable. Great acting always dances with danger.

"Stars are actors or creatures that look as if they are going to blow up any minute. They have an in-built violence within them."

British actor/director Richard Attenborough[7]

"When I go out there on stage I'm battling the world, I have to be the best."

Welsh actor Richard Burton[8]

Danger

Danger, then, is a virtual precondition for presence. If there is no danger at all, the performance cannot electrify an audience, cannot move them, cannot thrill or transport them. Sporting events are notoriously dangerous and their records of broken bones, concussive blows to the head, "spills and chills" are as frequently reported as are the heroics needed to win victory over those threatening catastrophes. Were it entirely safe, the skier's ride would be of no interest to us, no matter how fast or elegant. Similarly, the actor's performance has no great interest for us if the character we see is never threatened, never endangered. Something must be on the line, something must be risked. The fine actress Lee Grant, in accepting an Academy Award for her performance in the film *Shampoo*, thanked her director "who encouraged me to fly without a net."[9] That is the difference between "safe" and "dangerous" performing.

Yet how do we liberate that sense of danger into performance? Where do we find it? Again, we find it within ourselves. Danger is hardly unknown to our consciousness; no one is totally without an inner volcano of her own, without the boiling lava of primordial imagination. Theatre, as Antonin Artaud reported with insights sharpened but not defeated by psychosis, serves to remind us that the sky can always fall on our heads, and that the plague can always land with the next ship. As the struggle for victory must be played by the actor with single-minded absorption, so must her ever-present awareness of potential for catastrophe be planted as an obstacle to achieve her character's goals.

And we do not have to go very far afield to find that ever-present chasm, that catastrophe, always threatening to catch up to us, as the bear threatens to catch up and destroy the man running in the forest. We know the catastrophe by personal experience; it is vivid in our imaginations. It is, of course, mortality; the inevitability of death. Universal mortality is the final link between actors, characters, and audiences; it is the most fundamental sharing we experience – the basis of our deepest alignment, and perhaps the basis of theatre itself. The inevitable awareness of our mortality, far from draining our enthusiasm for life, can serve as an inspiring source of power and shared energy, a springboard for heroism.

It is wise, in this context, to examine the remarkable suggestion of N.S. Shaler that "heroism is first and foremost a reflex of the terror of death," a suggestion that lies at the heart of Ernest Becker's justly celebrated study, *The Denial of Death*.[10] In this latter work, Becker draws upon the entire range of twentieth-century psychological and philosophical literature to explore the "terror of death" which lies far more deeply and pervasively beneath human actions than most of us dare to admit, even to ourselves. Death, Becker says, is not at all a conscious preoccupation; rather it is a lingering unconscious dread that promotes our greatest energies in our attempts to deny it. The urge to action, suggests Becker, is an urge toward the denial of death, toward heroism.

Death, obviously, stalks us all. When the man in the forest runs for the safe haven of a cabin door, death is the bear that chases behind him. The man does not need to look back at the bear, or study the bear, in order to run from it. The bear may not even be there, in fact; the bear's presence in the man's imagination is sufficient to induce his speedy charge, his "driven-ness." As we have seen, the man is not even "afraid" of the bear when he is running from it; or at least does not, at that time, conceptualize his feelings as "fear." His fear only comes later, when he is safely in the cabin. Fear is Antonio Damasio's secondary emotion, one we entertain at leisure, yet it affects us whether we entertain it or not. In Becker's view, most of what we call "character" and most of what we call "behavior" is stimulated, at the deepest level, by the bear of death behind us. The bear to which we pretend, using all these mechanisms, to be oblivious.

If this is true – if this model is sufficiently in agreement with our own beliefs so that it can be useful – it provides the actor with two deeply telling points of collaboration with her character, or with any character. These are the unconscious terror of death, and the more conscious affirmation of life. The character, if she is real, is mortal. She represses her fear of death – by living, by acting. So does the actor. Through her behavior, her character, and her style, the actor affirms life and affirms the present. Like the character she plays, the actor will, in the words of William James, "plunge ahead in the strange power of living in the moment." In this case, the actor is not only aligned, in a profound way, with the fundamental situation, character, and style of the person she represents; she is aligned with her own life and the life of her audience. She is aligned with immediacy, with the present, and with the forces that converge on actor, character, and audience alike at every moment. By giving her character the potential to die, in other words, she creates the opportunity, even the necessity, to make her character live.

"It's very important to realize that we're up against an evil, insidious, hostile universe, a hostile force. It'll make you ill and age you and kill you. And there's somebody – or something – out there who for some irrational, unexplainable reason is killing us. I'm only interested in dealing with the top man. I'm not interested in dealing with the other stuff because that's not important. The only questions of real interest are the ultimate questions, otherwise who cares about anything else?"

American playwright, actor and film director Woody Allen[11]

Acting is affirmation

One of the greatest direct treatments of this affirmation of life is the theatrical masterpiece of Thornton Wilder, *Our Town*. At the end of the play the young heroine, Emily, dies. The townspeople gather around her grave and sing the hymn "Blessed Be the Tie That Binds." And as they sing, Emily's spirit rises from the grave to take its place in the town graveyard. It is, even in the most inelegant production, a terribly sad scene, deeply affecting to the audience. And yet what gives the scene its poignancy is not a preoccupation with death, but rather the converse. It is the muffled affirmations of the townspeople's singing. With every verse, the townspeople declare to each other, to their private audiences, and to their God, "I am still alive!" The scene is moving because the characters fight sorrow and they fight against death; not only Emily's death, but also their own – and ours, too, by the extension of our feelings. And rather than having the

224

choruses fading out into despair, Wilder has them increase to a crescendo. Mere living is, itself, a positive affirmation of life. Acting only intensifies the affirmation. Acting, or behavior, in other words, is the moment-to-moment conquest of death. It is "playing against" the biggest and profoundest of obstacles. Playing it as such can tie the actor to her deepest source of power.

Acting, therefore, is an affirmation of living, an exultation of life itself. Everything we do in life is an act intended to extend and improve our lives. It is this aspect of behavior, the positive aspect, with which audiences will identify. It is this aspect they will understand.

Jack Nicholson, the superb film actor, says "I'm at least 75 per cent of every character I play. For the rest, I try to find a character's *positive philosophy* about himself. You have to search out and adopt the character's own justifications and rationalizations."[12] This affirmation is the key to Nicholson's brilliant "good/bad boy" performances, and what character is not a "good/bad" character when all is said and done? The "justifications" and "rationalizations" which Nicholson finds are not objective behavioral descriptions; they are a person's – or a character's – distortions of the true impact of his behavior. Nicholson's findings are self-serving, but that is because his character is self-serving, and is finding ways to justify and rationalize his bad behavior. But while Nicholson thinks the behavior is bad, as do we, the character thinks it is just fine. And so Nicholson plays his good/bad characters as heroes. He plays them heroically, and as he does so, he affirms their life and the life within them.

Performing is an affirmation

And performing, too, is an affirmation of life. Performing is itself a form of action, a positive act. The townspeople at Emily's graveside are affirming life by their singing, but so are the actors who play those townspeople. The actors are affirming that they are alive simply by being in the play. They celebrate life at the same time they represent it. Even in the darkest tragedy, that affirmation can be joyous. Essentially, the actor says with every act: "I survive. I live!" Theatre exists on that vitality.

Robert Frost, the great American poet, wrote several witty and revealing essays on the nature of artistic performance. Certainly poetry is the most private of the public arts. And yet Frost wrote, with evident sincerity as well as wit:

> What do I want to communicate [with a poem] but what a hell of a good time I had in writing it? The whole thing is performance and prowess and feats…why don't critics talk about those things? I look at a poem as a performance. I look on the poet as a man of prowess, just like an athlete. He's a performer…You excel at tennis, vaulting, tumbling, racing, or any kind of ball game because you have the art to put all you've got into it. You're completely alert. You're hotly competitive and yet a good sport. Putting up the bar in the high jump, for instance. You

deliberately limit yourself by traditional, artificial rules. What you try for is effective and appropriate form. And success is measured by surpassing performance, including the surpassing of your former self.[13]

Frost, quite obviously, found in his art the alignment of the great athlete, or the great actor. He found the ability to make goals, obstacles, artificial rules, feats, prowess, and competition with – among others – his former self aligned with his creation of splendid artistic monuments. His writing, as a result, has not only insight and eloquence, it has power. It has undifferentiated impact. It speaks with its totality as well as with its parts. For Frost, the job of "performance" was both part of his artistic process, and of his artistic product. It is the same with the great actor.

As the actor affirms life through her character's actions, so she affirms life by the mere act of her own performance, and by the discipline of her training and her rehearsal. When the actor's alignments and concentrations are true, and her consciousness is not fragmented and inhibited, performance of even the darkest, saddest plays brings with it a wry feeling of glee, of satisfaction, of joy. Actors, like their characters, dance on their own tombs. As the poet William Butler Yeats observed:

> All perform their tragic play,
> There struts Hamlet, there is Lear
> That's Ophelia, that's Cordelia;
> Yet they, should the last scene be there,
> The great stage curtain about to drop,
> If worthy their prominent part in the play,
> Do not break up their lines to weep.
> They know that Hamlet and Lear are gay:
> Gaiety transfiguring all that dread.[14]

And the same goes for the performers who play Hamlet and Lear. They, too, are "gay" (in the original "gaiety" meaning of the word): affirming, filled with the power and spirit of life.

Defenses

Great acting is not easy; anyone who says otherwise is either shallow or a charlatan. And one of the hardest things about acting is admitting that it is, in fact, hard.

Peter Brook says, "Time after time I have worked with actors who, after the usual preamble that they 'put themselves in my hands,' are tragically incapable, however hard they try, of laying down for one brief instant even in rehearsal the image of themselves that has hardened round an inner emptiness."[15] Conditioned as we are to hide our vulnerabilities, to demonstrate "control" in interpersonal relations, to obliterate the fear of death and the fear of failure, and any showing of these, it becomes difficult or impossible to develop the sense of present-ness, of volcanic potential, that characterizes the truly talented actor. And the less-than-great actor (one hesitates to call her "bad," more likely she is simply, and stultifyingly, "good") has many rationalizations for her less-than-greatness. These are her actor defenses, and she can always, if she wishes, polish them to a high degree of sophistication.

Anti-intellectualism is one of the most common actor defenses, and it has a long history. It can be seen in the John Wayne remark, with which this book begins, and in similar remarks by highly elegant performers like Jason Robards, who once remarked, "I always felt I had to get up on a stage and perform before people; studying didn't matter." Many directors echo this attitude with the explicit command: "Don't think about it! Just do it!"[16]

It is easy, but rather foolhardy, to take these comments at face value. The vast majority of successful professional actors today, in America and around the world, have had extensive training and experience. And a great deal of the anti-intellectualism professed by the successful actor is, perhaps, as much a pose as a reality. Jason Robards, in fact, was the son of a famous stage and film actor (Jason Robards Senior); he grew up in Hollywood and studied acting at New York's American Academy of Arts and with famed New York acting teacher Uta Hagen. I once heard a prominent American actor being interviewed on a television talk show tell the audience that he had never studied acting and that his parents knew nothing about theatre; the actor, however, had graduated from a major drama school and his father was the artistic director of a professional theatre company. Many celebrated actors would like their fans to think that their celebrity status derived from their native genius rather than the rigorous training they had received; almost all of them, however, in private at least, are usually quite articulate, about the "intellectual" aspects of acting. Certainly, every actor knows how harmful certain kinds of thinking are to acting; thinking about how your voice sounds while you are on stage, for instance, or how your makeup looks, or whether you've got your lines right. But one cannot simply avoid these sorts of problems by abolishing thinking. The mind cannot be told to stop. We cannot *not* think. The mind simply rebels – it thinks in any event.

But the mind can be aimed. The goal of an acting theory – the goal of thinking about acting – is to find a way to aim, not to still, the actor's mind.

Reliance on a simple, single theory or "method" is another actor defense, one that is crippling both in the long and the short run. An actor refuses to study, because she claims that acting must be instinctual and nothing else. An actor refuses to learn scansion because she believes that verse must be spoken "naturally." An actor refuses to study the character's psychology because acting is simply a matter of "technique." An actor refuses to act out of himself because the character is "someone else." An actor refuses to act in a period costume or foreign dialect because "I jus' wanna be me." An actor does not think about acting, because she believes thinking stifles art.

The folly of these approaches need not be discussed at length. The author has pointed out in another book* that successful professional acting careers demand comprehensive and versatile greatness, not mere sufficiency. Earlier in these pages we have discussed alignments which can take into account, and that can synthesize, the great complexities of acting. The defensiveness of the blinded adherent of simplistic "methods" and clichés is simply and clearly that: defensiveness. The simplistic actor knows it – she knows that there are things about acting that confuse her, things she must somehow keep out of her mind, things about herself that she must consciously suppress (including the fact that there are things that confuse her that she is suppressing). She knows the trap she's in, but avoids the work on herself needed to get out, because it would amount to an admission of defeat. Her acting becomes scared, shallow, a cover-up for her hollowness. She is, finally, powerless; consumed by impotence and hopeful only of not being found out.

"One mustn't allow acting to be like stockbroking – you must not take it just as a means of earning a living, to go down every day to do a job of work. The big thing is to combine punctuality, efficiency, good nature, obedience, intelligence, and concentration with an unawareness of what is going to happen next, thus keeping yourself available for excitement."

British actor John Gielgud[17]

Acting Power: A summary

Power comes from alignment, and power builds upon power. The chapters and exercises in this book, whether the latter are performed or just read and mused about, are calculated to build – one atop the other like plates in a stack – the alignments an actor needs to enter a situation with the confidence that her characterization, her style, and her need for theatricality are her allies, not her enemies. As allies, they give the actor strength. That strength leads to

---

* *Acting Professionally.* The seventh edition is co-authored with James Calleri. London and New York: Palgrave Macmillan, 2010.

confidence. That confidence leads to more strength. It is the ultimate power feedback loop.

Jason Robards, who said that "studying didn't matter," also said (in the same article), "Acting is strange. You are split in many ways. You have about six things going on in your head. You have to be completely in it, yet aware of... the audience. It's all there if you trust yourself."[18] Self-confidence, finally, is its own reward. It is that which allows the actor full play of her tactics and full pursuit of her intended victory. It allows her to use the audience in the same way the skier, or the matador, uses his appreciative fans.

Self-confidence – faith in ourselves – unites our split personalities. It permits actors to be actors and at the same time characters, and lets audiences remain themselves and at the same time empathize with the fictional characters on stage. If acting is complex, it is because we are complex, because life and conceptualizations we may make of life are complex. It is the job of the actor to learn to manage that complexity, to learn to use it, and to create a powerful and subtle art out of it.

Theatre, after all, is the art we make out of ourselves. It requires, in the end, neither scenery, nor costumes, nor lighting fixtures, nor apparatus of any kind. It does not even require a text. It requires behavior within a context; people acting and people watching them, or in the French term Peter Brook likes to use, *assisting* them. Theatre is as vital as life, as cruel as death, and as unfathomable as unconscious experience. And acting that re-presents these – that puts them again "into the present," as the word "represent" essentially means – this is the acting that brings art and life to the stage, and to ourselves.

NOTES

PREFACE

1 James, William, *The Letters of William James*, Boston: Atlantic Monthly Press, 1920, p. 87.

INTRODUCTION

1 Burton, Hal, *Great Acting*, 1967, London: British Broadcasting Corporation, pp. 71–72.
2 Fadiman, William, *Hollywood Now*, New York: Liveright, 1972, p. 88–89.
3 Shaw, George Bernard, "The Art of Rehearsal," *Collier's Weekly*, June 24, 1922.
4 YouTube and espn.playbook online interviews.
5 Watzlawick, Paul et al., *The Pragmatics of Human Communication*, New York: Norton, 1967, p. 51.
6 Berne, Eric, *Transactional Analysis in Psychotherapy*, New York: Grove Press, 1961, p. 4.
7 The books your author recommends are Annie Loui, *The Physical Actor*, London: Routledge, 2009, and Dudley Knight, *Speaking with Skill*, London: Bloomsbury, 2012. I must mention that both authors are longtime colleagues of mine.
8 Ross, Lillian and Helen, *The Player: A Profile of An Art*, New York: Simon and Schuster, 1962, p. 381.
9 Gunn, Bob, "Stage Fright," *Strategic Finance*, 83:2, p. 12, July 2001.

CHAPTER 1

1 Robinson, Kevin, *The Actor Sings*, Portsmouth, NH: Heinemann, 2000, p. 25.
2 Jones, Edward E. and Richard E. Nisbett, *The Actor and the Observer: Divergent Perceptions of the Causes of Behavior*, New York: General Learning Press, 1971, p. 2.
3 McKittrick, Chris, *Daily Actor* (blog), December 5, 2011.
4 Heim, Michael and Simon Karlinsky (eds), *Anton Chekhov, Letters*, New York: Harper and Row, 1973, p. 122.
5 Swift, Clive, *The Job of Acting*, London: Harrap, 1984, p. 5.
6 Newquist, Roy, *Showcase*, New York: W. Morrow, 1966, p. 267.
7 Margolies, Danny, "Father (Now) Knows Best," *Backstage Magazine*, December 10, 2000.
8 Llinás, Rodolfo R., *I of the Vortex: From Neurons to Self*, Cambridge, MA: MIT Press, 2001, p. 3. Emphasis in the original.
9 Probst, Leonard, *Off Camera: Leveling about Themselves*, New York: Stein and Day, 1975, p. 39.

10 Knights, L.C., *How Many Children Had Lady Macbeth?*, Cambridge, G. Fraser: The Minority Press, 1933.
11 Sian Thomas's and Simon Russell Beale's quotations are both in *Performing Shakespeare's Tragedies Today: The Actor's Perspective*, edited by Michael Dobson, Cambridge: Cambridge University Press, 2006.
12 Watslawick and others, *The Pragmatics of Human Communication*, New York: Norton, 1967, pp. 44–45.
13 In an interview with Ernie Manouse on Houston PBS, January 28, 2010.
14 Pascal, René, *Pensées*, Paris: Mercure de France, 1670 (1976, p. 165.)
15 Weiner, Norbert, *Cybernetics: Or Control and Communication*, Cambridge, MA: MIT Press, 1948.
16 CultureVulture.net, May 4, 2011.

CHAPTER 2

1 Ramachandran's, V.S., *The Tell-Tale Brain*, New York: Norton, 2011, p. 252.
2 In interview with Patrick Healy, *New York Times*, Feb 15, 2011.
3 Ross, Lillian and Helen, *The Player: A Profile of an Art*, New York: Simon and Schuster, 1962, p. 378.
4 Kahneman, Daniel, *Thinking, Fast and Slow*, New York: Farrar, Straus and Giroux, 2011, pp. 22–23.
5 Louise Kelley, ed., *Issues Theory, and Research in Industrial/Organizational Psychology*, Amsterdam: Elsevier Science Publishers, 1992, p. 44.
6 Donnellan, Declan, *The Actor and The Target*, 2nd Edition, New York: Theatre Communications Group, 2006, p. 55.
7 Michael Tomasello, quoted by Nicholas Wade, *New York Times*, March 14, 2011.
8 Daniel Sullivan's quoted by Alexis Solosky, *New York Times*, April 11, 2012.
9 Jean Benedetti's translation of Stanislavsky's *An Actors Work*, London: Routledge, 2008, p. 231.
10 Martin Sheen's recollection appeared in "Roses Remembered: an interview with Martin Sheen," in the theatre program for the 2010 revival of Gilroy's *The Subject Was Roses* at the Mark Taper Forum in Los Angeles.
11 In interview with Lynn Hirschberg, *New York Times*, December 19, 2008.
12 Email to the author, August 22, 2011.
13 Horowitz, Simi, "Standing By," *Back Stage West*, May 31–Jun 6, 2007.
14 Agate, James *The Later Ego*, New York: Crown Puhlishers, 1951, p. 110.
15 Hirschberg, Lynn, "A Higher Calling," *New York Times*, December 21, 2009.
16 Goethe, *Rules of Acting*, in Russell Vandenbroucke, *The Theatre Quotation Book*, New York: Limelight, 2001, p. 165.
17 Rees, Mandy and John Staniunas, *Between Actor and Director*, New York: Heinemann, 2002, p. 51.
18 Ullman, Liv, *Changing*, New York: Bantam, 1978, p. 280.
19 Cook, Judith, *Directors' Theatre*, London: Harrap, 1974, p. 64.
20 Cottrell, John, *Laurence Olivier*, New York: Prentice-Hall, 1975, p. 388.
21 Rosenthal, R. and Jacobson, L., *Pygmalion in the Classroom*, New York: Holt, Rinehart & Winston, 1968.
22 Watzlawick, Paul et al., *The Pragmatics of Human Communication*, New York: Norton, 1967.
23 Christian, Brian, *The Most Human Human*, New York: Doubleday 2011, p. 174.
24 Newquist, Roy, *Showcase*, New York: W. Morrow, 1966, p. 264.
25 Berne, Eric, in *Transactional Analysis in Psychotherapy*, New York: Grove Press, 1961.

26 Satir, Virginia, *Conjoint Family Therapy*, Palo Alto, CA: Science and Behavior Books, 1967, p. 81.
27 The translation of this scene from *Woyzeck* is by the author.
28 In interview with Jenelle Riley in *Backstage*, January 20, 2010.
29 Shipman, David, *Brando*, New York: Macmillan 1974, p. 14.
30 Ross, Lillian and Helen, *The Player: A Profile of an Art*, New York: Simon and Schuster, 1962, p. 102.
31 Oatley, Keith, *Emotions: A Brief History*, Malden, MA: Blackwell, 2004, p. 4.
32 In interview with Mervyn Rothstein, *New York Times*, September 14, 2008.
33 Zarrilli, Phillip et al., *Theatre Histories: An Introduction*, London: Routledge, 2nd Edition, 2010, p. 65.
34 Diderot, Denis, *Paradoxe sur le Comédien*, written in 1773 but first published (posthumously) in 1830.
35 Clurman, Herbert, *The Fervent Years*, New York: Hill and Wang, 1957, pp. 44–45.
36 Blakeslee, Sandra, "A Small Part of the Brain, and Its Profound Effects," in the *New York Times*, February 6, 2007.
37 Damasio, Antonio, *Descartes' Error: Emotion, Reason, and the Human Brain*, New York: Putnam, 1994, p. 139.
38 James, "What is an Emotion?" first published in *Mind*, 9, 1984, pp. 188–205.
39 Damasio, Antonio, *Descartes' Error: Emotion, Reason, and the Human Brain*, New York: Putnam, 1994, pp. 140–41.
40 The three neuroscientists referred to are Elaine Hatfield, John, T. Cacioppo and Richard L. Rapson in *Emotional Contagion*, Cambridge: Cambridge University Press, p. 15. Emphasis added.
41 Ibid., pp. 56 and 51.
42 Cain, Michael, *Back Stage West*, February 28, 2002.
43 Krampner, Jon, *Female Brando: The Legend of Kim Stanley*, New York: Back Stage Books, 2006, p. 205.
44 Probst, Leonard, *Off Camera: Leveling about Themselves*, New York: Stein and Day, 1975, p. 167.
45 Donnellan, Declan, *The Actor and the Target*, 2nd Edition, New York: Theatre Communications Group, 2005, p. 55.
46 Ross, Lillian and Helen, *The Player: A Profile of an Art*, New York: Simon and Schuster, 1962, p. 36.
47 Perlstein, Rick, *Nixonland*, New York: Simon & Schuster, 2008, p. 419.
48 McGaw, Charles, *Acting is Believing*, New York: Holt Rinehart & Winston, 1962, p. 35.
49 Burton, Hal, *Great Acting*, 1967, London: British Broadcasting Corp., p. 29.
50 Ross, Lillian and Helen, *The Player: A Profile of an Art*, New York: Simon and Schuster, 1962, p. 134.
51 De Niro's comment was also published, in slightly different form, in Andy Dugan, *Untouchable: A Biography of Robert De Niro*, New York: Thunder's Mouth Press, 1996, p. 77.
52 Bannister, Robert, "Four Minutes that were an Eternity" in *Runners' World*, Volume 14, Issues 1-6, 1979, p. 67.
53 In interview with Jamie Painter Young in *Back Stage West*, June 7, 2001.
54 Winokur, Jon, *True Confessions*, New York: Dutton, 1992, p. 70.
55 *Evening Gazette*, September 24, 1926, page 4.

CHAPTER 3

1 *The New Yorker*, Vol 37, 1961, p. 109.
2 In interview with Charlie Rose, PBS, May 5, 2008.

3 Piaget quotations paraphrased from his writings by Howard Gardner, in *The Quest for Mind*, New York: Knopf, 1972, p. 63.
4 Redfield, William, *Letters from an Actor*, New York: Limelight, 1984, p. 30.
5 Probst, Leonard, *Off Camera: Leveling about Themselves*, New York: Stein and Day, 1975, p. 52.
6 Olsen, Mark, "Anything but Typical," article in the *Los Angeles Times*, November 29, 2007.
7 Ullman, Liv, *Changing*, New York: Bantam, 1978, p. 120.
8 Newquist, Roy, *Showcase*, New York: W. Morrow, 1966, p. 265.
9 Newquist, Roy, *Showcase*, New York: W. Morrow, 1966, p. 267.
10 Ross, Lillian and Helen, *The Player: A Profile of An Art*, New York: Simon and Schuster, 1962, p. 303.
11 Benedetti, Jean (tr.), *An Actor's Work*, London: Routledge, 2008, p. 210.
12 Burton, Hal, *Great Acting*, 1967, London: British Broadcasting Corp., page 133.
13 Brook, Peter, *Evoking (and Forgetting!) Shakespeare*, London: Nick Hern Books, 1994, p. 43.
14 Cottrell, John, *Laurence Olivier*, New York: Prentice-Hall, 1975, p. 392.
15 Perl's translation of Freud's dictum is in Joen Fagan and Irma Lee Shepherd (eds), *Gestalt Therapy Now*, Palo Alto, CA: Science and Behavior Books, 1970, pp. 16–17.
16 Esper, William and Damon DiMarco, *The Actor's Art and Craft*, New York: Anchor Books, 2008, pp. 110–11.
17 Eliot, T.S, "The Love Song of J. Alfred Prufrock," 1920, line 27.
18 Goldman, Michael, *The Actor's Freedom: Toward a Theory of Drama*, New York: Viking Press, 1975, page 92.
19 Efros' confirmation is "At one time Stanislavsky could say throughout an entire rehearsal: 'I don't believe you!'" in Antonio Efros, *Beyond Rehearsal*, tr. James Thomas, New York: Peter Lang, 2009, p. 190.
20 William Ball, quoted in his obituary by Eleanor Blau, *New York Times*, August 2, 1991.
21 Quintero, José, *If They Don't Dance They Beat You*, Boston: Little Brown, 1974, p. 113.
22 Camus' 1955 observations on this page may be found, respectively, in *The Myth of Sisyphus, and Other Essays*, translated by Justin O'Brien, Vintage International Edition, 1991, pp. 61 and 77.
23 *Screen Actor* (Spring 1974), pp. 21–22. Emphasis added.

CHAPTER 4

1 Newquist, Roy, *Showcase*, W. Morrow, 1966, p. 184.
2 St. Denis, Michel, *Theatre: The Rediscovery of Style*, New York: Theatre Arts Books, 1960, p. 71.
3 Felsenstein, Walter, *The Music Theatre of Walter Felsenstein*, London: Quartet Books, 1991, p. 18.
4 St. Denis, Michel, and Jane Baldwin, *Theatre: The Rediscovery of Style and Other Writings*, London: Routledge Theatre Classics, 2009, p. 67.
5 In interview with Patrick Pacheco, *Los Angeles Times*, November 20, 2011.
6 Guthrie, Sir Tyrone, *Tyrone Guthrie on Acting*, New York: Viking Press, 1971, p. 7.

CHAPTER 5

1 Cited in Holzman, Lois, *Psychological Investigations*, New York: Brunner-Routledge, 2003, p. 85. The quoted phrases have been reversed for greater clarity.

2 Stanislavsky, *An Actor's Work*, translated by Jean Benedetti, London: Routledge, 2008, p. 99. His lines about "responsibility" are from Vasily Toporkov's *Rehearsals With Stanislavsky*, translated by Christine Edwards, London: Routledge 1998, p. 200.

3 Ramachandran, V.S., *The Tell-Tail Brain*, New York: Norton, 2011, p.124.

4 Vasilij Toporkov, *Stanislavski in Rehearsal: The Final Years*, tr. Christine Edwards, pp. 200–201. New York: Theatre Arts Book and Routledge Press, 1998.

5 Kivisto, Peter and Dan Pittman, "Goffman's Dramaturgical Sociology," in *Illuminating Social Life*, Peter Kivisto (ed.), Thousand Oaks, CA: Pine Forge Press, 1998, p. 272.

6 Goffman, Erving, *The Presentation of Self in Everyday Life*, New York: Doubleday: 1959, p. 65.

7 Peter Brook's quotation from his *The Empty Space*, New York: Atheneum, 1968, p. 25.

8 Gardner, Howard, *The Quest for Mind*, 1972, New York: Knopf, p. 103.

9 *Antigone*, translated by Mark Griffith, Cambridge: Cambridge University Press, 1999.

10 Goldman, Michael, *The Actor's Freedom*, New York: Viking, 1975, p. 16.

11 Lahr, John, "Surreal Life: The Plays of Sarah Ruhl," in *The New Yorker*, March 17, 2008, p. 82.

12 Hotson, Leslie, *Shakespeare's Wooden O*, London: Hart-Davis, 1959.

13 West, Samuel, *Performing Shakespeare's Tragedies Today: The Actor's Perspective*, Michael Dobson (ed.), New York: Cambridge, 2007, p. 51.

14 *Back Stage West*, January 6, 2005.

15 Duerr, Edwin, *The Length and Depth of Acting*, New York: Holt, Rinehart & Winston, 1962, p. 490.

16 Willet, John, *Brecht on Theatre*. New York: Hill and Wang, 1964. pp. 92-93 and p. 227.

17 Stanislavsky, *An Actor's Work*, translated by Benedetti, London: Routledge, 2008, p. 19. His "What's false here?" comments are from Vasilii Toporkov's *O Technike Aktiora* (1958) translated by Jean Benedetti in his *Stanislavski: A Biography*, London: Routledge, 1988, p. 287.

18 John Willett, ed. and trans., *Brecht on Theatre*, New York: MacMillan, 1964, pp. 234–35.

19 Goffman, Erving, "Role Distance" in Goffman, *Encounters: Two Studies in Sociology of Interaction*, New York: Macmillan Publishing Company, 1961. Your author's full essay on this subject is available in "Role Distance: On Stage and On the Merry-Go-Round," *Journal of Dramatic Theory and Criticism*," Fall, 2004.

CHAPTER 6

1 In interview with Dany Margolies in *Back Stage West*, December 6–12, 2007.

2 Swift, Clive, *The Job of Acting*, London: Harrap, 1984, p. 5.

3 Bannister, Roger, *The Four Minute Mile*, New York: Dodd, Mead, 1962, p. 212.

4 Lahr, John, *Astonish Me!* New York: Viking Press, 1972, pp. 211–213.

5 Barrault, John-Louis, *Reflections on the Theatre*, London: Rockliff, 1951, pp. 126–129.

6 Hayman, Ronald, *Hayman's Techniques of Acting*, New York: Holt, Rinehart & Winston, 1971, pp. 142–43.

7 Richard Attenborough in *Dialogue on Film*, Beverly Hills, CA: American Film Institute, 1972, p. 56.

8 Richard Burton in *The Listener*, Volume 78, British Broadcasting Corporation, 1967, p. 203.

9 Grant, Lee, *Uniontown Morning Herald*, March 30, 1976.

10 Becker, Ernest, *The Denial of Death*, New York: Free Press, 1973, p. 11. His quotation from N.S. Shaler is taken from Shaler's *The Individual: A Study of Life and Death*, New York: D. Appleton, 1900.

11 Lax, Eric, *On Being Funny*, New York: Charterhouse, 1975, p. 45.

12 Jack Nicholson quoted in *Time*, August 11, 1974. Emphasis added.
13 Lentricchia, Frank, *Robert Frost*, Durham, N.C.: Duke University Press, 1975, pp. 167–168.
14 Yeats, W.B., "Lapis Lazuli" (1938).
15 Brook, Peter, *The Empty Space*, New York, Atheneum, 1968, p. 29.
16 Greenberger, Howard, *The Off Broadway Experience*, Englewood Cliffs, NJ, Prentice-Hall, 1971, p. 50.
17 Newquist, Roy, *Showcase*, New York: W. Morrow, 1966, p. 157.
18 Greenberger, Howard, *The Off Broadway Experience*, Englewood Cliffs, NJ, Prentice-Hall, 1971, p. 47.

INDEX